"Gloria's emphasis on the CBT author as pioneer will certainly set new course developers on the right track: aware of the importance of a carefully-charted journey, alert to the many dangers along the way (namely, the lure of executable, even appealing, but ineffective instruction), and always inspired by ever-changing horizons in learning technology. Gloria's extensive contacts in the training industry have enabled her to accurately define what CBT is today—and to envision for her readers what it might be tomorrow."

Carol Endriss
Chief CBI Author
The Hartford Insurance Group

"No one has seen more organizations through the process of setting up CBT development arms. Nobody has been involved in the creation of more CBT. This book bears testimony to those statements. It is an essential source book for those who wish to take the shortest and most effective route to the development of successful computer-based training."

Patrick Dillon
CBT Consultant

Amy Hughes

Making CBT Happen

Prescriptions for successful implementation of computer-based training in your organization

by Gloria Gery

WEINGARTEN
PUBLICATIONS

Boston
1987

MAKING CBT HAPPEN
Prescriptions for successful implementation of
computer-based training in your organization

by Gloria Gery

Copyright © 1987 by
Weingarten Publications, Inc.
38 Chauncy Street
Boston, Massachusetts 02111

Library of Congress Cataloging-in-Publication Data

Gery, Gloria, 1944-
   Making CBT happen.

    Includes index.
    1. Employees, Training of—Computer-assisted
instruction. 2. Computer-assisted instruction.
I. Title.
HF5549.5.T7G42   1987   658.3'12404   86-51671
ISBN 0-9617968-0-4

Printed in the United States of America

Book design by John Goodwin

First Edition

Acknowledgements

I have always read the formal acknowledgements in books because of my fascination with both how a thing like writing a book gets done and the associated support processes and individuals. My knowledge is now personal rather than vicarious. So I want to publicly thank my supporters without whom this book could not have been written or published.

First and foremost, of course, is my husband, Bob. He pushed me over the edge to make the commitment. He suffered through my moments of doubt. And he ate lots of Chinese take-out while the writing and editing were in progress. Bob, I promise you home-cooked Chinese food in the future!

A strong second is my publisher and very dear personal friend, Nancy Weingarten. She dragged me to the edge of making the commitment to write. But more importantly, through her publications and conferences, she has provided me with a forum for communicating ideas and information. In fact, without the reasons of making presentations and writing articles for Nancy and her wonderful staff, most of the ideas put forward in this book would never have seen the light of day.

Close by Nancy is my editor, Floyd Kemske. His patience, support, critical review, and creative input have put flesh around the bones and the finishing touches on the manuscripts. With deepest thanks for that—plus patient instructions on the details of using my word processing software!

Another Weingarten Publications editor, who has helped me with my articles, suffered through late deadlines, and extended a sense of humor through our relationship, is Rebekah Wolman. Thanks, and may your new writing career be as fruitful as you've made mine!

The entire staff of Weingarten Publications have been good soldiers in the cause of producing this book, but I would like to commend the following for genuine heroism: John Goodwin, who created the design, Adrienne Ross, who ran the typesetting and pagination system, Melinda Roman, who managed the production process from typesetting through printing and binding, and Catherine Sununu, who devised and carried out marketing plans. Cathy, let's hope it works!

There are many others. I can't neglect the following key people: Tony DePaolis of CSR, who worked with me at Aetna Life & Casualty and beyond to develop my knowledge of CBT; Joe Campisi and Irv Sitkin at Aetna who gave me my "technical chance" and offered me the lifeline of a new career in data processing, CBT, and beyond; Mike Beer of Harvard Business School (and formerly Corning Glass Works) who imbued me with both personal confidence and a sense of professionalism and responsibility about developing ideas and communicating them in whatever field I was working in; Daryl Conner of O.D. Resources for the magnificent concepts on sponsorship and for educating me in consciously managing change; my peers in the industry, including Marsha Seidman of Crwth Computer Coursewares, George Owens and Harold Wolfe of Helios Custom Training, Pat Dillon and Jesse Heines, independent consultants, Wallace Judd of ComTrain, Chet Delaney of Chase Manhattan, Barbara Sealund of Sealund & Associates, Travis Piper of Creative Approaches—and many more. Thank you all for your ideas, critical review of my thinking, and generous professional support and friendship!

Of course, my many and wonderful clients have provided me with a forum and even paid me to develop my ideas. Particular thanks go to Bill Sebrell of the Hartford Insurance Group and Pat Meyer of Unisys.

And finally, but not least, thanks to my wonderful family for the love and support that gave me an accelerated kick start on life and the fuel of whatever talent, motivation, skills, and energy it took for me to get this far. Mom, I love you. Dad, I really miss you and wish you were still here to share this moment. I hope you're both very proud!

Gloria Gery
West Hartford, CT
January, 1987

Contents

Exhibits

Exhibits, Figures, and Charts

Introduction

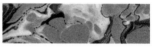

To those who say CBT is a dream,
we say, "thank you."

The capability to create practical interactive learning experiences has existed, in varying degrees, for over a decade. The idea to do such has been around much longer (remember B.F. Skinner and his teaching machines?). The need for interactive learning has *always* been present. And we've been able to meet it for given individuals but not for the masses—until now.

The forces of need, technology, and the market are all converging. A critical mass of installed systems, previous success, and skill is approaching. But the body of knowledge, to date, has been fragmented, inadequate, and generally inaccessible to those charged with meeting the increasingly diverse and complex training and learning needs in complex organizations.

But we are finally getting there. We have an installed base of computers and networks. Our present and future users and learners are becoming familiar with the technology and either have experience with computers or are expecting, if not looking forward to, it. The technological development environments are adequate. Of course, they never are completely "there," but we have adequate authoring systems, design tools, productivity software, and media that can be integrated (such as videodisc and audio technologies) enough to get started.

Many of us have been working to "get educated." Conferences, articles, user and professional groups, seminars, and evangelists abound. We are on the threshold. Commercial CBT and interactive video programs are just rolling off the production line. Publishers, trainers, line managers, and individual creators are experimenting with and producing programs that work. Critics have appeared. Some malign the present and offer no alternatives except the past. Some observe and critically evaluate the present and see a vision of what could be. Others disregard the present as initial and exploratory activity: R&D. They dream and try to describe the future.

I write this book with a foothold in the past based on many years of successful experience as a trainer and training manager. I have another foot in the future, encouraging clients and colleagues to minimize the limitations of current mind-sets and technology, to define what is possible, and to make a leap of imagination to what could—if not must—be done. Emotionally, I walk the fine line between exhilaration and terror. We tread in virgin territory. The terrain is complex and filled with unexplored and unknown dimensions: we are attempting to apply computer technology to one of the most complex and unfamiliar applications— human learning. Our current technological tools and conceptual frameworks are primitive in relation to what they will be. Our experience in using even the primitive tools is low. Many, if not all, of our current products are criticized as being inadequate to the task. Of course they are! Would you have decided to stop working with computer technology based on the very first transaction-automating programs?

Some would have. And where would the world of operations, communications, transportation, and information be today? Others dreamed—and toiled. And we are now at a very sophisticated level in applying the computer to manage our world. But the development of software to address the application of "human learning" is where traditional data processing applications were twenty-five years ago: at its beginning. Developing software to achieve learning has many parallels in applications software development. The parallels relate to the fact that CBT is essentially software development, and we should borrow from other software development fields to facilitate the process, conceive of technological possibilities, structure development tools, and generate design frameworks. The differences, on the other hand, lie in the complexity, non-linearity, and individual nature of the human learning process in relation to current data processing applications.

Some say we need artificial intelligence or expert systems technology before CBT can be created in a meaningful way. I say hogwash. We can do meaningful things now. Frankly, I believe our limitations are largely in our minds. Yes, of course, there are technological issues to deal with. But with CBT, as with other technologies, the technological solutions will be found. It's easier to do that than to change the frame of reference of an instructional developer from the present to some possible state.

There are "religious" beliefs about training that have institutionalized themselves in such disciplines as criterion-referenced instruction, among others. Instructional designs begin with statements such as "At the end of this lesson learners will be able to. . ." My experience is that "At the end of this lesson adult learners will have learned what they damn well choose to." And it is our job to provide those flexible learning experiences and, more importantly, to create the motivation to learn. Well, CBT has the potential to do more things in greater frequency and intensity than many traditional linear instructional strategies or logistically-bound media permit. We can compress time and conditions, we can simulate situations. Computer-based training can allow learners to manipulate variables in low risk situations and to control their learning experiences to meet their personal learning style and needs. And we can do these things—and more—in an affordable and timely way. I'm convinced.

Do I have all the answers and techniques? Of course not. If I did I'd be rich and at the beach rather than managing my cash flow and sitting at this computer! Do I have ideas that might help move us individually and collectively along the learning continuum? I hope so.

And so, I offer you my thoughts. Some have already been proven through a range of experiences and situations. The ideas on sponsorship and management (Chapter One) and how to develop CBT software (Chapter Five) fall into that category. Others are observations based on a blend of experience and ideas of how it should be. The comments on technology (Chapter Four) and author development (Chapter Eight) fall into that category.

And then there are the visions! I think they are possible. But I don't know for sure. I sometimes see flashes of genius in interactive learning design, but I don't see them translated into production. Some of my comments on interactivity (Chapter One) and software proficiency training (Chapter Eleven) fall into this "dreaming" category.

I have organized my thoughts in the form of answers to the questions I most often hear about CBT. It may surprise you to see these questions are exactly the ones you asked or are asking about the implementation of computer-based training in your own organization. It shouldn't surprise you, however. These are the same questions everybody has. We are all exploring this CBT territory together. We share common blank spots on our maps. Nor should you be surprised at the length and complexity of answers to apparently simple, nontechnical questions. When all is said and done, the technical questions are the ones that have short, simple answers. Nontechnical questions are another matter entirely, and long answers are necessary. I do hope you find the question-and-answer format helpful in the reading.

Regardless. . . I hope some of what you're about to read helps. That's what makes the effort in communicating worthwhile. And as you develop these and your own ideas further please let me know! I want to place an order for the book you're going to write to help the rest of us along.

CHAPTER **1**

Interactivity and Related Matters

We will be able to consistently
create give-and-take between
learner and computer when we
learn how to talk about the
process and measure it.

Just what is computer-based training?

You know, for years, that's been a difficult question to answer. And I'm not sure we're much closer to adequately and completely defining it today than we were during the 1970s when CBT was just becoming technologically feasible. As a matter of fact, the first articles about CBT that appeared in the literature focused primarily on definitions and distinctions among the various possible terms. My "Chinese menu" (See Exhibit 1.1) allows you to mix and match the possibilities to find something suitable to your mood and tastes.

In my view, the main reason CBT is so hard to define is that we haven't yet seen many of its possibilities beyond simple tutorial instructional programs. And tutorials take least advantage of the computer's unique and powerful capabilities to be applied to one of the most undefined and complex applications, human learning.

We need to have a common definition to proceed, however, so for our purposes, I'll be using "computer-based training" (or CBT) to mean

An interactive learning experience between a learner and a computer in which the computer provides the majority of the stimulus, the learner must respond, and the computer analyzes the response and provides feedback to the learner.

In the process, one of them learns something—we hope. Perhaps it will even be the learner!

This definition includes interactive video and other multimedia programs when they are computer-driven. Frankly, all kinds of visual and audio media can be configured effectively and coordinated through computer-based programs. Conceptually, however, we are talking about interactive (with a capital "I," if you will) programs with a computer at the central nervous system control level. You can translate the concepts and techniques in this book into any and all interactive learning technologies. I refer to this throughout as CBT. You can assume that the more media involved, the more complex the development and implementation situation, however.

Note that the definition specifies "interactive learning experience" and not "course" or "training program." We are not trying to create jargon here, just clarity. The words *course* and *training program* have particular implications:

• A whole body of knowledge, organized in a particular way

• A defined sequence of material with a beginning and an end

• Information presented in a lecture or video

• Specific learning objectives

- One path through the material, typically decided on by the instructional designer

- Tests for knowledge at the end

- Something you take all or none of, with very little provision for experiencing a part of it

- Typically, an event in which you learn *about* things that you really learn *how to do* in real-life situations, such as on the job.

In fact, when you add all of the components of a "course" together, they frequently don't fit well into the capabilities and limits of the computer (although *some* of them fit very well indeed). But some of the activities associated with human learning *do* match the computer medium perfectly. And so, I try not to limit my thinking with words like *course* that have such comprehensive implications. The term *interactive learning experience* includes what we traditionally think of as a whole training program, plus specific (possibly more limited) learning activities that better exploit the medium.

These interactive learning experiences can take different forms, many of which don't resemble a traditional course at all. They would include

- interactive practice exercises to incorporate a skill (such as practice problems with applications software, application of a formula or procedure to a given set of circumstances, and so on);

- interactive case studies simulating situations in which the learner applies previously acquired knowledge (e.g., management or sales situations);

Exhibit 1.1
PICK YOUR OWN TERMINOLOGY

A	B	C
Computer	Assisted Aided Managed Based Enhanced Mediated Interactive	Instruction Learning Education Training Teaching Development Study
Select one from each column		

7

- interactive role plays in which people can practice new behaviors, approaches, or techniques (e.g., personal development activities) without the risk of doing so in real life;

- interactive drills in which learners can improve mastery levels and move along the learning continuum from familiarization to automatic operation or fluency (e.g., applying formulas, identifying or solving problems, repetitions of procedures, troubleshooting situations);

- interactive tests in which learners can interactively assess their own progress to demonstrate competence or achieve confidence in their knowledge or skill; and

- many others yet to be discovered.

So, when should I use CBT?

I think the computer should be used in training only when it *adds value* to the training. There is still a world of possibilities for traditional media. If learners are motivated and able and willing to learn by reading, why add the complexity and restrictiveness of the computer to the process? Give them a book. If you just want learners to see something happen, show them a movie or give them a video tape.

But if there are things that they can't do with a book or a film (or a workbook, a mimeographed case study, a short discussion, or whatever), then consider the computer. If you want learners to do repetitive activities in real situations, CBT might be the best alternative. If practice problems in a video tape provide only linear visual sequences when, in fact, conditionally branched alternatives are more desirable, consider interactive video. If classroom instruction provides only limited workshop situations that result in limited skill acquisition through role-playing or practice problems, consider supplementing with interactive workshops or case studies via computer. When learners require self-directed tangible experiences that help them comprehend abstract concepts, consider inquiry-based activities or activities in which they can manipulate variables, administered by a computer.

My philosophy is one of minimalist training: do as little as possible in as simple a medium as possible to achieve the objectives.[1] The key is understanding both the learner and the trainer's objectives clearly. More often than not they are different—but the learner always wins. Adult learners learn only what they want, when they want. And it's time we as trainers stopped kidding ourselves into thinking that we can force people to be at a particular learning outcome following completion of a learning sequence. We'll discuss more about these philosophical issues later under design.

A "whole training program" is not always necessary to achieve your objectives. Let's look at some examples.

Sales Training. A national bank was experiencing difficulty in getting its personal bankers to sell any products other than its traditional first mortgages. It would be tempting to write off the problem to ignorance of the new products, but the bankers were scoring well on the product knowledge course tests. A secondary needs analysis, in fact, determined that the problem was not product knowledge—the target of all of the training programs—but the bankers' ability to identify "qualified" candidates for the complex products when faced with unfolding situations. The trainers had focused primarily on the cognitive components and not on the learning transfer components, which is where the payoff in the knowledge lay.

A defensive instructional developer argued that the product knowledge course contained paper-based case studies in which the bankers determined appropriate product "fit." The bankers argued that in real life they never saw an entire case on paper before they made their judgments. Their "cases" unfolded with dialogue from the clients, one sentence at a time. Bankers were, in fact, having to make judgments based on partial information. The instructional developer argued that it wasn't possible to achieve learning transfer with conventional classroom or self-paced media. Every learner would have to experience a carefully constructed and executed set of situations. This meant a great deal of role-playing: learners would have to experience the situations a sufficient number of times to internalize the application of the cognitive knowledge to particular cases. Otherwise, no instructional strategy could train the bankers to qualify customers. Every possibility seemed either too expensive (e.g., one-on-one situations, such as joint calls, with learners) or too cumbersome to create (e.g., branched case studies in programmed instructional mode).

During the secondary needs analysis the training department also learned that the bankers, even when faced with sales quotas for the new products, didn't sell them. When they were not confident in their ability to identify a prospect, they stuck with the tried-and-true products they were familiar with. They wanted to avoid inappropriate matches, embarrassment at lack of knowledge, conflict, and so forth. They maintained acceptable performance levels by overselling in the traditional product lines. Who could argue with them? Clever folks, we are.

Enter the computer and its possibilities. The bank continued to teach product knowledge through traditional means. The bankers were motivated and could and would learn from simply reading product announcements, marketing guidelines, and whatever they had always relied on. When the more comprehensive needs analysis was completed, the training solution was a bank of interactive role plays written in "play" form: giving scenario, characters, and dialogue. Following exposure to limited

Exhibit 1.2
AN INTERACTIVE TRAINING EXPERIENCE FOR BANKERS

Situation

Banker Jim Grover is conducting an exploratory interview with Bob and Kim Anderson to identify the best type of first mortgage product for them.

Their current financial situation is clear, but future income and liabilities are not.

Press Return

Dialogue

Jim: Things look good for the mortgage. Let's see which type best fits your situation.

Kim: We've been assuming a traditional 30-year, fixed payment mortgage. Why not?

What would you say next?

a. Well, our balloon payment program is a popular one with young professionals and I thought you'd prefer it.

b. O.K. Then 30-year, fixed payment is what we'll arrange.

c. Well, that may be best, but I'd like to be certain. So if you don't mind, I'll ask you a few questions so we can determine that based on information.

Select A, B, or C

Feedback

If A... Not a good response. While we want to sell more balloon payment mortgages, the fact that it's popular doesn't mean it's right for the Andersons. "C" was the best choice. Defaults are high when balloon mortages are sold incorrectly.

Get more information before you mention specific alternative products.

If B... You couldn't go wrong giving them what they asked for, but you might miss the opportunity to provide them with more flexibility with their cash now. Ask more questions before you concede. The Andersons probably need to be educated about options to conventional financing.

If C... Good choice. And a tactful way to handle their preference without offending. Remember, we want to sell more balloon payments without alienating customers. We also want to be sure it's the right type of mortgage for the customer. Defaults are high on balloon mortgages, and we have to assess future income and liabilities carefully before we recommend it.

CONTINUED

AN INTERACTIVE TRAINING EXPERIENCE FOR BANKERS (cont.)

Dialogue

Bob: O.K., but you should know we're not high flyers. Kim's MBA tuition has been high.

Jim: Don't I know. But will your financial situation be different in five or ten years?

Kim: It'd better be after all of this study! Plus, in five years, I get $100,000 from a trust established when I was a kid.

Press Return

Situation

Bob looks uncomfortable and frowns at Kim.

Dialogue

Jim: What's wrong, Bob?

Bob: That trust is irrelevant. We want the house now.

What would you say next?

a. Well, you certainly can have the house now, but the fact that you are certain to have a large income in five years gives you more options with payment schedules.

b. Kim, do you consider that trust income money that you would want to use toward the house, or do you expect to keep it separate from your joint finances?

c. You're right. That's Kim's money and she probably wouldn't want it to go toward the house.

Select A, B, or C

Feedback

If A... That may be true in some cases, but not all. Kim may not consider her trust money joint property. Don't assume it's available for the mortgage. But don't stop here. Ask Kim how she views that money. "B" was the best choice.

If B... Good choice. You didn't make assumptions and you didn't offend Kim. You have a good chance to find a better match.

If C... Not a good choice. You're making assumptions about how Kim views the money and you may be very wrong. Ask Kim directly. It wasn't Bob's decision to say that the trust money is irrelevant.

Situation

After some discussion, you determine that Kim prefers not to use the money toward the house. But you find that Bob's income is almost certain to increase dramatically after three years, due to exercise of stock options. The probing has led to far better information.

And you successfully educate Kim and Bob and reduce their anxiety about overextending themselves. Everybody wins in this situation.

Press Return

11

information, bankers were asked to judge how to proceed, just like in real life. (See Exhibit 1.2 for an example of the script). Essentially, the instructional strategy used was drill and practice. The learning objective was targeted: to develop skill in identifying candidates for the product. And the sequences were crafted by "subject matter experts" in the field application of the product. Once instructional templates were developed, experienced or skilled bankers wrote the scripts, which were edited and then incorporated into the interactive program by trainers. The trainers set up a structure for learning that couldn't have been achieved otherwise. There was value added because of the computer's unique ability to offer individualized learning materials an infinite number of times, with unending patience, in a cost-affordable manner. And the learners loved it. Most important, they finally started selling the new products because they were both competent and confident in their knowledge and skill.

Field Engineering Training. A major computer manufacturer's new and flexible customer-configured computer system presented serious field engineering (i.e., customer service) training problems. The new computer configurations were too expensive to install at centralized training centers or local branches in sufficient number; troubleshooting practice therefore wasn't available on any significant scale. Even if they could be installed, the various customer combinations of the central processor and peripherals made all the likely combinations impossible to represent. In addition, the actual diagnostic tests took significant time to execute in a "real" system, and even if the hardware were available, learners would be able to troubleshoot only one bug in any given course. Finally, each machine had to have bugs reinstalled following successful learner practice and thus required the presence of a training coordinator. All in all, not a desirable situation.

An additional complicating factor was the diversity of field engineers' knowledge and the amount of experience they had with various systems. Some learners required extensive practice; others would essentially be learning "differences" from other systems. A single learning path would over- or undertrain FEs, with all that implied in terms of increased costs.

The typical field engineering training program consisted of reading lots of manuals and then practicing on a live system. While referencing technical manuals might not be attractive to some of us, the engineers were used to it and didn't mind. Plus, one of the learning objectives was understanding of and skill in using the product documentation, since it would be their primary resource in the field. Nobody ever intended that lectures, videos, or any other instructional medium be used to repeat or lecture on the documentation content.

The company evaluated CBT. Initially, the training staff considered developing tutorials about the "content," which the learners had previously spent two and a half days reading. Even if this idea were instruc-

12

tionally desirable (which it wasn't), it was a herculean task and would not have been doable in the time allotted—thank goodness! Finally, the trainers decided to structure complementary interactive exercises that each learner could experience until self-evaluation demonstrated sufficient competence and confidence for the master case and competency certification.

The final program had four levels:

- Level I. Cognitive content about the product and related troubleshooting procedures with high course control (as opposed to learner control) and presentation of material with questions and guided practice activities.

- Level II. Guided practice activities with an available on-line coach for "hints," direction, and feedback—and more learner control.

- Level III. Simulations, practice problems, and exercises with little cognitive content but lots of learner experience in applying knowledge, however it was learned.

- Level IV. Mastery testing in installing, configuring, and repairing the system.

The overall training course still had heavy doses of reading and working with the system documentation, which were necessary. But due to the computer's ability to simulate and to compress time, it had many more practice problems, troubleshooting situations, and learner self-assessment labs than any traditional course could have had in the same period of time. Field engineering effectiveness improved dramatically because the learners had time to practice and increase skills during the learning process and not on the job at a customer site. This was a much more practical, affordable, and effective alternative than was either the previous situation or an entire course of computer-based training. And it was a powerful interactive learning experience.

Applications Software Training. An information center manager was faced with training and responding to large numbers of geographically dispersed users of an integrated personal computer package for spreadsheet, data base, and graphics. As use of the package spread, the users became increasingly diverse in knowledge, skill, motivation, and the level of learning needed. Some needed to learn the whole package; others needed to know limited functions. Workshops were inadequate for skill acquisition. Schedules were jammed. Timing of training was a problem: too little too late or too much too soon. Hot-line calls and individual consulting were killing her staff because people wanted to learn when they wanted to learn, not when it was expedient. Commercially available CBT tutorials could provide a "kick start," but lacked specific content relevant to her learners' needs. The information center manager knew she could not spend her own resources creating the complex software simulations and practice activities to address the needs. A hopeless situation? Should she update her resume?

Enter the possibility of creating on-line job aids, glossaries, and reference materials to permit "on-line coaches" to serve as a first-line defense for information needs. She purchased some commercial products and acquired a concurrent development tool to develop supplementary on-line materials for the applications. (See Chapter Eleven, "Software Proficiency Training," for further detail on concurrent development tools.) She created workshops: some would familiarize new users with the integrated software's capabilities, limits, and potential applications; others would introduce the on-line help workstation aids. Learning what they wanted when they wanted it because they needed it increased user skills at a reasonable cost. The information center staff was freed up for advanced consulting by power users and for working with users to identify applications with a high payoff. Another success story.

Would that I had a simple formula for deciding when to use the computer to provide training! It's not possible to make simple judgments when our experience in using this medium is just beginning. One good way to start evaluating whether the computer fits your training situation would be as follows: look at the computer's unique capabilities and limitations, look at interactivity and its various dimensions, and then look at your particular application. In the process you'll have to consider some learning and instructional design issues to put things into context. I will outline those issues for you in this book, although we won't be exploring them in depth.

Can you precisely define and describe interactivity in CBT? Everyone talks about it, but it's not at all clear.

Well, you've asked the $64,000 question! Interactivity is truly the heart of the CBT matter. It's what the computer permits that no other instructional approach can approximate except for a one-on-one Socratic dialogue between an expert and a learner. Interactivity eludes description, and many people have their own personal definitions of it. For our purposes, however, let's begin with some basics and proceed to the more intangible and complex.

The dictionary definition of an interaction is a "mutual or reciprocal action," that is, "to give and take mutually." It is directed by each toward the other. These abstractions might sound confusing, but I believe they address the essence of CBT. A CBT interaction is either a course-initiated or learner-initiated stimulus-and-response cycle with the added dimension of having either the learner or course *evaluate* the response and then take another action that requires some response.

14

In straightforward terms, interactivity is the incorporation of repetitive, frequent, and meaningful iterations of a stimulus-response-analysis-feedback cycle into material that is presented in a medium that permits it (see Figure 1.1). Essentially, creating an interactive learning experience is the process of structuring and sequencing variations of this cycle into a series that, when experienced by a learner, results in progress toward knowledge or skill acquisition. Typically, the more interactivity the better, particularly when the interactions are systematically chained together by either the learner or the course to move the learner along the knowledge continuum.

Figure 1.1
THE INTERACTIVITY CYCLE

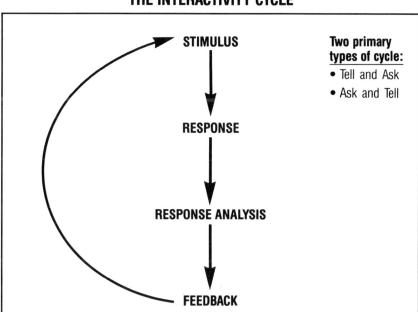

The definition gives us a lot of room to maneuver. Classroom training can be interactive or it can be passive. Computer-based training can be either as well. It's purely a function of the presenter's (or program developer's) style and the ability or willingness of the learner to demand it or respond to it. But let's examine the implications of the definition for CBT.

Program-Initiated Interactions. A stimulus is something that incites activity (or a response). The stimulus in a CBT program or course-initiated interaction can be a command to do something, a choice or decision to be made, or a question to be answered. For example, in a CBT tutorial on how to use software, examples of interactions are as follows.

15

Commands or Action Requirements

"Enter the appropriate command to. . ."
"Practice X procedure now."
"Press X keys."
"Complete the X screen."

Choices or Decisions

"Which of the following commands would do X?"
"Select which procedure you would like to learn next."
"What would you do next?"

Questions

"Type in the correct command to do X."
"Which of the following functions does X software perform. . .?"
"Is it True or False that you can window X when doing Y?"

Learner-Initiated Interactions. But the stimulus-response cycle works two ways. The learner can initiate an interaction, too. He or she can make an inquiry or command to get more information (e.g., hints, details, HELP, examples), proceed down another learning path (e.g., a menu choice, additional practice, problems), repeat a sequence, or review a previous page.

In most of today's CBT environments, learners "command" the courseware or make inquiries against it by using menus or by pressing specific keys to learner options, such as F1 for HELP, R for review, and ESC for escape. In the future, some courseware will allow learners to make inquiries or express their wishes through either natural language (e.g., "Tell me how to. . .") or specified commands (e.g., "Repeat Module X.") Then again, things move fast in CBT, and it's entirely possible that such courseware already exists in some form or other.

Imagine the varieties of learner-initiated interactions that could take place if courseware permitted:

Commands

"Tell me more."
"Repeat section X."
"Define X."
"Display the procedure for. . ."
"Display a bar chart illustrating these relationships."
"Show me a picture of. . ."
"Rotate this image."
"Give me more detail."
"Provide me with practice problems to improve my skill in X."
"Test my knowledge of or skill in X and prescribe a sequence of learning modules to address my needs."

16

Seek Advice or Query the Program
"Help me with this. . ."
·"What's the best way to. . .?"
"Give me a hint."
"How do I. . .?"
"How am I doing?" (with credit to Mayor Koch!)

Variable Manipulation
"Let's see what would happen if I selected X vs. Y"
"What if. . .?"
"Change this variable to X and that variable to Y and show me the consequences."

While my examples are in narrative form, many of these learner options are possible now. They can be built into CBT programs with frame-based systems even without natural-language inquiry by using "go-to lists," function keys, key presses tied to options like "Glossary," and so on. What limits current programs to offering the learner so few options is largely the logic and branching requirements of authoring languages or frame-based authoring systems. If it were easier to permit such options technically, the number and type of learner-initiated interactions would dramatically increase.

For example, imagine a glossary that could be accessed within a course when the learner simply typed a word or term. But, in fact, most technical environments for authoring will permit only an arrangement such as a menu from which the learner chooses "glossary," then a listing from which to select the word. Even when developers include such glossaries in courses, they are sometimes too time-consuming for the learner to access or the learner can't remember how to do it because the procedure is so complex.

An excellent example of learner-controlled instruction is that of providing learners with on-line natural language inquiry access to documentation when they are taking a program or using applications software. Chapter Eleven explains this concept in much more detail as it applies to applications software. When there are memory-resident terminals, sufficient storage, and tools to develop such on-line documentation, we will probably see this concept spread to areas like product knowledge, engineering, customer service, and troubleshooting training.

The Power of Learner Control. Learner-initiated interaction options are extremely powerful and desirable in adult learning situations, since learning is so needs-driven. The learner can initiate whatever he or she needs to advance rather than wait for things to come along in a course-controlled program. In addition, providing varied and easily-accessible learner options permits much more individualized learning while substantially reducing CBT development time. Programs with high

17

learner control also improve learner satisfaction by taking away the restrictions and cumbersomeness of much of today's CBT.

Interactivity levels. We characterize interactivity levels as low, medium, or high based on the nature and frequency of the Interactivity Cycle (Figure 1.1). The more frequent and demanding of the learner are the course-initiated interactions, the more they are likely to instill the training through a combination of repetition and thinking. Additionally, the more the learner can control the rate, sequence, repetition, approach to learning, practice exercises or problems, and access to hints and help

Chart 1.1
INTERACTIVITY DIMENSIONS

NATURE OF THE INTERACTIONS
Questions
Choices or Decision Points

COMPLEXITY
Number of fixed vs. open-ended options for the learner
Inherent complexity of the stimulus/response required
Whether learners must "think" or simply react to stimulus

RESPONSE ANALYSIS
Anticipated responses programmed
Unanticipated responses programmed
Tolerance for variable input (in relation to anticipated/unanticipated responses)

FEEDBACK
Nature (e.g., a consequence vs. a comment)
Depth
Number of conditional responses

BRANCHING
Amount
Conditional vs. non-conditional

LEARNER CONTROL
Amount
Nature
• Learner mobility through and around the course
• Options
• Inquiry
• Pathing

to accommodate personal learning style and needs, the more likely the learner is to like the experience and to integrate the material. In my experience, the fact that learners enjoy the learning experience is not necessary to their learning the material, but it certainly helps. And when they enjoy it, they are less likely to resist it.

The Interactivity Continuum. Exhibit 1.3 depicts the relationship of learner control and course control and its effect on interactivity. The degree to which the CBT program or the learner controls the learning experience is a result of the program's design. And the control dimension of program design must consider several things including the following.

- Nature of the material

- Learner knowledge and confidence levels

- Learner preferences

- Instructional strategies employed

- Programming or authoring complexity

How would you measure interactivity?

A good question with a complex answer! I'm sure more will emerge as we collectively gain experience with interactive design, but for the time being, I have identified twelve interrelated variables in eight categories. Let's look at them in detail.

1. Nature and Frequency of the Interactions. Essentially, we are looking here at the categories of interactions described in the beginning of this chapter. Is the interaction a course-controlled command to do something, question to respond to, decision or choice to make, or is it a learner-controlled inquiry or direction to the CBT program (e.g., request for a hint)?

The sheer number of these types of interactions contributes overall to the course interactivity level and resultant learning. Appropriateness is as important as frequency, however. The more appropriate these are to the content and the desired learner outcomes, the better. For example:

- True-false questions about the correctness of a specific software command might add something to a learner's knowledge about using specific software. They are not, however, as powerful in promoting skill acquisition as is requiring the learner to input (or recall) the command, with HELP an available learner option.

- Multiple-choice questions asking *why* the learner made the choice more effectively assess analytical capabilities than does asking a "what" question.

19

Exhibit 1.3
LEARNER CONTROL AND PROGRAM CONTROL

CBT Program Control

High levels of CBT program control are recommended when

- Learners have little or no knowledge of the subject matter content
- Learners have low motivation to learn the content or acquire the skill and see little relevance to or anticipated use of the material
- Learners are inexperienced in learning this specific content or type of subject matter or skill
- Learners are used to highly structured and directed learning experiences
- Learners have little experience in independent learning
- Learners don't know what they need or want to know about this content
- Learners have low confidence in themselves or their ability to learn this (or any) material relatively easily
- Learners have little or no experience with CBT programs, particularly with learner-controlled programs
- Learners are used to or prefer being told what to do
- Progressing through program content and structure is dependent on having learned or experienced material presented in a specific sequence
- There are limited or no competency tests or pre-tests available for learners to assess their existing knowledge level before making decisions about what content or sequence to choose
- Requirements exist to be certain that learners have experienced specific material (e.g., safety certification)

Learner Control

High degree of learner control is recommended when

- Learners know what they want or need to learn
- Learners are motivated to learn and see personal relevance to learning the material or acquiring the skill
- Learners have experience in learning this or similar material or in acquiring similar skills and know how they best learn it
- Learners have experience and comfort with self-directed learning
- Learners resist structure and have a high preference for individual freedom
- Learners have high confidence in their ability to learn
- Learners are experienced with CBT and have become comfortable with learner mobility options
- The program content is not necessarily linear and the learning sequence is not critical

CONTINUED

LEARNER CONTROL AND PROGRAM CONTROL (cont.)

- Learners can assess existing knowledge or mastery through competency or knowledge tests within or related to the program so they are capable of selecting learning paths
- Post-training knowledge or competency is all that matters, there is no requirement that learners must be certified or validated in having seen certain content
- Learning the content is largely discretionary rather than required

- Learners tend to achieve well when asked to perform a procedure, with access to interactive on-line job aids such as a glossary, procedural HELP, and error message definitions. It is much less efficient to demonstrate procedures with screen displays overlaid with narrative descriptions in windows followed by an occasional cognitive question.

Insufficient interaction is the basis of major complaints by users and evaluators of CBT courseware. Furthermore, those interactions that are included are usually assessed as trivial or of little worth. Typically, such interactions don't demand enough of the learner (i.e., they are not sufficiently complex) or are inappropriate to achievement of the learning goal. For example, multiple-choice interactions don't assess recall, only recognition or chance selection.

2. Placement and Repetition of Interactions. Users react to how appropriate the placement of interactions is in relation to material presented. Frequently questions are asked immediately following exposition of material and assess only short-term memory. Or they are not repeated later.

3. Interrelationships of the Interactions. Much of the material we must teach is complex, and the elements are interrelated. Much of the CBT currently available includes interactions that relate to single modules, but the interactions rarely build and interrelate in complex sequences. Of course, complex interactions demanding integration by the learner are difficult to develop, but the learner still needs them.

4. Complexity of the Interactions. Complexity of an interaction relates to the number of its "parts" and the degree of difficulty associated with analyzing the components in relation to the task. For example, selecting among four closely related alternatives is more difficult than choosing between two very different alternatives. The sheer number of variables in an option make it more or less difficult. Clearly, it is more difficult for a learner to recall and order a sequence of activities than to order activities that are presented. The former task is more difficult because it requires a greater depth of knowledge about several elements (i.e., both the tasks *and* their correct sequence).

Complexity of the interactions is a function of the following.

- The number of options presented to a learner

- Whether the options are fixed or open-ended

- The inherent difficulty of making the required or desired response

- The number of variables that must be considered in order to make the response (i.e., how many and what things the learner must think about)

- The nature of the cognitive processes required to respond (e.g., recognition versus recall versus analysis versus synthesis).

5. Response Analysis. Response analysis is the process by which the CBT software accepts and evaluates whatever the learner inputs either in response to a course-generated interaction or a learner-generated request, inquiry, or command. Essentially, response analysis describes the programmed process by which the software compares the learner input or request against a set of programmed possibilities, "judges" them as acceptable or unacceptable in relation to the requirements of the interaction (i.e., are they right or wrong?), and then feeds back a programmed response to the learner.

The learner judges the program as more or less interactive based on the program's tolerance of variable input (e.g., different spellings, close answers) and on how the program handles anticipated and unanticipated unacceptable responses. Naturally, this variability of response analysis is closely tied to the nature and depth of the feedback provided. For the most part, the more possibilities the CBT accepts and appropriately handles, combined with the relevance and complexity of the feedback to the learner, the more interactive the program appears to be.

Courseware that accepts only a single alternative in a form prescribed by the developer and then simply beeps or says "try again" as feedback is seen as less rich than CBT that accepts alternatives and gives appropriate feedback. I experienced a software tutorial that accepted only one way of executing an activity during a simulation. As an experienced user of such software, I had put in a different, but entirely correct, command. The course told me I was wrong. The experience had a significant effect on my judgment of the course.

A simpler but equally illustrative example is how a program handles learner responses to a question. A goodly number of learners will respond "yes" or "no" when asked if a statement is true or false. If the program accommodates those answers, learner satisfaction is increased.

In looking at such elements, we are not talking technically about interactivity; rather, we are discussing how learners perceive interactivity.

But I assure you, these considerations are no less important when learners make their judgments. After "boring," the second most frequent complaint about CBT courseware is that going through it is "frustrating." Typically learners are referring to the rigidity of responses required or lack of flexibility to move around the program.

When we examine response analysis in relation to learner inquiry, we are looking at similar but slightly different components. Essentially, the greater the flexibility the learner has for alternative ways of requesting specific options from the CBT, the more satisfying the experience. For example, the more easily learners can return to menu options or page back, the more powerful the program. Of course, there's a point of diminishing returns after which the sheer number of options is overwhelming. But there's an optimum number of alternatives that has yet to be established, somewhere between one and ten. Experimentation and evaluation of learner reactions will tell us more.

6. Feedback. Feedback is the evaluative or corrective information about an action, choice, or inquiry that the learner has made within the program. Feedback can be generated for actions in response to a course requirement or to a learner inquiry.

The critical dimensions associated with feedback include the following.

- The nature of the feedback (e.g., a judgment, comment, further direction, hint, command to further action such as "try again," a consequence such as what would actually happen in a piece or software or role-playing, or a branch to another or previously completed sequence)

- The depth of the feedback (e.g., amount of new or previously covered information, related material, reasons for the judgment about the learner's response)

- The number of conditional responses to various learner inputs (i.e., do all unacceptable responses get the same feedback or is each feedback display contingent on exactly what the learner input?)

- The quality of the feedback (e.g., a beep to indicate an unacceptable response versus a word versus presentation of acceptable alternatives versus a hint)

When appropriately structured, feedback provides evaluative information to the learner about progress and competency levels and as a result increases confidence and decreases anxiety levels. It provides reinforcement of content, which results in further internalization of the material. It can provide additional related information. And it can significantly increase understanding of consequences of actions when appropriate to the material.

7. Learner Control. We've looked at the issue of learner control levels and alternatives in several ways already. In summary, there are several dimensions of learner control that contribute to interactivity, including:

- The nature of learner control and the degree and ease of learner mobility through and around the CBT program

- The number and depth and flexible access to options such as "Review," "Escape," "Skip," "More Detail," "Examples," "Glossary," "Procedures," "On-line Documentation," "HELP," "Hint"

- The number of and flexibility of access to alternative learning paths at menu choice points or within learning sequences

- The nature and amount of "inquiry" by the learner into the program.

Again, the proper balance of program control versus learner control in relation to the learner population can have a considerable impact on learner satisfaction with interactivity levels and on the learning outcomes themselves.

Figure 1.2
INTERACTIVE LEARNING EXPERIENCE
LINEAR STRUCTURE

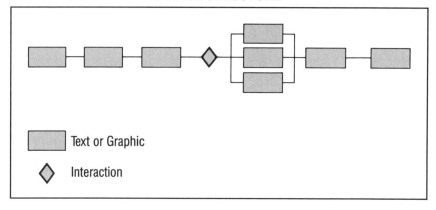

Text or Graphic

Interaction

8. Branching. The conditional branching capability of the computer is one of the most important components of interactivity. By conditional branching, I mean the presentation of various feedback or learning paths that are specifically related to the learner's input. Let's look at the two major ways conditional branching is used within CBT programs: conditional feedback and conditional pathing.

Conditional feedback is the most basic use of the computer's power to be dynamic. Essentially, the CBT program evaluates learner response and then branches to specific feedback that relates to that response using basic conditional if-then-else logic. The specific feedback then is displayed on the screen. Figure 1.2 is a flow chart representing such a linear learning path with conditional feedback.

The process of developing conditional feedback can be very simple or quite complex, depending on the nature of the interaction and the desired feedback. Essentially, what complicates development is the number of variables involved in various alternatives.

This is where we get into "richness." At the very least, conditional feedback incorporates a judgment (i.e., yes/no, correct/incorrect, good/better/best) and possibly a restatement of the content or additional information.

Sometimes, in an effort to save development, scripting, and programming time, courseware developers try to create "cheap" interactions by using the same feedback to all acceptable and unacceptable responses without incorporating judgment of them. To put it mildly, learners hate this. For a number of reasons they want to know whether they were correct or not. At times the feedback is a consequence to an action (e.g., the next screen appears in a software simulation when the learner inputs the correct command). In these cases, learners like to have a judgment displayed and some narrative description of what happened when they first performed the activity. After several repetitions, however, the feedback is inherent in the software's execution; that is, people see the system screens progress and know that they did the correct thing. Learners then become intolerant of the judgment and just want the simulation to proceed.

In my experience, most existing CBT courseware is linear, and any branching is limited to conditional feedback. This is due to author inexperience, the complexity of developing conditional learning paths other than options through menu choices, or limits in available development time and budget.

On the other hand, CBT that incorporates conditional learning paths includes alternative paths of progression based on one or more of the following dimensions of learner performance:

- Learner selection of a path through menu options

- Learner performance on a given interaction or combination of multiple interactions or test items

- Learning rate as indicated by actual time between presentation of an interaction and the learner's response

- Conditions defined in a pre-course on-line questionnaire (e.g., learner title, job grade, expressed learning objective) or scored pre-test evaluating knowledge level, skill, or fluency.

Conditional branching points can be determined before the learner

25

begins the course, at selected points within the program, or throughout the program based on either course- or learner-controlled options. Figure 1.3 flowcharts a general conditionally branched program.

Essentially, a decision tree is created in a conditionally branched program. These trees can be very simple or enormously complex to script and then program. The ability to conditionally branch a learner's progress based on knowledge, preference, performance, or given conditions is the very promise of CBT. But it is rarely realized because it is so difficult to do with a frame-based authoring system or a programming language, and there's always too little time to do it. It isn't so much complex as it is time consuming to define and label all the alternative paths

Figure 1.3
INTERACTIVE LEARNING EXPERIENCE
CONDITIONALLY BRANCHED STRUCTURE

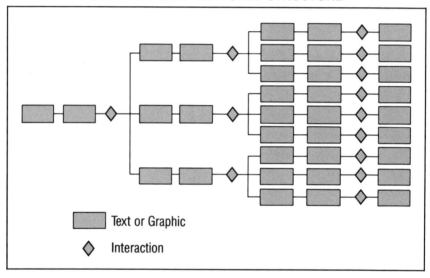

☐ Text or Graphic

◇ Interaction

and then to program them. From a learner perspective, an intermediate level of multiple pathing is desirable. Too many paths result in learners getting "lost" in the course and having difficulty maneuvering their way through and out of the program. In addition, they aren't confident that they have covered all the material.

There is another, dramatically different, model that relates to learning path branching. Understanding it will require you to shift your frame of reference. You must let go of predefined sequencing, flowcharting, and so forth to appreciate it. I'm referring to a learning data base model (see Figure 1.4) in which learners access various learning elements that they want or need while they are solving specific problems, performing case studies or role-playing, using a piece of software, or whatever the program is trying to teach them to do.

Let's explore an analogy from data processing to make understanding a little easier. Historically, early data processing systems were designed and programmed to address a given application, task, or problem. Specific sequences of activities, events, and conditions were defined and programmed to result in a desired outcome. Typically these early systems were transaction-oriented. They processed payrolls, paid claims, issued checks, or counted inventory. They were not flexible in design. Any conditions or needs not accounted for in the original system either couldn't be met or the system had to be enhanced by professional systems staff to include them. Their structure was essentially linear and the capability was defined by the initial customer or, in the absence of user involvement, by the system developer. Over the years, this has resulted in efficient application programs that perform specific activities. But it has been accompanied by enormous expense and time required to address changing needs and diverse user priorities as well as user dependency on MIS. Maintenance consumes up to eighty percent of many MIS/DP budgets, and new development is on the back burner. Many users aren't even in the development queue. As a result, many DP departments and staff suffer from credibility problems and are not seen as adding required value to the business.

Along came data base technology and concepts. Essentially, data base design permitted the definition of a commonly defined and agreed-on set of data items that could be accessed by multiple diverse users with varying objectives and needs. They use various tools such as report generators, graphics software, and so forth.

The data conforming to the definitions is collected and maintained, and it is fed into or fed by various transaction systems. It can be inquired against and manipulated at will by authorized users. And it permits timely, flexible applications development by individuals or user departments.

It's possible to conceive of and develop a learning data base that would operate similarly. Learners with varying learning needs, styles, priorities, and time frames could configure their own preferred learning sequence by inquiring against the learning data base, once they understand how to access and manipulate it. For example, learners who want to be told *about* something before they answer questions could select a tutorial before answering questions. Learners who prefer to test their knowledge level before going through a tutorial could choose a competency test first. Within a more structured linear interactive tutorial, other learners could request additional practice problems or review procedures before performing required activities. Learners with a low tolerance for structure could use purely exploratory techniques and wander through the data base at will. Much like in its data processing system analog, once the learning data base is established, course developers and learners could create specific applications or paths much more quickly.

The data base learning model has several limitations. Some are developmental. Developing such a model is currently limited by developer frames of reference, authoring system limitations, and learner expectations.

Most instructional designers have a frame of reference based on course control as the optimal structure, and their criterion-referenced or learning objective-related instructional development process requires specified learning outcomes to be defined by the developer for achievement by the learner. For example, most instructional developers set objectives for each lesson or course and then develop content to achieve them. That's fine as far as it goes, but it presumes a homogeneous learning population with homogeneous learning objectives—a rare situation indeed. The concept of having the learner define his or her objectives— which, I submit, each does anyway—and then permitting the learner to configure his or her own learning experience, is foreign to most corporate trainers and managers. Actually, they consider the concept more than foreign: it's a mortal sin.

Second, authoring systems are frame-based and are not designed to

Figure 1.4
LEARNING DATA BASE MODEL
(FOR INTERACTIVE LEARNING EXPERIENCE)

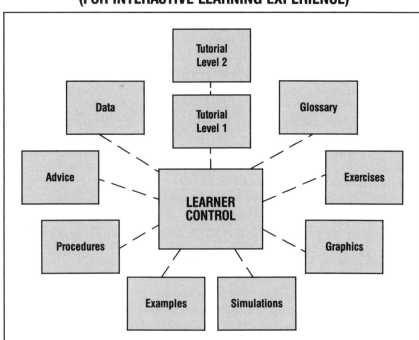

Learner or Course Controlled Through Inquiry or Sequencing

permit such learner flexibility other than through limited choices at given points through menu options, hints, review options, and skip options. No currently available authoring system permits the development of a relational learning data base with flexible inquiry or configuration capability. In order to incorporate some of the above concepts into a CBT program using most currently available frame-based authoring systems, developers must do an "end run" around the system. Or they must program or include enormous amounts of conditional branching options from many more screens and lesson segments. This, of course, dramatically increases development time and cost. And those are already at marginally tolerable levels.

Finally, most learners have particular expectations. School and previous training programs have taught them how to learn things through a combination of tutorial and drill and practice. For the most part their learning experiences have been passive: information has been presented in a linear sequence by either an instructor, video presentation, or book. Following the linear presentation, learners review the material repeatedly until they are either confident in their knowledge or their time runs out and they have to take the test. Then they are tested with a series of questions or presented with an activity to carry out. Following the test, they are graded or given a score. Remediation in the form of alternative presentations may or may not occur. For the most part, learner-directed review and repetition of previously presented material is the primary alternative available.

When learners take tests, they presume that the material will have been formally presented before they are tested on it. They view it as "unfair" for a teacher to ask a question that wasn't covered in class, even if it was in assigned readings. When teachers ask learners to synthesize material to form new patterns or to extrapolate on their own, learners react negatively. It's not until graduate school or advanced college seminars that learner-controlled study with little or no formal presentation occurs. Even then, this type of learning experience is only effective for (or appealing to!) mature and sophisticated learners who have specific learning objectives in mind.

Some schools or teachers teach exclusively through case study or exploratory learning. It's a much tougher model to develop and execute. But it produces some of the most powerful learning experiences available, because "real-world simulation" is the basis for the learning experiences.

Simulation, case study, or primarily exploratory learning strategies are frustrating to the learner with limited ability or motivation, or to those who are unclear about their learning objectives or inexperienced in self-directed learning. These kinds of learners are frustrated by the lack of structure and seek refuge from the ambiguity.

Even when given such limited options as selecting the learning sequence, they seek structure, whether they are in a traditional environment or using self-paced CBT. "Tell me what to do and in what order," they plead. If you simply present them with a learning data base, show them how to use it, and say "go and learn what you want," it will drive them to distraction. Most learners are so conditioned by their previous learning experience that you initially have very little success using any kind of strategy based on the learning data base, even one that incorporates a certain amount of structure. For example, you could give the learners an activity such as completing a troubleshooting exercise, analyzing a sales situation, or solving a business problem and then show them how they can inquire against the learning data base for the necessary information. But even this compromise is too much for all but the most motivated or intuitive learners.

But there is a place for this model of the learning data base. It is very powerful as a follow-on to traditional instructional sequences of "tell and ask." It can be effectively incorporated at advanced knowledge levels or with learners who have very specific and conscious learning objectives, as do advanced software users. Or it can be used in conjunction with learning transfer activities such as practicing software use, product knowledge training, and so forth, when learners might wish to inquire or request specific information that they are aware of but have not yet internalized. There is an example of this concept in the use of concurrently executing interactive job aids in conjunction with the use of applications software, either a learning version or live production version.

Blends of Conditional Branching Structures. In fact, most courses probably do or should incorporate a blend of all three branching approaches: conditional feedback, conditional branching, and the learner-controlled data base. In fact, even in linear CBT there is usually some learner-controlled access to a limited "data base" of hints. The design and programming challenge is to achieve the appropriate balance of structure and freedom to permit configuring the optimal learning experience within required time frames and budgets. My observation, however, is that we over-structure the learning and limit learners far too much. A shift of several degrees toward more freedom seems in order for most of our adult learners!

The definitions and dimensions of interactivity seem so straightforward. Why is there so much difficulty in designing effective, highly interactive instruction?

Well, I wish it were easy to translate abstractions into operational programs. It's not, however. Frankly, there's been very little articulate discussion of interactivity at all. So we haven't been aware of which variables to incorporate into program design in order to create interactive

Exhibit 1.4 Table A

LEVELS OF INTERACTIVITY
FOR CASE STUDY PRESENTATION STRATEGY

LEVEL	LEARNING OUTCOME	TECHNIQUE
Level I	• Awareness • Familiarization • Recognition	**VIGNETTE** Single-screen narrative vignette with 2–4 variables described. **Learner Options:** Select among 2–3 alternatives (i.e., True/False, Yes/No, identify). **Feedback:** Response evaluated (i.e., right or wrong) with informative feedback.
Level II	• Understanding • Knowledge • Discernment, distinction, discrimination among alternatives	**SCENARIO** 1– or 2–screen scenarios with 6–8 variables described. **Learner Options:** Select among 3–5 alternatives. **Feedback:** Response evaluated (i.e., right/wrong, good/better/best) with informative feedback.
Level III	• Experience, skill in application/use	**UNBRANCHED BASE STUDY** 4– to 10–screen case study with 10–16 variables. **Learner Options:** Four or more opportunities for selection among 2–5 alternatives. **Feedback:** Response evaluated (i.e., right/wrong, good/better/best) with informative feedback. Program progresses linearly as structured by developer. "Scored" scenario with point values associated with learner options.
Level IV	• Integration/synthesis of knowledge • Advanced experience in application of content to complex situations	**BRANCHED CASE STUDY** 4– to 10–plus screen case study including 10–25 variables. **Learner Options:** Six or more opportunities to select among 2–5 alternatives. **Feedback:** No evaluative response at learner choice points. Consequences of each learner choice influence the variables/dialogue/outcome/options in subsequent case/content/choices. "Real world" consequences of chosen actions are simulated. Summary feedback is given at conclusion.

learning experiences. But we're making progress. To date, a number of issues have limited our creativity in interactive design:

Lack of Models. Creating models and structures for interactive instruction takes experimentation by creative individuals. It also requires time. Let's face it: very little time has passed since the forces have converged to make possible interactive instructional development in normal business environments. And to date, only a few people have been given the time, money, and freedom to experiment with design. There-

Exhibit 1.4 Table B

LEVELS OF INTERACTIVITY
FOR INTERACTIVE PRESENTATIONAL STRATEGIES

LEVEL	LEARNING OUTCOME	TECHNIQUE
Level I	• Awareness • Familiarization • Recognition	**BASIC PRESENTATION** 1– or 2–screen narrative or graphic/text presentations with 2–4 ideas, facts, or units of information to provoke learner interest or awareness of the importance of a topic. **Learner Options:** Select among 2–3 alternatives (i.e., True/False, Yes/No, identify). **Feedback:** Response evaluated (i.e., right or wrong) with informative feedback, plus the information that the question introduced. OR Consequences of choices or inputs are presented or displayed, depending on nature of stimulus (e.g., a question selection vs. "do something" with a graphic display).
Level II	• Understanding • Knowledge • Discernment, distinction, discrimination among alternatives	**INTERMEDIATE PRESENTATION** Multi-screen narrative presentation/description or graphic/text presentation of 3–5 ideas, facts, or units of information. **Learner Options:** Select among 3–5 alternatives or respond to an open-ended stimulus (e.g., "fill-in-the-blank" or completion question) or a "generative" response (e.g., identify or name) without alternatives from which to select. **Note:** Complex open-ended or learner-constructed responses with two or more variables/word inputs or a large number of potentially acceptable responses moves this to a Level III presentation. **Feedback:** Response evaluated (i.e., right/wrong) with informative feedback plus additional information or restatement of previously displayed information. OR Consequence of choice/input displayed narratively or graphically, depending on nature of stimulus (i.e., a question or selection vs. "do something" with a graphic display) to the learner. The sequence is not conditionally branched.
Level III	• Understanding • Knowledge • Discernment/discrimination among complex or closely related alternatives • Application/use	**IN-DEPTH PRESENTATION** All of the above applied to more complex situations, a larger number and broader range of alternatives that are more closely related to each other and harder to distinguish. **Learner Options:** Constructed responses require a deeper knowledge of the material—i.e., they usually require analysis, synthesis of ideas, judgments or decisions about more complex ideas or concepts (i.e., responses require more than naming something). Learners could also choose among closely related alternatives.

32

CONTINUED

LEVELS OF INTERACTIVITY
FOR INTERACTIVE PRESENTATIONAL STRATEGIES (cont.)

LEVEL	LEARNING OUTCOME	TECHNIQUE
Level III		**Feedback:** Evaluative (i.e., right or wrong, good/better/best) plus informative feedback to reinforce previously displayed information plus expanded presentation of related knowledge (i.e., going beyond previously displayed information). OR Consequences of choice or input displayed (narratively or graphically, depending on nature of stimulus). Learner could be conditionally branched to further consequences and choice points (repetitively). **Note:** Any number of branched alternatives moves this structure up to a Level IV. This begins to approximate a "real world" simulation.
Level IV	• Analysis/synthesis • Advanced application	EXPLORATORY PRESENTATION OR GRAPHIC SIMULATION All of the above (Levels I–III). Situations and ideas are more complex or abstract and require greater depth of knowledge from learner. Alternatives are more closely related; situations are more complex; situations are less obvious or clear. **Learner Options:** Simulations are of graphic models or realistic situations and problems. Learners must complete or generate more complex processes, configurations, or procedures. **Feedback:** Situations and models have a higher number of branched responses in which consequences to actions are displayed and learner must then choose among alternatives that are a result of previous choices. More "discovery" or exploratory learning is incorporated with the learner directing the learning path or "inquiring" against "data bases." A major strategy is learner-controlled "browsing" through information based on interest or need.

fore, there are few available models to serve as interactive structures to emulate or to build upon. When new developers review commercial products or attend authoring system user group meetings to get ideas, there are few interactive models for them to see.

What's needed are models, including descriptions and representations of the logic involved. Such a compendium would make a best-selling book in the CBT world. In the meantime, developers must communicate with each other through user groups, review commercial courseware, clearly document their own ideas, and work actively to generate new structure. These models will come, in time. Until then, let's continue with systematic trial and error in our design process. And let's communicate!

Mind-Set Based on Past Media Limitations. All new technologies

Exhibit 1.4 Table C

LEVELS OF INTERACTIVITY
FOR APPLICATIONS SOFTWARE SIMULATIONS

LEVEL	LEARNING OUTCOME	TECHNIQUE
Level I	• Awareness • Familiarization • Information processes	**NONPARTICIPATIVE DEMONSTRATION** Partial or full application screen display. Narrative description (in window) of formats, function, input requirements/options, fields, data elements, etc. **Learner Options:** No actual learner input to simulated screens. Simulations, changes, and results are "performed" by the course, demo, or interactive job aid. Interactions are questions or judgments learners must make about the software function, input, or information (e.g., Yes/No, True/False, Either/Or, Select one). Open-ended or fill-in response options push this to Level II. **Feedback:** Response evaluated (i.e., right or wrong) with reinforcing information.
Level II	• Knowledge • Understanding of function, uses, limits • Limited experience or skill in using the knowledge within the software	**INTERACTIVE WALKTHROUGH** Narrative description or instructions to learner (e.g., "now do this," generate a command) appear in a window overlapping a partial or full application screen display. **Learner Options:** Largely learner "performance" or execution of described actions in the simulation under close "guidance" or control by the course. Narratives with questions about the software or appropriate user responses can be included. **Practice Exercises:** Multiple choice: "what should you enter in this field?" (pick one) with courseware giving feedback (right/wrong, appropriate/inappropriate, what error message would result). **Feedback:** Response evaluated (i.e., right/wrong). If response is wrong, feedback gives another try or hint, then gives correct response and reinforcing or additional information.
Level III	• Understanding of software functions • Features • Capabilities and limits • Relative complexity of performance • Intermediate and high skill levels in operating the software • Structuring applications • Generating reports	**GUIDED SIMULATION** Differences from Level II relate to: • degree of complexity, number of variables, degree of learner autonomy from course guidance • number and complexity of practice problems • number of "open-ended" responses required of learner (e.g., "what would you do next?" or "enter the command to do X") vs. "which of these options would result in X?" **Practice Exercises:** Adequate in number, scope, and complexity to develop skills; usually "open-ended" or task-oriented. Student actually types content of field within the simulation to get response showing misspelling, inappropriateness, probable error messages, etc. **Feedback:** Response evaluated (e.g., Right/wrong). If response is wrong, feedback gives another try or hint, then gives correct response and reinforcing or additional information.

34

CONTINUED

LEVELS OF INTERACTIVITY
FOR APPLICATIONS SOFTWARE SIMULATIONS (cont.)

LEVEL	LEARNING OUTCOME	TECHNIQUE
Level IV	All of the above, plus "automatic operation" (i.e., high skill) while using actual software. • Synthesis of knowledge/understanding/skill	CONCURRENTLY EXECUTING LEARNING PROGRAMS IN CONJUNCTION WITH "LIVE" SOFTWARE All of the above plus operating within the actual applications software simultaneously with limited, if any, course guidance. Software "performs" and gives error messages as it normally would. Learner can access HELP, glossary, procedures, and on-line documentation at will. **Note:** Depth of knowledge and skill achieved are a function of numbers, complexity, and relevance of practice problems, depth of feedback, and learner need or motivation to learn some or all of the software. **Practice Exercises:** Actual use of the software, typically with off-line exercises, using test system and learning data base. Concurrence of software and learning material to develop high skill level; usually synthesis-oriented. **Feedback:** Response evaluated (e.g., Right/Wrong). If response is wrong, feedback gives another try or hint, then gives correct response and reinforcing or additional information.

go through various stages of application. The initial stage inevitably is "automating the past." Essentially, this means that the mind-sets of the early adopters are based on their experience with and knowledge of past technologies and processes. Early television simply replicated previously successful radio formats, with images attached. Remember the early newscasts? They were essentially the same as radio newscasts, but with a picture image that went with the voice. Compare them to today's newscasts, which are filled with graphic representations, "windows" with multiple images, and dynamic movement between full motion images.

The same thing happened in data processing, where initial applications mimicked paper-based processes. Early systems analysts essentially tracked the manual methods and automated them. Sophistication in both thought processes and technologies, plus critical examination about whether the "old way" was the best way, changed the frame of reference or mind-set of developers to such approaches as data base and expert systems. Of course, some of the limits were technological, but more were psychological (i.e., how developers viewed the technological environment).

Pioneers of CBT are in the same situation as the pioneers of business data processing. They are essentially automating previous linear approaches to instruction using the classroom tutorial or programmed instruction model with limited conditional feedback. For the most part, we haven't begun to exploit the computer's unique capabilities for conditional branching, data storage, and variable manipulation. I personally have seen only one program that teaches entirely through simulation and permits the learner to make quantitative decisions while the CBT program stores the data and lets the learner then use it in a spreadsheet or graphics package for further, and more sophisticated analysis.

Why not more *real* use of the computer's capabilities? Yes, there are some technological limits, such as authoring system structures (which, in turn, are based on developers' limited frames of reference and historical teaching or learning models!) and computer memory constraints. But the most critical limit is the one most difficult to break: limited and confined thought processes, outlooks, and imagination of the new developers. We must make a giant leap of imagination and redefine what's possible now that we have powerful and radically different tools.

There's another mind-set limitation discussed earlier: the mind-set of learners who have learned in environments characterized by linear instructional strategies based on the "tell-and-ask" model. These learners become anxious and frustrated with nonlinear learning models. As they gain experience with them, comfort levels will increase. There is a "chicken and egg" trap here. Which comes first, learner comfort or developer creativity? Time will tell, but I favor the developer creativity path since it will give learners the opportunity to experience an alternative.

The Creative Process. Creativity is difficult to create! It's an unstructured, frequently unconscious process. Achieving creativity requires a combination of capability and orientation in the developers *and* the time, resources, and a low-risk political environment. Essentially, without models to "create" from (i.e., implement and expand upon in our particular CBT application), most development is trial and error within *very* limited time frames, due to production requirements. Little or no CBT research and development goes on in business or industry. And for all of the traditional reasons, precious little interaction takes place among the business developers and university researchers in the CBT field. These trains are running on different tracks.

Unique and creative work is usually expensive because of the amount of "footage on the floor." Creative film producers take shot after shot until it's "perfect" or "right." And they combine lots of unrelated film footage during the editing process, even though they've carefully worked from scripts and storyboards. There's rarely a situation where the first take is printed and stands. Similarly, creative and flexible CBT typically requires many writing-editing-review and revision cycles. And more often than not, time and money limits in the real-world business environment put a stop to the very process necessary for excellent results.

Lack of a Language to Express Interactions and Design. In traditional instructional development, a common language has developed over the years that permits us to clearly express certain design struc-

36

Figure 1.5
THE INTERACTIVITY CONTINUUM

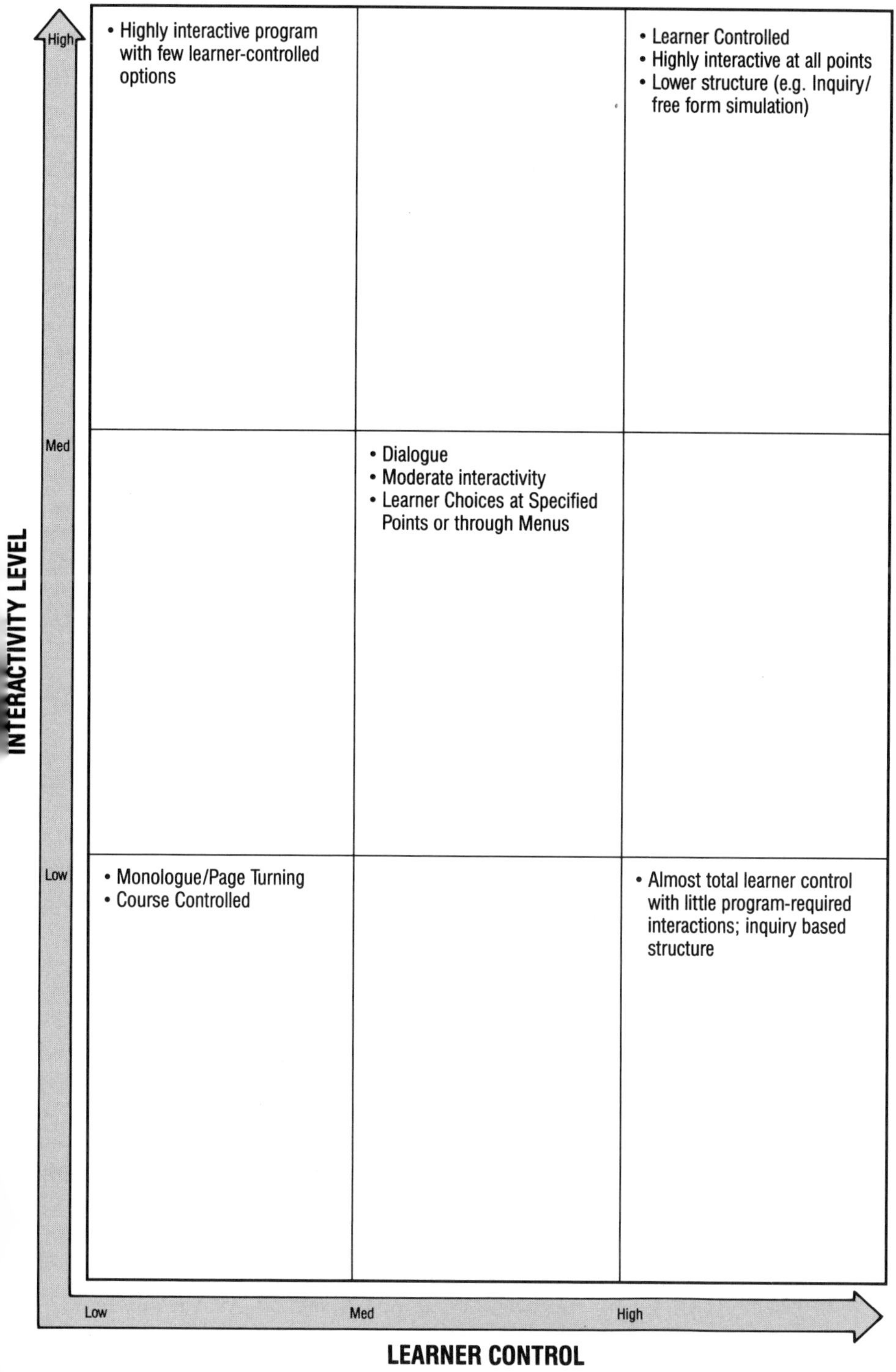

	INTERACTIVITY LEVEL		
High	• Highly interactive program with few learner-controlled options		• Learner Controlled • Highly interactive at all points • Lower structure (e.g. Inquiry/ free form simulation)
Med		• Dialogue • Moderate interactivity • Learner Choices at Specified Points or through Menus	
Low	• Monologue/Page Turning • Course Controlled		• Almost total learner control with little program-required interactions; inquiry based structure
	Low	**Med**	**High**

LEARNER CONTROL

tures and conventions. We use commonly understood terms such as *role-play*, *guided group discussion*, *lecturette*, and *frame* to present abstract ideas. When we try to express the varying types and complexity of interactions in CBT development, things fall apart. We can't simply say "interaction," because it can mean too many things. It is too imprecise for reviewers, managers, or developers to comprehend the specific details intended. Developers can't script easily from it. It leaves too much room for error. We need an agreed-on language (agreed on among the members of a particular development team, at the very least) to express interactive sequences incorporating various learning strategies.

Exhibit 1.4 is a start in that direction. It represents a continuum of interaction levels of complexity (Levels I-IV) for three fundamental instructional strategies or techniques: interactive presentations (i.e., tutorials), case studies/role-playing, and applications software simulations. None of these is rigid. All can be and are mixed together with drills of either these strategies or strings of practice problems or questions to result in interactive learning experiences.

These naming conventions can be used to express design approaches. For example:

> *Introduce the situation through a Level I Case (vignette). Develop the problem/solution/benefits model using multiple Level II Cases (scenarios) until such-and-such content is covered.*

Or:

> *Introduce software system using a Level I Interactive Presentation. Proceed to demonstrate software using a Level I Application Simulation (Guided Walkthrough). Progress through Level II Applications Simulations (Interactive Walkthroughs) to achieve familiarization. Using Level I Cases (vignettes) representing such-and-such business function, combined with six Level III Applications Software Simulations to achieve Level I skill. Present 50 paper-based practice exercises to be performed on a test version of the system, with learners able to access Level IV Simulations (on-line interactive job aids) until proficiency is achieved. Retain on-line job aids with the production software for user access as needed or desired.*

There is certainly room for further development and refinement of this or other language or naming conventions associated with interactivity. I offer this as a departure point. I hope it will assist you in structuring meaningful representations of your CBT design.

Design Representation. Representing interactive design structures involves not only describing *narratively* what strategies will be used to present given content and in what sequence they will occur. The precise expression of logic, branching, and learner options must be articulated for both scripting and programming or authoring system input

38

to occur. The program must be designed to teach, but it also must be designed to execute on the system.

Traditionally, tools like content outlines, narrative descriptions (hopefully using a language to express interaction!), and flowcharting have been the tools of the trade. These work fine for simple, linear programs with either conditional feedback or limited conditional branching through menus or straightforward alternative learning paths that return to the main course path relatively quickly. Once complex branching, numerous learner options, and nonlinear design structures are employed, flowcharting breaks down as a technique. It just doesn't fit the structure—and it gets too complex to manage, even when automated flowcharting software is used. When developers try to fit narrative instructional strategy descriptions and content listings of topics to be covered within a sequence on the same pages as the flowchart, paralysis sets in. And they go back to scripting without design because they don't know how to integrate the narrative and logical expression of design in a meaningful, concise way.

This, of course, affects the quality of interactivity directly since we retreat to simpler and linear designs. A vicious cycle.

In Chapter Five, "Development," various design documentation approaches are discussed in more detail. Suffice it to say for now that the inability to adequately and clearly express highly interactive nonlinear design models is an inhibiting factor to us in designing effective interactive instruction and in modifying the programs as better methods of interaction become clear.

Available Time and Money. There's not much more to say: time and money are generally far too limited for the CBT development task at hand, particularly in light of learner needs and management expectations. The following examples illustrate:

- A training staff was given a deadline for creation of a standalone CBT course to teach hotel staff about and how to use a property management computer system. Trainers were not given access to the system. They got only a demonstration session, during which they were able to print screens. Programming and systems staff were so busy dealing with system development problems and schedules that they were unavailable for the required consulting. The project deadlines were not changed.

- Trainers developed a CBT product training course on a new telephone system to be ready and available to salespeople when the product was announced. The product name changed twenty-six times during development while the CBT was being scripted and programmed. Product management was unwilling to change product introduction dates to wait for the training to be revised and completed.

39

- Trainers developed interactive role plays for use by sales reps in mastering marketplace realities with customers. The trainers had never been sales representatives and needed significant input by skilled and experienced salespeople to create realistic scenarios and dialogues for the role-playing. The salespeople would not commit the time to discussions with the trainers. Technical subject matter experts in the product area were not experienced in sales. Deadlines remained firm.

- A management team budgeted thirty-five hours per linear CBT hour based on the authoring system vendor's claim that "anyone can develop CBT" in that amount of time on this system. When developers brought reality-based estimates into the discussion, they were criticized for padding estimates and their credibility suffered. Development ratios were not modified.

- Trainers were asked to develop CBT for the first time for users of a large telecommunications system. The trainers had previously had only classroom development experience. None of them knew anything about CBT, authoring systems, or managing the effort. The project manager requested budget to hire an external CBT consultant to help educate them and structure and monitor their initial development efforts. After much discussion, they were given a budget of $1500 for the total consulting effort.

These scenarios are typical. Such conditions can only breed limited, linear CBT with limited conditional feedback. There's clearly no room for innovation. Most of the developers in these stories would be lucky to get content organized and structured once, never mind go through a creative process. Most of their design efforts will be limited to the simplest conventions within authoring systems in order to limit programming or input requirements. Vanilla CBT. Electronic page turning. Boring stuff, after which people will criticize the CBT medium or the developers. The circumstances drive the result. There's never time to do it right, but always time to do it again, and again, and again.

Courseware Development Process Employed. The CBT development process includes a blend of freeform creative activities and the very precise disciplines associated with scripting and programming the program. Instructional designers and training managers apply the instructional systems design approach in varying degrees. More talk about it than actually do it.[2] Ironically, when it comes to CBT, many are even less disciplined than with the more flexible and less rigorous environment of classroom instructional development. I have seen authors sitting in front of a terminal filling in menu screens without so much as a basic design document, never mind a detailed script with explicit branching and programming notes. This, of course, affects interactivity since developers can't hold complex conditional branching or flexible learner options in their heads in sufficient detail to input them into the authoring system. They are also trying to design, script, and "program" at the same time, an impossible combination of complex tasks.

New CBT developers or their managers rarely, if ever, have knowledge of, experience with, or commitment to the rigorous disciplines associated with the structured techniques necessary for effective and controlled software development. The methodology I recommend is detailed in Chapter Five. It can dramatically improve interactivity levels and quality by virtue of the disciplines and team process involved.

Authoring System Limitations and Subsequent Programming Requirements. Authoring systems and the assumptions underlying them are discussed elsewhere in this book. It's important to know, however, that the frame-based systems, particularly the very simple menu-driven ones, limit the nature and complexity of the interactions in a course. For example, if a system does not permit you to conditionally branch a learner to another learning path based on performance in several given exercises, that branching alternative is not available to the CBT developer. Or if an authoring system does not permit data from learner decisions in a business simulation to be held and manipulated mathematically, that design is not possible. Or if the authoring system does not permit paging back from a screen on which an interaction appears, too bad. The fact that the designer *wants* to permit the learner to review the material before responding can't be incorporated into the design.

These limitations dramatically limit the interactivity models that developers are creating, unless the developers are able and willing to program the interaction instructions using a general-purpose or authoring programming language. Sometimes it's lack of programming knowledge that limits that possibility. In other cases, it's time. In others yet, the authoring system won't permit the developer to call an external program into use.

Inability to integrate CBT programs with applications software to permit concurrent execution of tutorials and interactive help forces developers into full applications software simulations. Developing such simulations is a time-consuming and tedious task that typically limits the number, complexity, and representativeness of learner practice exercises. The inability of authoring systems to integrate with such productivity tools as spreadsheets, word processors, and graphics packages makes innovative design more difficult and time-consuming to implement.

Some say we won't have effective CBT until expert systems or artificial intelligence-based authoring systems or development tools are in place. I disagree. I'm certain that in the future we'll look back at our current efforts and consider them primitive. But that should not preclude our developing interactive CBT programs to meet today's training needs.

We can't wait and must proceed to work with currently available tools. When there is commitment, it can and is being done.

The Law of Diminishing Astonishment. Harvey Long of IBM's instructional technologies group coined this phrase to characterize the constantly increasing learner expectations we face as developers and trainers. Displays and sequences that generate a "gee whiz, golly" response one minute result in a "ho hum" reaction the next. The Law of Diminishing Astonishment is part of the human condition; it's the very thing that spurs us on to further growth. When learners and developers say, "Why can't I do X?", we must respond to maintain satisfaction and achieve learning. Rather than despair of filling them, listen to the needs. If you don't meet them, someone else will.

In Summary. Interactivity is CBT's *raison d'être*. Without it, what's the point? Your challenge is to understand interactivity, define it, create it, push the limits of current thinking and development tools, and make interactive CBT happen. The rest of this book is dedicated to helping you do just that!

NOTES

[1] For a good explanation of this concept, see John M. Carroll, "Minimalist Training," *Datamation*, November 1, 1984.

[2] See Ron Zemke, "The Systems Approach: A Nice Theory, But..." *Training*, October, 1985.

CHAPTER

Sponsorship and Management

Too many CBT programs founder
on the shoals of politics and
inadequate management control.
Before you lay your reputation
on the line with a new
technology, make sure your
organization is ready for it.

As a manager, I'm concerned about the managerial issues: deciding whether to use CBT, developing political support, establishing an appropriate organizational structure, creating controls, and selecting and developing staff. What are the key issues I should be concerned about?

Just realizing that there are managerial issues is a giant step. Many folks concentrate exclusively on the technological or the educational aspects. Let's look at the key managerial issues as I see them.

Gaining Sponsorship for CBT. Whenever there are new undertakings proposed in an organization, the first critical step is to obtain an adequate level of sponsorship for the activity or project. *Sponsorship* is defined as the political, logistical, and economic *funding* of an activity.[1] Because of its newness, the investment it represents, and—in some cases—its business implications, CBT requires such sponsorship. Essentially, the advocate of CBT as a medium must identify the individual(s) or group(s) who are in a position to provide such funding. The sponsor(s) must be at a high enough organizational level and position to control the resources (and establish the priorities) so that the project may proceed. In addition, sponsors must provide adequate public and private political support.

Inexperienced advocates sometimes think that getting dollars in the budget is all they must do. That's an incomplete, and somewhat naive, view. Experienced advocates know that they must build other support as well. Let's look at some of the roles and activities and see why gaining sponsorship for CBT is sometimes difficult.

Key Roles in Introducing Change. Introducing CBT is essentially introducing change to an organization. It requires new technology, new roles and responsibilities, new skills, and a different instructional development process (i.e., software development is superimposed upon instructional development). In some cases, significant amounts of desired power and control are at stake: it must be decided which group will have corporate responsibility for decision making about CBT direction, technology, standards, use, staff, and so on. Companies and departments differ. In some organizational situations, no one wants to touch CBT because of the real or perceived risks involved. In yet other organizations, no one cares enough to even become involved in a discussion about it.

Let's look at the general roles involved in planning the CBT change:

Sponsor. The individual or group in control of the logistical, political, and economic resources necessary to implement the change.

Change Agent. The individual or group charged with implementing the change.

Target. The individual or group that must change or adopt the change.

Advocate. An individual or group trying to get sponsorship.

These seem straightforward enough when looked at in the abstract.

The reality in most business or government organizations, however, is that these roles are overlapping and not always clear (see Figure 2.1). And when roles are unclear, or people involved don't understand that their roles are shifting, the right behaviors aren't likely to occur systematically.

Figure 2.1
CRITICAL ROLES IN THE CHANGE PROCESS

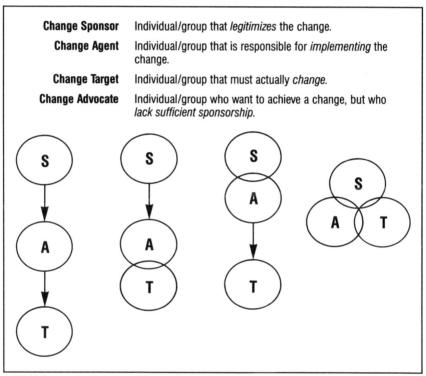

Change Sponsor   Individual/group that *legitimizes* the change.

Change Agent   Individual/group that is responsible for *implementing* the change.

Change Target   Individual/group that must actually *change*.

Change Advocate   Individual/group who want to achieve a change, but who *lack sufficient sponsorship.*

© 1986 O.D. Resources, Inc. Used with permission.

In large, complex organizations, necessary players are frequently in different departments with different sponsors. And training or data processing functions (typically the source of CBT advocacy!) are fragmented and decentralized (i.e., there's sales training, management training, product training, and procedures training) and often lack the ability or credibility to sponsor CBT other than in their own organizational unit. For example, the data processing department might have economic resources like a budget for CBT authoring systems or staff, but it cannot initiate a training project to support a specific business need without line management approval and involvement. Or the training department can initiate and sponsor any training project, but it may not be permitted to acquire any software without review and approval by data processing, which controls all DP acquisitions.

Understanding and Leveraging the Relationships. Figure 2.2 graphically depicts the three primary types of relationships in introducing and managing change: (1) the linear or "hierarchical" relationship, (2) the triangular or "staff" type of relationship, and (3) the square or "matrix" relationship.

Figure 2.2
THREE BASIC RELATIONSHIPS IN THE CHANGE PROCESS

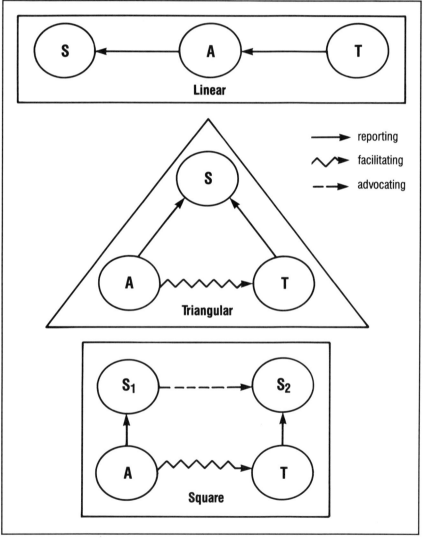

If you advocate CBT (or if you are a sponsor in one part of an organization, such as corporate training, trying to get sponsorship in another organizational unit, such as a line or sales department) you must understand your role. In any given situation, you might be a sponsor, a change agent, or an advocate. In addition to understanding the roles, however, you must understand the structure of the relationship you are involved in (i.e., linear, triangular, or square) to leverage the time and resources you expend in trying to build commitment.

To build commitments, you must become a *change facilitator*. What are the characteristics of the effective change facilitator? First of all, he or she is comfortable with the organization's overall business. If you simply consider yourself a training professional and never give any real thought to banking, travel, government, or whatever business your organization is in, you will never be able to exert the necessary influence on upper levels of management to secure sponsorship. Next, the change facilitator is a *manager*; that is, he or she must be comfortable in a realm where departmental objectives (and certainly individual objectives) are often in conflict. As a change facilitator, you must thoroughly understand the relationships between training, business decisions, and management principles. Finally, you must be multidisciplinary, operating equally well in the technical-procedural and human relations environments. You must know what the CBT systems are capable of, but you must also know how to understand the personal interests of your targets and how to appeal to them.

The Linear Structure. The easiest organizational structure in which to implement CBT is the linear structure. The CBT advocate needs only to convince the sponsor that CBT is a good idea and worth the trip. Once that sponsor is committed, he or she can direct and institutionalize activities moving toward CBT implementation (e.g., building it into objectives, funding it with budget dollars, establishing its priority in relationship to other objectives, and publicly and privately wielding political might). Naturally, sponsors usually work to build commitment among those who report to them who must carry out the task of implementing CBT so that full enthusiasm prevails. But when resistance is encountered within a sponsor's chain of command, there are always sanctions, pressures, rewards, and consequences available to increase momentum.

Whenever possible, working within a linear structure is the way to go, because it's politically simplest, since ultimately all of us within organizations play to the priorities of the people we report to if we want to survive and prosper. But frequently the CBT advocate, or the person who has been charged with implementing CBT across organizational lines (such as the CBT staff person or department), must work from outside the organizational structure he or she wishes to influence. That makes things much more interesting (read "difficult").

The Staff or Triangular Relationship. This relationship will be clear from an example. Suppose you are the CBT change agent ("A" in the chart in Figure 2.1) and you report to a sponsor who says, "CBT Change Agent, get Lee (the 'T,' or Target, in Figure 2.1) to use CBT." Now Lee reports to your sponsor, but not to you. Unless your sponsor tells Lee that it's something that he (the sponsor) wants Lee to do, you are reduced to persuasion, political debt, or charisma to get Lee to use CBT—unless Lee was already planning to do it. This last, coincidental, situation is one I wouldn't count on. Key rules in this type of situation:

1. Be certain the sponsor communicates expectations to the target and clearly legitimizes your role as a facilitator, educator, doer, or whatever else is involved.

2. Get the ground rules clear on which of you is responsible for what (e.g., technical development, subject matter expertise, project identification). Use your organization's standard procedures to ensure that responsibilities, expectations, time frames, and accountabilities are fulfilled. For example, if your organization operates with formal written performance plans or objectives, be sure CBT is included. If a simple memo does it normally, use one. Include results in your business activity reporting.

3. If the target's priorities shift or interest wanes, but yours aren't changed by the sponsor accordingly, know when to go back to the sponsor for political, logistical, or economic support. Of course, it's best to work one-to-one with the target. If you can't make progress, however, you have no way of reestablishing momentum: the target doesn't report to you.

4. If you don't have adequate sponsorship, you have four choices: educate your sponsor, get a new sponsor, try to get out of the assignment, or prepare for failure in the form of your expending a lot of effort with little or no meaningful result. Sorry, I wish there were another message. But there's not.

Frankly, savvy staff people try to assess the adequacy of sponsor commitment before they take on the task. They don't confuse positive comments from a prospective sponsor with the ability and willingness to fund the project logistically, politically, and economically. Less sophisticated, inexperienced, or overeager CBT advocates take any interest—or even a request to "do something with CBT around here"—at its face value. Staff people, who typically lack traditional forms of organizational power, naively jump at anything that smacks of power. Be cautious and careful. And remember, the first thing to do is to accurately assess sponsor commitment levels (see Chart 2.1).

Chart 2.1

SPONSOR COMMITMENT DIMENSIONS

The following dimensions must be assessed to determine CBT sponsor commitment. The more intense the sponsor feels about these issues, the greater the commitment.

Dimensions are not weighted equally. You must factor in relative importance in relation to both the situation and the sponsor's value system.

When commitment is not adequate, your strategy must include tactics to increase sponsor commitment on the more important (or the majority) of the dimensions. Only with adequate commitment will you succeed.

1. Sponsor Dissatisfaction with the Status Quo. The degree to which the sponsor is dissatisfied with the current or anticipated training situation.

2. Vision of the Desired State Employing CBT. The clarity of the sponsor's vision of what CBT will look like, cost, and how it will be administered. Your sales strategy will be even more effective if it addresses the reasons behind the prospective sponsor's dissatisfaction with the present situation.

3. Need for the Change. The degree to which the sponsor feels that CBT is needed (versus simply useful, nice to have, or not necessary).

4. Resources Necessary for CBT. The degree to which the sponsor understands the organizational resources (time, money, people, and so on) required for successful implementation of CBT, and to which he or she is able and willing to commit what is necessary.

5. Organizational Impact. The degree to which the sponsor understands the true effects of CBT on the training and user organizations.

6. Human Impact of CBT. The degree to which the sponsor can appreciate and empathize with what the people involved with CBT are being asked to change about the way they operate.

7. Scope of the Change Associated with CBT. The depth of the sponsor's understanding of the size of the group to be affected by CBT.

8. Sponsor's Public Role. The degree to which the sponsor is able and willing to demonstrate the type of public support necessary to convey strong organizational commitment to CBT.

9. Sponsor's Private Role. The degree to which the sponsor is able and willing to meet privately with key individuals or groups in order to convey strong personal support for CBT.

10. Consequence Management. The degree to which the sponsor is able and willing to promptly reward those who facilitate the implementation of CBT or to express displeasure with those who inhibit it.

11. Monitoring Activities. The degree to which the sponsor will assure the establishment of monitoring procedures that will track progress or problems occurring during CBT's implementation.

12. Importance of Sacrifice. The degree to which the sponsor realizes that he or she may pay a personal, political, or organizational price for implementing CBT; the degree to which he or she will support CBT despite the costs.

13. Sustained Support. The degree to which the sponsor demonstrates consistent, sustained support for CBT and rejects any course of action with short-term benefits if it is inconsistent with the CBT implementation.

The Matrix or Square Relationship. The matrixed sponsor, agent, target, and advocate relationship just complicates things further. Here's an example of this type of situation: The DP training manager uses CBT within her organization and likes it. She appoints someone (CBT change agent) to get trainers in another area, like sales training, to use CBT. The sales trainer doesn't report to, and may never have even heard of, the DP training manager. A CBT change agent on a suicide mission runs over and tries to get the sales trainer to deal with the CBT agenda (which, typically, is built into the CBT change agent's objectives). It's a complete waste of time unless, as mentioned earlier, the sales trainer is predisposed and willing to accept the CBT change agent's help, the sales trainer owes something politically to the CBT change agent, or the CBT change agent is so charismatic that anything he suggests to anyone is done right away. If so much charisma existed, my guess is that person would be in politics or in a very powerful management or sales job—not slaving away at the middle level of an organization like the rest of us only slightly charismatic folks.

For this scenario to work out well, the CBT change agent must convince his manager (sponsor) to serve as an advocate to the sponsor in the *other* department, thus building his or her commitment to CBT and the things necessary to accomplish it. The situation is similar to the tale above. Without the ability and willingness to truly sponsor something within a chain of command where the sponsor can use incentives, sanctions, pressures, and rewards toward a given objective, the CBT change agent is better off going to the beach. Nothing is likely to happen in the office without that sponsorship.

Evaluating Sponsor Commitment Levels. There are thirteen key dimensions of sponsor commitment to CBT. Think in terms of these dimensions when assessing sponsor effectiveness. The greater the number and intensity of these factors, the greater the commitment. Chart 2.1 lists the dimensions.[2] If commitment levels are low or inadequate to the CBT implementation task at hand, you can use various strategies to build commitment by focusing on the most critical of the items listed in the chart. Not all are equally important, so you'll have to make some subjective assessments of the key factors with each individual(s) in your organization. Understanding the specific areas that are lacking is an excellent first start at picking a commitment-building strategy that is likely to pay off.

Remember, no one sponsors a change—particularly an unfamiliar one—unless he or she sees sufficient benefit to make necessary risks worthwhile. Building commitment is an educational and sales activity. Many of the items included in the CBT strategy outlined in Exhibit 3.1 in Chapter Three will help you assess and foster sponsorship.

In spite of all of the reasons for developing and using CBT in my organization, we just don't get going on any scale. What's wrong?

Well, each organization is different, so I can't diagnose yours in particular. But your situation is not unusual. Gaining and maintaining momentum for CBT is not easy. Some organizations never jump on the bandwagon; others fail to keep it rolling once they've begun. I've seen lots of activity but little movement in many places. For example, authoring systems are installed but not used. A pilot project is begun and is not finished, or is the last CBT undertaken. Or CBT development is put in performance and business plans, but every year there's a reason for not doing it. Most frequently, CBT doesn't progress because sponsorship is inadequate, not coming from the right sources, or both (see the beginning of this chapter). Often, the key motivator that can move sponsor interest in CBT beyond the level of attending conferences about it is the feeling of gaining *control*.

Risks and Control Mechanisms. Every undertaking in life has risks. Risks are the most tangible in physical activities such as sports where injury (or even death) is possible, especially when those involved are inexperienced and the challenge is great, like in mountain climbing or skydiving. In organizational life also, risks are everywhere, although they are not as tangible as a broken leg.

When new activities such as CBT are undertaken, the risks are personal, political, and financial. Reputations are at stake. Credibility can increase or decline based on the outcomes. Business results can suffer if adequate courseware is not delivered for such critical efforts as new systems installations or product introductions. And all involved can be hurt. In addition, when we are at risk, anxiety increases dramatically. Not a pleasant working situation, to say the least: tensions and tempers rise, management controls tighten, and so on.

For those learning new and risky sports, instructors frequently teach basic competency and survival or risk-management techniques very early on. They also emphasize the control mechanisms so that the new learners don't give up because they feel overwhelmed or not in control. For example, in skiing you're taught the snowplow to slow yourself down. You're also taught how to fall. Usually these instructions occur on nearly-flat ground or on the "bunny" slope. In white-water kayaking, you're taught how to right yourself while still in the kayak. You learn this in a swimming pool—not in a cold and raging river with rocks in every direction. In skydiving, there's a reserve chute that automatically opens.

Beyond the basic survival techniques, every sport also has control mechanisms and "tricks of the trade": in ice skating, edges give control; in bicycling, it's cadence; in running, it's pace. Control mechanisms exist in CBT also. One of the difficulties experienced by organizations getting started is identifying and developing control mechanisms. Often,

51

they reject the task itself, or they spin their wheels in unproductive activity trying to avoid them. The problem is much like the one I experienced recently while in London.

"Blimey, Get Out of My Way." I was in London and wanted to take a day trip to Bath, about a two-hour drive away. I explored my many alternatives for getting there. The train wouldn't permit exploration of little towns. Besides, the schedule didn't fit my terms. Guided bus tours stopped at tourist shops, and I don't like traveling in a mob. I seriously considered hiring a car and driver. I'd done it before and found it a very pleasurable way to go. It's a bit expensive, though, and I decided to "save" some money by renting a car and driving myself. No problem. I'd driven on the left side of the road many times in the Caribbean and had no trouble in adjusting quickly. So I called Avis and away I went. If only it had been so simple! I hadn't counted on a *huge* difference between my past and this experience. London is slightly larger than St. Thomas and has more traffic. The car rental company was out of maps and gave me oral and handwritten directions. The car was a standard shift with the shift on my left (of course the steering wheel was on the right). London drivers park both facing and against traffic and I kept panicking, thinking I was either in the wrong lane or the wrong way on a one way street.

My navigator (now a *former* friend!) missed directing me to the right exit from a rotary ("traffic circus" as it is known in England) with six exit roads, and we got sidetracked into downtown London at rush hour. I thought the speedometer and road signs were in kilometers and they were really in *miles*, so I was going even faster than I thought in my efforts to maintain the proper speed. I couldn't find first gear and so had to start in third: a noisy and disturbing situation, to me and everyone nearby.

When I acted on my instincts, they were all wrong: I wound up on the wrong side of the road or in the wrong gear. As I got more and more distressed, I thought of abandoning the car, turning back and forgetting the trip, killing my navigator, applying for more insurance, or stopping cold and calling someone for help. The last alternative was out of the question because I was would be damned to let my husband know about this—and he was the only other person I knew in England.

My goal was becoming less important. As a matter of fact, I began to wonder what was so interesting about Bath in the first place. I cursed the people who suggested the trip and began to rationalize that the more expensive alternative of hiring a car and driver was probably less expensive in the long run. Nightmares of paying a $3,000 deductible played in technicolor. The one good decision I'd made was to purchase the additional insurance. But then I wondered if my medical insurance would pay if I got into an accident abroad. The truth of the matter is that there were simply too many variables for me to manage and feel control of. Any one of the differences from my normal situation would have been enough to handle, but I wouldn't have felt so overwhelmed.

Finally, I stopped and one-by-one reduced the difficult contributing variables that I could influence. I bought a map and got confirmation of the directions, including key landmarks, from a knowledgeable local. I asked a gas station attendant how to find first gear, got on the highway instead of taking the heavily trafficked and confusing "charming" side roads. I asked about the miles versus kilometer situation and reduced my speed. Essentially, I reduced the number of unfamiliar variables I was dealing with to two: driving on the left and a left-hand shift. I also realized that I should have asked for an automatic car in the first place, but I couldn't do anything about that mid-trip. Next time. . . All in all, it turned out to be a pleasant and worthwhile day.

IMPLICATIONS FOR CBT

The above may be a long-winded way to introduce my thoughts about controlling your CBT development activities, whether you're a first-time or relatively experienced traveler. In my experience, many CBT activists have initial or ongoing feelings of lack of control. Those who stay with it learn, as I did with my London driving, that the way to decrease anxiety and increase control (and consequent quality, timeliness, and cost-effectiveness) is to identify the controllable variables and reduce the uncertainty associated with them. Let's look at the critical control mechanisms now.

CBT Management Control Mechanisms. There are several primary control mechanisms associated with the CBT development process that, when consciously and carefully managed, increase the likelihood of quality and timely courseware development. Most of these control mechanisms are discussed in detail in the following chapters. I've combined them here to place a managerial perspective on them.

Knowledgeable Team Members and Limited Development Team Size. Clearly, having people involved who know what they are doing increases control. I include among these people a project manager and department management with knowledge about what should be done, in what sequence, and so forth. In Chapters Seven, "Roles," and Eight, "Fielding a Team," the required knowledge, skills, and characteristics are covered in detail. There's also a discussion of ways to improve them all. In the absence of knowledge or experience within the team itself, it's frequently desirable to employ an expert external resource, such as a consultant, to work with the team at least through its initial courseware development projects. The fewer people you have with the requisite skills, the more control you achieve, simply because communication is easier. Have enough people—and no more—with enough skill and time.

Clear Roles, Responsibilities, and Accountabilities. Put someone in charge. Define roles and expectations. Clearly articulate the decision-making process. Identify when you want to be involved and establish that you expect questions and discussions when there is conflict among team members, uncertainty as to how to proceed, or need for additional perspectives. "Legitimize" ignorance and establish a requirement that uncertainties be expressed. Make it unacceptable for people to proceed using their own assumptions or when uncertain.

Chapters Seven and Eight detail the roles, responsibilities, knowledge, skills, personal characteristics, and experience required, and some ways to develop them.

Structured Development Process. Here, the establishment and use of a structured development process, including clear role definition, steps, quality control points, and evaluation criteria can't be overemphasized. It's the highest leverage item available to training managers. The process, including strict adherence to the walkthrough of clearly defined deliverables at the end of each phase, is detailed in Chapter Five, "Development."

Standards. Establishing, communicating, building commitment to, and enforcing standards provides up-front control. Such standards also tend to compensate for less experienced development team members (see Chapter Six).

Third-party Perspectives: Insurance. Expertise external to the team can be an important quality-control mechanism. Either knowledgeable external CBT consultants or more experienced CBT developers or project managers from other groups within the organization can serve as a check and balance to the team's or project manager's self assessments. Consultants can be used for education, advice, review and evaluation, supplementing the project manager, participation at stages where the team could use input (e.g., design phase, establishing standards), technological expertise, and validation of activities such as time and cost estimating, design, technological decisions, development methodology.

Using External Contractors. Sometimes it makes good sense to contract externally for initial or pilot courseware development. This is particularly true when much up-front work on standards development, structuring a development process, or establishing design conventions need to be done in addition to designing the program. For contracting to work well, the person you hire must have the relevant experience and knowledge.

When external contracting is done, I strongly urge clients to have their anticipated internal CBT developers serve as active members of the team to learn from and contribute to the activity. Working with a knowledgeable individual or group is a very good way to decrease risk and get results relatively quickly, even while you are gaining knowledge and getting productive work done.

Understanding and Consciously Making Trade-offs. In CBT development, understanding the specific trade-offs in your situation and consciously analyzing and deciding about them is an important control mechanism. If you don't recognize the trade-offs, you will make them anyway, but unconsciously.

Trade-offs will fall into three general categories:

• power versus simplicity

• structure versus freedom

• productivity versus creativity

There are likely to be others, but these apply specifically when you are selecting technological environments, establishing the depth of the CBT course, determining specificity of standards or the development process, or deciding how rigidly you will enforce standards and process. Careful examination and conscious decision making and communication about desired trade-offs give you up front control in CBT.

Project Scope and Complexity. Limiting the project's size and complexity from a perspective of structure, content, or learning objectives can dramatically increase control. Some of the biggest failures I have seen result from the development team biting off more than it can chew while it is simultaneously learning how to develop CBT and creating the initial CBT infrastructure (e.g., standards, templates, and so forth). We have a long history of traditional data processing projects to learn from: both failures and those that are merely out of control.

One of the main causes of failure is too ambitious an objective. Structure a modular project rather than a complex integrated design. During initial development activities, avoid higher-order learning objectives (such as analysis, synthesis, and extrapolation) and stick to lower-order objectives (awareness, knowledge, or application skills). If possible, try to address a limited and homogeneous learner population. When you're just starting to learn about CBT, attempting to meet all heterogeneous learner needs predestines you to failure.

Limit design complexity when you begin CBT. Avoid complex situations where multiple and interrelated variables combine with complex logic or branching structures. You can take these on after you've got the basics under control.

Time- and Cost-Estimating Methodology. A structured approach to gathering information on the project and estimating development time and expense goes a long way toward gaining sponsorship for it and controlling it during development. When estimates are not clear and reality-based, pressures and anxiety increase, tempers flare, credibility suffers, shortcuts are taken, quality declines, and so on. Chapter Nine, "Cost Estimating," details the elements that must be articulated and assessed as a part of the estimating process. Managers should be certain to test the proposed estimates against these dimensions to be certain that overenthusiastic developers aren't setting up an uncontrolled and doomed situation. That's reason enough to refuse to sponsor a project. If estimates don't fit with desired or required schedules or costs, then the required trade-offs must be made intelligently to ensure up-front control. That's the only way to fly.

Other Critical Success Factors. Sponsor commitment and control mechanisms detailed above are, in effect, elements that are critical to success. In addition, several other critical success factors are worth discussing:

Realistic Expectations. When all players involved—and particularly sponsors—have reality-based expectations, there are few disappointments. Any product, concept, or medium is doomed if it is oversold on outcome, cost, schedule, resource effectiveness, ease of implementation, or how people will feel about it. There is skepticism and even cynicism about implementation schedules, expenses, and the actual outcomes for almost any computer-based project today. Information processing has a long history of delivery failures: failure to deliver on time, failure to deliver within budget, failure to deliver the product as everyone expected it to be. Computer-based training has a special problem because many people's initial experiences have been limited to linear tutorials on the one hand, or Star Wars-type flashy interactive video-based simulations on the other. As a result, people expect too little or too much relative to the investments.

There's a fine line between making someone excited about the concept of CBT and overselling what can be delivered in your world. Enough said.

Training Applications Where Interactivity or the Computer Delivery Environment Adds Business Value. Selecting the "right" applications means choosing projects with payoff. Payoff or value is interpreted in the eye of the buyer, not the seller. If I see the personal payoff in spending $7,000 on a mink coat and you would rather own a horse, my expenditure is a complete waste to you. That would be particularly true if you believe animals shouldn't be killed for human ornamentation! So underlying values like "computers are negative" can certainly be a stumbling block.

The sales strategy most effective in gaining and maintaining sponsor commitment and organizational and learner acceptance is that of showing people that the CBT program enables them to do something they can't do now. The benefits or value-added components traditionally associated with CBT are

- decreased cost for delivery (economic advantage)

- ability to train previously "unreachable" or difficult-to-reach learners (logistical, economic, and political advantage)

- improved rate of learning (economic and educational advantage)

- decreased learner costs (economic advantage)

- increased retention of learned material (educational and economic advantage)

- increased control (logistical and political advantage)

- improved training program maintenance (logistical advantage)

but...

The big bang is *business value*, making a difference in business results. Many of the items above are the traditional benefits attributed to CBT. With the exception of costs, however, few are seen as directly tied to business results. And most business people feel that CBT will cost more than traditional alternatives and that many of the educational benefits are unproved. My feeling, however, is that the big ticket is the ability to truly effect learning transfer through affordable simulations (see examples in Chapter One) and to increase skill levels through sufficient practice in a concentrated period of time. We are talking about employee competence with all of the attendant business benefits:

- ability to sell more volume of a new product faster;

- decreased use of hot-line support by customers;

- decreased service call costs and "call backs" by customer service or field engineers due to improved competency;

- decreased number of employee grievances because supervisors truly understand and have skill in applying carefully thought-through employee relations policies; and

- improved product quality with fewer product returns or less waste of materials.

Let's be honest. Managers and professionals seriously involved in the primary business of their company couldn't care less about the advantageous training benefits. They care about what it does for them. They frankly would prefer never to spend a dime on training for its own sake. And for the most part, the corporate platitudes on desire for employee development are translated into serious commitment only when managers see that the development translates into some meaningful business results. When managers see *business value*, arguments about the relative costs per delivery hour completely disappear and out come the checkbooks. They now see value for the money spent from a *business* rather than a training perspective.

Good sales people know that customers buy benefits and solutions, not features. Sponsors of CBT buy business payoff, not training process. Just show them what it does for them that's advantageous from their frame of reference, and you've got the sale and lots of follow-on sales. If you can't show the benefit, be prepared to be making presentations about CBT's wonderful features for years (if you last that long) and to watch your personal and professional credibility declining with each sexy pitch.

Availability of Technological Design and Development Tools Appropriate to the CBT Task at Hand. Finally, having the right tool for the right job as described in Chapter Four, "Technology," is key to success from a development, design, cost, educational, and business perspective.

Putting It All Together. "Easy for you to say," my critics exclaim. "You can sit on the sidelines as a consultant and tell us what to do." Well, I suppose it could look that way, but in fact, I have developed CBT within a large corporation. And I work daily helping others learn how to manage the many and complex variables involved in it. I have seen this process again and again and I can say that while learning to manage any complex activity takes time, if you concentrate on the critical factors and master the control mechanisms we've discussed, you can put it all together for your organization.

---

[1] This material on sponsorship, key organizational roles in implementing a new activity, and commitment building is based on materials and instruments that are a part of the "Managing Organizational Change" training program owned by O.D. Resources, Inc., 2900 Chamblee-Tucker Road, Atlanta, Georgia 30341. Models and content are incorporated and reproduced with permission of O.D. Resources, Inc.

[2] A quantitative instrument (paper) that structures the process of evaluating sponsor commitment to a given change may be ordered at a modest price from O.D. Resources, Inc., 2900 Chamblee-Tucker Road, Atlanta, Georgia 30341. Telephone (404) 455-7145.

CHAPTER

Strategy

Without a clear understanding
of what your organization
wants to accomplish with CBT,
you'll never produce anything
but activity.

You emphasize having an appropriate and complete strategy as a critical success factor in CBT implementation. What do you mean by strategy?

A *strategy* is the science and art of employing the political and economic forces of a group to afford the maximum movement toward a goal. Webster adds that it's "a careful plan or a method." I agree. At the next lower level, *tactics* are "the art or skill of employing available means to accomplish an end." Typically tactics are smaller-scale actions serving a larger purpose.

In my consulting work, I see a broad range of strategies and tactics. Some are conscious, deliberate, and well planned. Others are random and reactive. Some support carefully thought-through objectives for using CBT to address business training problems. Others don't relate to the business per se but support a goal of "using the computer for its own sake." Frankly, using the computer for its own sake seems to me irresponsible, irrelevant, or both. Using it to address real unmet business needs is a necessary condition for success in most organizations. But regardless of your goal, strategy is the key.

Whether it's conscious or unconscious, planned or reactive, every organization has a strategy. Successful organizations, vendors, or advocates for a particular activity clearly and consciously articulate objectives, formulate a general approach to getting there, and develop specific tactical plans to move themselves toward the goal. Managers monitor conditions and goals as they implement strategies and tactics, making changes when appropriate. Frankly, I don't see a lot of conscious strategy development in the CBT world. I don't even see many defined objectives other than being "state of the art." What I do see is lots of activity, much of it not leading anywhere. And therein lies the problem.

Activity is important. But it's relevant only when it moves you toward a goal or toward fulfilling a previously unmet or inadequately met need. I've seen organizations that are in a CBT "activity trap." They are very busy evaluating authoring systems or bringing in courseware or attending conferences. But when you step back and look at what they've gotten for their time and money (and remember, time is money!), it's not much. All the activity should lead somewhere.

I'll summarize the general components of an effective CBT strategy, and then I'll go one step further by describing one for you to use as a departure point in thinking through your own. A successful CBT strategy should contain

- clear, achievable results or products in the business, educational, technological, political, or psychological arenas (e.g., solving business problems, creating technological architecture, building commitment levels)

- alternative general approaches to achieving these results or products

(e.g., educating, developing commitment levels, creating a technological architecture)

- identification of key sponsors (see Chapter Two for a comprehensive discussion of "sponsorship") whose political, logistical, or economic support is necessary to legitimize the activities throughout the organization (e.g., key information systems managers who must support mainframe CBT installation and management; line department management who must supply subject matter experts to the course development team)

- specific tactical plans for activities to achieve strategic goals (e.g., conducting an in-house CBT conference to familiarize a broad base of trainers with the technology; identifying three priority business problems that interactive training can solve better than current practice or traditional training; funding a CBT pilot project)

- clear definition of roles and responsibilities (of sponsors, facilitators, "doers," managers, vendors, and consultants)

- identification of possible resistance sources in the organization; accompanying strategies to manage that resistance

- monitoring and evaluating activities.

To see how these elements fit into a plan, examine the accompanying exhibit. It is a sample three- to five-year strategic plan for an organization that already believes CBT will pay off. This comprehensive plan was developed from the perspective of a staff person functionally responsible for implementing CBT as a medium. If it had been written by a line manager whose concern was solving a particular business problem and for whom the rest of the organization's needs were irrelevant, the plan would be different. A plan, of course, must fit the objective of the person or group who develops it.

For an organization unsure of how actively or whether to pursue CBT, a simpler plan would be more appropriate. You can limit your strategy simply by selecting elements from the exhibit. Learn what constitutes a strategy, build one appropriate to your organization, and get necessary sponsorship to make it work. Then, determine whether and when you should go the next step.

Use the components of the comprehensive strategy in Exhibit 3.1 as a laundry list of ideas for your more limited strategy. Or think up entirely different things. Remember, the strategy must fit the nature and magnitude of the goals—and defining specific goals is where you start. These are necessary conditions for success.

Exhibit 3.1

A SAMPLE THREE- TO FIVE-YEAR STRATEGY
FOR COMPUTER-BASED TRAINING

Objectives

To investigate and evaluate currently available and future training technologies, including computer-based training

To identify potential applications for interactive learning within the company

To develop an understanding of the technological, organizational, educational, and human resource requirements associated with the development of interactive learning

To recommend a technological architecture for development and delivery of interactive learning programs, including hardware and software

To develop knowledge of effective commercially available courseware products for evaluation by internal training staff

To identify, evaluate, and recommend vendors for interactive learning development under contract

To evaluate the effectiveness and acceptability of interactive learning by trainers and learners

To build knowledge and understanding of viable interactive learning tools and products among company trainers and line managers with needs

To recommend an internal organization within the training department structure, including roles, responsibilities, and required skill components, to result in effective use of interactive training technologies within the organization

Strategy

Develop the CBT manager or coordinator's knowledge and understanding of interactive technologies, development requirements, and commercially available tools.

Tactics

Retain external consultants with specific knowledge in CBT for one-on-one educational activities with CBT manager. Concentrate on building knowledge levels about technological alternatives, strategy components, marketplace issues, appropriate educational applications for CBT.

Attend national Data Training CBT Conference annually.

Participate in local training group or professional association programs or other CBT related conferences and seminars.

Identify public seminars with targeted objectives that relate to the required knowledge.

Purchase or borrow commercially available or customer-developed CBT programs for review and evaluation to increase understanding of applications, effective and ineffective design, instructional strategies, and learner

CONTINUED

62

A SAMPLE THREE- TO FIVE-YEAR STRATEGY (cont.)

perspectives when experiencing CBT programs. Whenever possible, evaluate programs developed in, or intended for, our industry. Sources: consultants, authoring system vendors, peers in other companies, commercial courseware vendors, customer courseware vendors.

Read:
- *Making CBT Happen* by Gloria Gery
- *Authoring* by Greg Kearsley
- *Screen Design Strategies for Computer-Based Training* by Jesse Heines
- *Teaching Computers to Teach* by Esther Steinberg
- *Computer-Based Training: Evaluation, Selection and Implementation* by Greg Kearsley
- *Data Training* (monthly publication)
- *Training News* (monthly publication)

As CBT development tools are identified as appropriate, bring them in-house for pilot evaluation.

Attend and become moderately active in the authoring user group or other local authoring system meetings. Attend the national users' group meeting.

Maintain communication with internal staff who are piloting or evaluating CBT authoring systems or courseware.

Make a presentation on internal CBT activities at a major regional or national conference.

Strategy

Build general knowledge, understanding, and commitment to CBT among the organization's trainers and line managers.

Identify key CBT sponsors within the training and line management organizations and target activities toward building their commitment and solving their training problems.

Develop and maintain knowledge about and communication of internal results among departmental and divisional training management.

Tactics

Develop among targeted sponsors specific understanding of the training issues and problems. Identify driving and restraining forces associated with use of CBT. "Qualify" targets based on need, potential for commitment-building, available resources, and technological delivery possibilities. Target activities toward areas and people of high success probability.

CONTINUED

A SAMPLE THREE- TO FIVE-YEAR STRATEGY (cont.)

Structure educational and commitment-building activities toward targeted units. Provide formal and informal learning opportunities for training and line management personnel with training needs where CBT might apply. Activities include:

- Annual or periodic internal CBT conference.
- Develop an internal CBT library of books and journals accessible to interested people on a loan basis.
- Develop and distribute a quarterly newsletter focusing on marketplace developments, descriptions of relevant new courseware or authoring systems, issues, internal CBT activities, including courseware development and acquisition, case studies, and educational activities.
- Distribute specific articles, books, and marketing literature to targeted internal trainers and line managers.
- Conduct periodic demonstrations of development tools, authoring systems, and courseware for both general and targeted audiences.
- Develop an internal library of courseware for evaluation or use by internal trainers and line managers.
- Schedule periodic seminars and workshops addressing management, design, technical, and other issues (e.g., authoring system skill workshop, CBT design seminar).
- Provide broad access to external consultants hired for general discussions, specific problem-solving activities, education, or "motivation" to internal trainers.
- Conduct one-on-one meetings and demonstrations with targeted potential trainers or line managers with CBT potential. Place priority on the most likely "buyers" and those most likely to solve business problems not currently being addressed by conventional training alternatives.
- Develop an internal CBT users' group or task force for ongoing relationship development, education, and communication by internal CBT users.
- Develop ad hoc study groups or teams for specific CBT activities (e.g., recommendation of technological architecture, evaluation of development tools, courses, etc.).

Report monthly on activities, results, issues, and problems to information systems management.

Strategy

Gain experience with CBT courseware development. Use experienced custom courseware developers to assure successful pilot courseware development.

CONTINUED

A SAMPLE THREE- TO FIVE-YEAR STRATEGY (cont.)

Tactics

Establish criteria for pilot courseware projects.

Identify high payoff courseware applications.

Establish a specific and controlled development process to assure timely and high-quality courseware development.

Fund the development from centralized funds, but assure investments and sponsor commitment within targeted organization (possibly shared funding).

Establish criteria for external vendor selection.

Jointly evaluate vendors and proposals with client organization.

Jointly manage courseware development, including standards development, and project activities, with client organization.

Retain external consultants as appropriate to maintain control and participate in design.

Evaluate resulting CBT courseware, including critical evaluation of the courseware development experience, learning effectiveness, and learner reactions.

Strategy

Identify organizational, administrative, and policy issues that must be addressed for effective CBT implementation.

Tactics

Identify training policies that need study regarding CBT (e.g., rotation of training staff, student registration, record keeping). Determine whether they are positive, negative, or neutral in relationship to CBT's use in this organization.

Evaluate their impact on CBT with appropriate training and management staff.

Develop recommendations on organization and administration.

Obtain management sponsorship for any required new or changed policies and practices.

Strategy

Evaluate and recommend a CBT architecture that is compatible with the organization's existing hardware and software architecture. Identify and evaluate any short term issues or limitations that affect CBT development and implementation.

CONTINUED

65

A SAMPLE THREE- TO FIVE-YEAR STRATEGY (cont.)

Tactics

Obtain formal and informal documents regarding internal information systems hardware and software architecture and future plans.

Evaluate alternative CBT technological development and delivery alternatives. Articulate trade-offs.

Capitalize on research and work done by other organizations, including targeted. Use external consultant resources as necessary.

Involve internal data processing, training, and line managers in the study, and evaluate.

Recommend short and long term CBT development and delivery architecture, including hardware, and design, authoring, programming, and delivery software.

Gain appropriate management sponsorship to the recommendation, including those who are able and willing to enforce the policy.

Control vendor access to trainers to limit proliferation of incompatible tools and duplication of expense. Communicate company policy to internal trainers, line managers, and vendors.

Monitor internal and external technological activity, including evaluation of tools and recommendation of new tools as they emerge.

CHAPTER

Technology

Authoring and presentation
systems are the most obvious of
the CBT tools, but they are by
no means the only ones.

What are the technological aspects of developing and delivering computer-based training?

The world of CBT is afflicted with technological myths. In fact, a lot of my work as a consultant consists of shooting down the fantasies that people have about the technological components of developing and delivering computer-based training programs. I'm convinced these myths spring from a combination of vendor marketing hype, new user inexperience, the fact that many trainers looking at CBT alternatives have had little reason in the past to develop technological expertise, and the inevitable human propensity to believe what we wish were true. Hope is not an effective strategy, however. Realistic and informed expectations of CBT technology are crucial to success.

I'll list some of these myths—many of which will look like the CBT chapter in a book I'd like to write someday on "the greatest lies in the world." Some will be new, others familiar. We'll debunk them in this chapter, and I'll elaborate on some of the realities of CBT technology.

MYTHS ABOUT TECHNOLOGY

- An authoring system is all you'll need to address all the technological issues involved in CBT design and development.

- You can design effective CBT with our authoring system after little or no training.

- The authoring system is easy to use.

- Anyone can do CBT with our authoring system.

- Lessons developed on our authoring system can run on any equipment. The code is transportable.

- You can design on-line with our authoring system, no need to bother with storyboarding or scripting beforehand.

- Our authoring system prevents you from designing boring or ineffective CBT.

- Our authoring system permits development of all types of instructional design strategies.

- The internal graphics and text editors have as much power as you'll ever need. You'll never need other external editors.

- CBT development ratios using our authoring system can be as low as 20 hours to develop an hour of instruction.

- We're committed to ongoing system enhancements and full user support.

- The first thing you should do is select an authoring system—and you should use the most popular one on the market.

In fact, some of these statements are all or partially true as they relate to some specific authoring systems, tools, or vendors. For example, many vendors *are* committed to maintaining and enhancing their product and to excellent user support. But *caveat emptor* particularly applies when evaluating the full range of technological tools associated with CBT development and delivery.

REALITY (AS I HAVE SEEN IT)

- You'll need several technological tools for productive and creative CBT development—and an authoring system is just one of them.

- One size *never* fits all. You may need several authoring systems in a diverse organization to address very diverse training needs, delivery hardware, and the range of knowledge, skills, and motivation that different authors will possess.

- Unless it's so simple it does hardly anything, no software is ever easy for inexperienced people to use. This is especially true with trainers, given their lack of familiarity and, sometimes, the lack of inclination toward software use. Learning the capabilities and limits of the technological tools and developing proficiency in using them always takes significant amounts of time and motivation.

- There are lots of trade-offs, and you must know what you need before you can select a technological development environment. Buying an authoring system is not the place to start, although many people do start there.

- Interactive CBT design takes lots of time. Automated design tools help in that process. Don't confuse the time it takes to input what you've designed into an authoring system with the time it takes to actually design and script it. They are two very different activities.

What are the technological components relating to CBT?

The technological components relating to CBT projects include hardware, authoring systems, general programming and authoring languages, graphics development software, automated design tools, word-processing software, other productivity software, lesson presentation systems, and student administration (or CMI) systems.

Each technological component plays a role during the various development stages. Understanding the features, capabilities and limitations, and interrelationships among these tools is critical to both creative and productive courseware development.

Hardware. The hardware involved in CBT development can include

- computer processor

- video display terminal or monitor

- keyboard

- videotape or videodisk player

- audio player

- printer

- communications network

- input devices (such as mouse or light pen)

Sometimes people need to (or can) select hardware dedicated to CBT. Other times, they must live with what exists. The hardware you have in-house or select for CBT development and delivery in many ways defines your options for development software, courseware features, learner interfaces, and delivery display characteristics. There are many trade-offs in hardware evaluation and selection. Considerations are well developed in Greg Kearsley's book.[1] Read it especially if you will be acquiring hardware dedicated to CBT development and delivery. You have much homework to do.

Most of us, however, must—and *should*—live with the hardware we have already installed. The reasons are economic, administrative, and logistical. It's true that some of the "dedicated" CBT systems have more bells and whistles on them, but most of us don't absolutely need all these features, especially in relation to the additional cost and complexity of adding yet another type of incompatible computer to our technical environment.

For our purposes, we will assume you will be using your organization's existing hardware architecture and will be piggybacking CBT applications on equipment installed for other purposes. I'll move on to software issues, but first, here are some recommendations to keep in mind when you do have hardware choices to make.

- Select the highest-resolution monitor possible.

- Select microcomputers that can ultimately be integrated through networks with available mainframe computers.

- Avoid dedicated CBT delivery hardware if possible.

- Select color over monochrome displays.

- Select hard disks over floppy diskettes.

- Select faster over slower machines.

- Plan for adequate disk space for mainframe course storage and access.

- Have printers available at learning delivery stations.

- Select as much on-line storage as possible.

- Select as large an internal RAM as possible.

- Don't presume a touch screen or light pen input are most desirable. Sometimes keyboard input is much faster and less fatiguing.

Software. CBT software components can be standalone (like an authoring system) or used in combination, as when you write with a word

Chart 4.1

TECHNOLOGICAL TOOLS AND THEIR USE
IN THE DEVELOPMENT PROCESS

TECHNOLOGICAL TOOLS	DEVELOPMENT PHASES
• Idea Processors • Outline Processors	• Project Definition • Design
• Word Processors	• Project Definition • Design • Development (Scripting)* • Script Revisions
• Automated Design Tools • Flowcharting Software	• Design
• Authoring Systems	• Prototyping • Development (Scripting)* • Programming • Revisions
• Programming Languages or Authoring Languages	• Programming • Revisions
• Graphics Software	• Prototyping • Design • Programming
• CMI/Recordkeeping Systems	• Evaluation • Implementation

*Based on your development philosophy, power of the internal text editors, and the nature of the project, Development (Scripting) can be done with either word processing or authoring system software.

71

processor and then input ASCII text files in batch mode to the authoring system (an excellent technique, by the way, because it allows you to create the text faster than you could with most authoring system internal editors, and makes for a more maintainable product). Different software tools are appropriate at different stages of the design and development process. I've summarized the tools and when they should be used in Chart 4.1. Further details about software tool use during each development stage are addressed in Chapter Five on CBT development. Always remember, however, that the right tool for the right job makes things easier all around. Before we look at the various tools, an important observation:

Software components are almost always operating system-specific (i.e., they require a specific operating system such as MS DOS, Unix, or whatever). If a vendor claims the authoring system can be "used on any hardware or operating system," watch your pockets. While this might someday be true, it's only a dream today for most of us. Don't let a dream turn into a nightmare by basing your delivery plans on the assumption that the code is easily transportable.

There are hardware, user, courseware application, and expense issues associated with selecting and using various software alternatives. Each selection decision should be specific to your particular situation. Don't choose a tool simply because someone you know has it. It might not fit for you.

Just what is an authoring system?

Authoring systems are enabling software products (commercially available or internally developed) designed to make courseware developers more productive. They are like other productivity tools such as electronic spreadsheets or word processors. But they are designed with instructional needs in mind. Just as you load your individual data or words into spreadsheets and word processors, you load or input your lessons or learning activities into an authoring system. And just as spreadsheet and word processing programs vary in features, functions, ease of use, user interfaces, and ability to integrate with other software, so do authoring systems.

Each authoring system developer makes assumptions about general instructional functions and structures, features, capabilities, and required user interfaces. These are essentially "preprogrammed" so that course developers avoid repetitious programming and can focus on CBT content and design. For example, the developer decides how many possible acceptable responses instructional designers will want to permit and builds that assumption into the authoring system. The developer of *any* application must make assumptions about it; for example, in a spread-

72

sheet program, the developer has decided how many rows and columns of information a user will need, and has programmed in that number of options.

The major difference between software for spreadsheets and for instructional design is that there is general agreement about components for spreadsheets (e.g., all the rows and columns must total horizontally and vertically). Instructional design requirements have many more philosophical and discretionary considerations—and the diversity of products in the marketplace reflect the range of philosophical assumptions. For example, some authoring systems require you to state learner objectives at the beginning of each lesson whether you want to or not. Other leave that option up to the courseware designer. Some systems permit learners to review previously seen material while in the middle of an interaction, and others do not. Some systems require you to use predetermined screen displays; others provide total freedom.

Necessarily, each product has its structural and functional capabilities and limits, and it's critical to know what you will be requiring of a system before you select it. Selecting an authoring system can be successful only when you know your needs and who will be using it. In fact, many organizations producing a range of CBT courseware (e.g., applications software, product, process, technical, or sales training) use more than one authoring system. They choose the right tool for each job. Think about how many data base environments probably exist in your organization. It's a perfect analogy!

There are numerous types of courseware applications, instructional design philosophies, developer knowledge of and skill levels with computers and software, budgets, and media requirements. This means there are more options available than most of us need or care to evaluate. Again, the situation is analogous to the word processing or spreadsheet software marketplace. Each product has its devotees, and some people aren't satisfied with *any* option and choose to develop their own unique package— something I caution you against. For the most part, adequate tools are available. The marketplace sorts out the core alternatives, and it is wise to keep on top of both the formal and informal information networks when preparing to select a system.

Remember, authoring systems are effectively used during the design phase for creating prototypes of design alternatives or screen displays. Currently, most design and scripting activities are best done with other software (i.e., word processors for scripting). As a matter of fact, authoring systems *slow things down* during design and writing, and I don't recommend their use at that point except for prototyping.

Also, know whether the authoring system you are considering requires a separate presentation system (discussed below). If so, important economic, administrative, and delivery issues come into play.

Chart 4.2
AUTHORING SYSTEM FEATURES CHECKLIST

MAJOR FEATURES

Does the system permit:	Yes	No	Optional	*Dependent on editor
1. Tracking of student progress?	☐	☐	☐	☐
2. Reporting of student progress?	☐	☐	☐	☐
3. On-line course listings?	☐	☐	☐	☐
4. On-line student registration?	☐	☐	☐	☐
5. Interface with the programming language?	☐	☐	☐	☐
6. Interface with other software packages?	☐	☐	☐	☐
7. Interface with videodisc?	☐	☐	☐	☐
8. Interface with videotape?	☐	☐	☐	☐
9. Use of a mouse?	☐	☐	☐	☐
10. Use of a light pen?	☐	☐	☐	☐
11. Multiple input fields on a single screen?	☐	☐	☐	☐
12. Superimposition of text over graphics?	☐	☐	☐	☐
13. Batch input of files?	☐	☐	☐	☐

Does the system include:	Yes	No	Optional	*Dependent on editor
14. Editor for unresolved branches?	☐	☐	☐	☐
15. Random test generator?	☐	☐	☐	☐
16. Touch sensitive screen?	☐	☐	☐	☐
17. Color?	☐	☐	☐	☐
18. Sound?	☐	☐	☐	☐
19. Lower case characters?	☐	☐	☐	☐
20. Variable character sets?	☐	☐	☐	☐
21. Animation?	☐	☐	☐	☐

Does the system accept:	Yes	No	Optional	*Dependent on editor
22. Multiple correct answers?	☐	☐	☐	☐
23. Close answers?	☐	☐	☐	☐
24. Is a separate presentation system required?	☐	☐	☐	☐

Is vendor support provided:	Yes	No	Optional	*Dependent on editor
25. By phone?	☐	☐	☐	☐
26. On site?	☐	☐	☐	☐

Can the presentation system be used for:	Yes	No	Optional	*Dependent on editor
27. Vendor-written courses?	☐	☐	☐	☐
28. User-written courses?	☐	☐	☐	☐
29. Third-party courses?	☐	☐	☐	☐

Microcomputers only

Can the system:	Yes	No	Optional	*Dependent on editor
30. Be networked?	☐	☐	☐	☐
31. Be uploaded to a mini or mainframe?	☐	☐	☐	☐
32. Allow multiple diskettes for large courses?	☐	☐	☐	☐

Minis and Mainframes

	Yes	No	Optional	*Dependent on editor
30. Does the vendor support timesharing?	☐	☐	☐	☐
31. Does the authoring system run on a micro?	☐	☐	☐	☐
32. Does the presentation system run on a micro?	☐	☐	☐	☐
33. Is the system installed by vendor?	☐	☐	☐	☐

* For authoring languages only: dependent on graphics and text editors used with the system.

CONTINUED

AUTHORING SYSTEM FEATURES CHECKLIST (cont.)

MAJOR CAPABILITIES

1. Describe flexibility of response analysis (how many specific responses can be accepted, how many characters per response, how many wild card characters, etc.?). _____

_____

_____

2. Describe branching (number of paths, conditions, etc.). _____

_____

_____

3. Describe internal editing capability (line, screen, full text). _____

_____

_____

4. Describe prompting (pre-formatted menus, self-developed templates, bypass menus, no menus).

_____

_____

5. Describe any limitations on screen use (text screens, questions screens, response input, amount of screen used). _____

_____

_____

6. Describe graphics capability and input methods. _____

_____

_____

HARDWARE

1. Describe hardware configuration required for authoring. _____

_____

_____

Micros only

2. What microcomputer(s) does the system run on? _____

_____

3. What operating system is required? _____

_____

Minis and Mainframes

2. What terminal(s) does the system run on? _____

_____

3. What operating environment and compatibilities? _____

_____

What are the primary features of authoring systems?

The number and type of features in authoring systems change almost daily! Currently, there are dozens of features you can look for. Chart 4.2 summarizes and defines many features.

While vendors scramble to incorporate as many features as possible in their products, few contain all. And each system has its own strong and weak points. Some systems are special purpose tools emphasizing particular types of design. Others are more general and can consequently sometimes lack specific capabilities required for a particular kind of application (e.g., simulating applications software screens). Choosing an authoring system *always* requires trade-offs. You'll make them even if you aren't aware of it. To be sure you optimize the situation, do the following before making a decision:

- Know your educational, technological, and development needs and priorities.

- Understand the definitions of features and how they relate to your needs.

- Establish selection criteria and know which are the most important to you.

- Be prepared to make conscious trade-offs.

- Don't expect everything in one package.

- Take off your rose-colored glasses and put on your hearing aid when listening to sales reps or "born again" users.

- Talk to peers who've looked at systems.

Keep in mind these other considerations when you are evaluating authoring systems. Ask yourself who is going to use the system to develop software. What educational applications are you going to develop and what capabilities are critical to effective courseware development? Who is the vendor? Can the vendor organization provide support in both the short and the long term? What are your technological requirements for development and delivery? Under what priorities and constraints are you operating?

The key considerations to take into account are summarized in Chart 4.3. You may have others. All your trade-offs should be conscious ones. And, again, don't look for one tool to meet your many (and sometimes conflicting) needs.

Chart 4.3
SELECTING AN AUTHORING SYSTEM: POINTS TO CONSIDER

When you start to evaluate CBT systems, you need to ask yourself a number of questions. The two most important ones are, "How critical is the training need I propose to address with this system?" and "How dependent will I be on the system to meet this need?"

The more dependent you are on your CBT system, the more important it becomes to find good vendor support and to match hardware capability and system function with training needs. The less dependent you are on a particular system, the more you can afford to risk experimenting with complex technology or to trade off vendor reliability for sophisticated function.

Once you have answered these initial questions, you should consider the system features, authoring requirements, and organizational variables outlined below. Naturally, they are not all of equal importance, and the weight you assign to each one will depend on organizational goals and circumstances. You will probably have to make trade-offs, since each system will have both advantages and disadvantages relative to your environment and needs. Some items may not be of any concern at all, but they should be omitted consciously rather than by oversight.

Remember, training needs must drive the selection of a system. A system's features and functions may be attractive, but if they don't address the training needs, CBT won't be successful in your organization.

Training Needs
- What is the nature of the training (e.g., information transfer, simulation, skill building, conceptual)?
- What instructional design strategies will be needed and used?
- Is the material linear or open-ended?
- How much is the material subject to precise definition or accurate and specific responses to questions and tests?
- What benefits, if any, are associated with standardization of training?
- Can learning be evaluated in terms of knowledge or skills acquisition or is the outcome general "education" or awareness? What types of test questions or activities are needed to evaluate learning or knowledge?
- Are there other training materials, like videotapes and text, that can be integrated effectively with CBT through computer-managed instruction?
- Will the training be enhanced by increased interactivity?
- How important is immediate/timely availability of training?
- Of what value is increased ability to control, monitor, and evaluate training?
- What needs for evaluating individual knowledge/skill/competence exist?
- What problems currently exist with production, distribution, and updating of training materials?
- Will CBT help or complicate the situation?

Training Audience
- Who is in the training audience? What is their experience with and receptivity to computers?
- How many students require training? Will the population grow or be increased by significant turnover?
- What is the geographic distribution of the training audience?
- What are the learner expectation/tolerance levels for various types of instructional design strategies, hardware limits, time spent in training, control and freedom for moving around the instructional material?

CONTINUED

SELECTING AN AUTHORING SYSTEM (cont.)

• Do learners require non-keyboard interaction (e.g., light pen, joysticks, touch screen)?

CBT System Features, Function, and Requirements

• What are the capabilities, functions, and features of the CBT systems (branching, screen, design, interaction/question design, response/answer analysis and feedback, graphics, color, interface with other software, programming language interfaces, ability to batch input text files, etc.)?

• How do the system's functions relate to your training needs? Which critical needs would or would not be met by the system?

• What hardware, software, and networks are required by the CBT system? Is the equipment standard or must it be especially configured? Can it be used for other purposes?

• What is the operational performance of the system? How much computer resource does it require? What is the system's response time? What storage is required?

• What is the nature and size of the storage for the authoring system and courseware in relationship to your anticipated course size and response time requirements?

• What is required for in-house installation and support (i.e., technical expertise, systems programming, software, lead times, etc.)?

• How reliable is the system (average downtime, service records)?

• Is authoring and presentation combined or can each be leased separately? If a micro system, does it require a separate presentation diskette or is the presentation code embedded in the lesson diskette?

Authoring

• What type of authoring software exists? Is it menu-driven, command level programming language, or complex programming language environment?

• How complex is the authoring for the specific training applications in question (e.g., how difficult is it to generate screen simulations, special characters, graphics, etc.)

• What editing capabilities exist?

• What skills and knowledge are required of authors? Must they understand programming logic? To what degree? Is a sophisticated programmer required? Is one available?

• What are the attitudes, skills, and experience of your anticipated authors? Are they motivated to learn if their current skills and knowledge are less than required by the authoring system?

Author Training and Support

• What author training exists?

• What is the nature of the training (workshop, manual, CBT courses, etc.)?

• How long is the training course?

• How long does it take for authors to become proficient in using the system? At basic levels? For the most complex functions/training situations?

• Is training at your location or at the vendor location?

• How much does author training cost per student or per training session?

• What resources are available for author training from the vendor? From consultants?

CONTINUED

SELECTING AN AUTHORING SYSTEM (cont.)

- What support or consulting exists to support authors with questions about or problems with design, technology, debugging, or system performance?

Costs

- What does each component of the CBT system cost: hardware, software, authoring system, line costs?
- Are there discounts for purchase of multiple systems?
- If the software is licensed, what is the cost per copy or per CPU the system runs on?
- Can the system be leased?
- Is the system available for a fee for a test/evaluation period? What is the cost?
- Are there any installation expenses?
- What are the costs necessary for supporting software on a mainframe?
- How much do service contracts cost? Would a multiple site installation affect costs?
- What is the cost of converting courseware from another system to this system (if applicable)?

Vendor Capabilities

- How experienced is the vendor with CBT?
- What commitment does the vendor have to the support and enhancement of the system?
- What technical support is available?
- What service capabilities does the vendor have for hardware/software (e.g., location of service personnel in relationship to your geographic installations, number of service personnel, historical/anticipated service response time)?
- How financially stable is the vendor?
- How many systems are currently installed? What is the experience of other users with authoring, vendor support, service?

Available Courseware

- What courseware has been developed and is currently available from the vendor, software houses, consultants, or other users?
- What is the cost of the software? Is it available for purchase or lease?
- Are costs per mainframe or for the course itself?
- Can courseware be duplicated to run on a number of internal systems/mainframes?
- How relevant is the courseware to your training objectives?
- What is the quality of the courseware? How does it conform to your internal standards for design, format, etc.?
- Can courseware developed for other systems be converted for use on this system?
- Can courseware developed for this system be converted to other systems? What are the constraints?

Consultants

- What consultants are available with skills/resources for custom course development?
- Where are they located?
- What costs are associated with development (time, travel, and living expenses)? Are contracts on a time spent or fixed cost basis?

I hear the term "frame-based authoring systems" quite a bit. What does this mean and what are the implications for me?

That's an important concept to understand. Frame-based systems have very definite design implications and involve a specific aspect of authoring system selection and use that is worth a separate and expanded discussion. In fact, the concept of the frame-based system reflects the fundamental assumption underlying most authoring system structures.

In frame-based systems you create "frames" or "screens" of instruction through which learners proceed. You then connect all "frames" presenting text, graphics, interactions, and feedback by numbering each frame and creating linear or branched paths to and from them. This means that each numbered display is "called upon" to be displayed to the learner based on the author's definition of conditional relationships. When the author is creating the programming or authoring system "logic," she tells the program to "branch to" or "go to" and display a specific screen when the learner does certain things. For example, if the learner inputs one response, the system displays screen 32. If another learner inputs a different response, the system displays screen 36. Each overlay, including boxes and windows or partial screen display, typically has a different frame number. The requirements to program the overlays vary, based on the authoring system's structure.

"So what?" you ask. Well, the reason I bring it up is that the underlying design structure that frame-based systems generate is essentially linear. This means that practically speaking, the authoring system "defaults" you into a linear tutorial instructional mode. Look at Figure 1.2 that illustrates a linear instructional design sequence that fits the numbering structures of frame-based systems. If this is the best instructional strategy for your course, there's no problem. But if you intend to use simulation of situations, with multiple and interrelated variables that the learner individually manipulates (such as that represented in Figure 1.4), frame-based systems make the courseware difficult to construct at best and impossible at worst. Essentially these frame-based systems almost require you to design with sequences that look structurally like this.

Text display (Frame 010): "This dress is black."
Text display (Frame 020): "These shoes are red."
Question display (Frame 030): "What color is this dress?"
Choose
a: red;
b: black;
c: white.
If a, Response screen display (Frame 040): "No, try again."
If b, Response screen display (Frame 045): "Good. You're onto your colors!"

Chart 4.4
AUTHORING SYSTEM TRADE-OFFS

PRODUCTIVITY

- Ability to develop in a word processor and batch input text files into authoring system
- Internal text editor capabilities within the authoring system
- Savable screen templates
- Screen partitioning/windowing
- Ability to interface with other software
- Answer analysis, macros for response analysis of questions (e.g., multiple choice, responses)
- Branching based on conditional performance with predetermined course structure
- Glossary access
- Help access
- Hard copy of screen display
- Printout of branches
- Editors for unresolved branches
- Printout of frames by name
- Automatic frame numbering
- Spellcheck

CREATIVITY

- Ability to interface with programming language or bypass menus and use authoring languages
- Ability to use the full screen for text, responses, feedback, graphics
- Screen partitioning and windowing
- Graphics capability
- Multiple font/character sizes
- Color
- Ability to program course structuring, incorporate volume and diversity of learner responses into answer analysis and feedback
- Learner-controlled progression through course

STRUCTURE

- Menu-driven
- Formatted macros
- Pre-determined answer analysis
- Limits/definitions to screen space use, font size, character types, line graphics or predetermined graphics configurations (e.g., circles, boxes, etc.) vs. free-form graphics creation
- Testing macros and answer analysis

FREEDOM

- Command language programming
- Flexible response analysis and conditional branching in formats
- Unlimited use of screen for text, responses, graphics, feedback
- Ability to set learner start/restart points at will by author or learner

POWER

- Command level authoring/programming or ability to interface with such
- Flexible (not pre-programmed) answer analysis
- Author-controlled branching
- Powerful internal text editor or ability to create in a text editor and batch input files into the authoring system
- Ability to interface with other software

SIMPLICITY

- Menu-driven structure/input
- Limited number of acceptable/unacceptable responses
- Ability to interface with other software
- Linear course structure with limited (if any) branching based on conditional performance
- Basic/structured graphics editor (e.g., lines, circles)
- Screen partitioning/windowing
- Editors for unresolved branches (e.g., verifiers)
- Limited testing (e.g., numbers/types of questions)
- Predetermined learner progression: limited learner control of start/restart points

Each partner in the three major trade-off pairs is characterized by certain capabilities and functions. Sometimes these features are mutually exclusive; sometimes they coexist.

Figure 4.1
STRUCTURE AND FREEDOM
AUTHORING SYSTEMS TRADE-OFFS

STRUCTURE (vertical axis, from Low to High)

FREEDOM (horizontal axis, from Low to Med to High)

	Low	Med	High
High	• Menu-driven • Formatted screen macros • Pre-determined answer analysis • Limits/definitions to screen space use, font size, character types, line graphics or pre-determined graphics configurations (e.g., circles, boxes, etc.) vs. free form graphics creation		• Ability to bypass menus and program
Med		• Testing macros and answer analysis • Command level programming	
Low			• Command language programming • Flexible response analysis and conditional branching in formats • Unlimited use of screen for text, responses, graphics, feedback • Ability to set learner start/restart points at will by author or learner

Figure 4.2
PRODUCTIVITY AND CREATIVITY
AUTHORING SYSTEMS TRADE-OFFS

PRODUCTIVITY	Low	Med	High
High	• Strictly menu-driven • Defined screen formats • Limited no. of acceptable responses • No/limited conditional branching • No/line graphics • No color • Limited no. of test questions		• Ability to interface with other software • Bypass menus and use authoring languages • Savable screen templates • Ability to develop in a word processor and batch input text files into authoring system • Editors for unresolved branches (e.g., verifiers)
Med		• Answer analysis (macros for response analysis of questions) • Internal text editor capabilities within the authoring system • Branching based on conditional performance with predetermined course structure • Ability to use the full screen for text, responses • Screen partitioning and windowing • Graphics capability • Multiple font/character sizes • Color	
Low			• Ability to program course structuring/branching, incorporate volume and diversity of learner responses into answer analysis and feedback • Learner controlled progression through course • Ability to interface with programming languages

CREATIVITY

If c, Response screen display (Frame 046): "No, try again."
After two incorrect tries, display (Frame 050): "Sorry, the correct response was black. Study your colors carefully."
Text display (Frame 060): . . .
And so on.

Of course, the above interaction is contrived and trivial, but you could look at that typical sequence of instructions required in a frame-based system and then compare it to the possibilities suggested in Figure 1.4. You could see that the very things that the computer is best for—flexible conditional branching and manipulation of variables—are not called upon with these tools. In part, frame-based systems are one of the reasons for CBT courseware that could replace Valium as the drug of choice! Of course, the designers have major responsibility for soporific CBT as well.

The frame-based structure (and the "mind-set" of most developers) result in linear and therefore not very flexible or engaging learning material. Frame-based systems can limit developers' thought processes to tutorial sequences. There are other course design alternatives (e.g., gaming or conceiving of the program as a data base with each learner configuring his or her own "view" through a combination of course-controlled and learner-controlled options). Most existing systems must be "gotten around" to permit such alternative design structures. The key point is that the tools "limit" as well as "enable" what you can build.

You keep mentioning trade-offs. Just what are the major trade-offs I will face in making my authoring system selections?

The three primary and interrelated trade-off dimensions are productivity versus creativity, structure versus freedom, and power versus simplicity.

Each dimension has essentially a zero-sum relationship between the extremes; that is, the more of one variable you have, the less you get of the other. For example, if you want very creative and unique components and strategies throughout your CBT course—including sophisticated graphics, clever analogies, games, and the like—you won't be able to produce large amounts within short periods of time (productivity). If you want developers to have only simple menu-defined options and to operate in the lowest level of design and programming options within the authoring system (simplicity), they won't be able to do many complex things or use some of the advanced system features, like exiting to a specially written program (power).

The trade-off variables within each dimension are listed in Chart 4.4. In addition, Figure 4.3 shows how representative authoring system features relate to these trade-off dimensions.

Figure 4.3
POWER AND SIMPLICITY
AUTHORING SYSTEMS TRADE-OFFS

POWER (vertical axis: High, Med, Low)

SIMPLICITY (horizontal axis: Low, Med, High)

POWER \ SIMPLICITY	Low	Med	High
High	• Command level authoring/ programming or ability to interface with such • Flexible (not preprogrammed) answer analysis • Author controlled branching • Ability to interface with other software		
Med		• Powerful internal text editor or ability to create in a text editor and batch input files into the authoring system	
Low	• Basic/structured graphics editor (e.g., lines, circles) • Screen partitioning/windowing	• Limited testing (e.g., numbers/types of questions) • Predetermined learner progression, limited learner control of start/restart points	• Menu-driven structure/input • Limited number of acceptable/ unacceptable responses • Linear course structure with limited (if any) branching based on conditional performance

One way to illustrate the trade-off concept dramatically is to explain the characteristics of general programming languages, authoring languages, and authoring systems. CBT courseware can actually be written in any general purpose programming language, such as Basic, Pascal, or assembly language. In fact, many courses are. For most of us, however, the knowledge, skill, and time required to program an entire course—particularly a complex one—is not practical. So authoring systems were developed to "preprogram" the routine, repetitive functions. Actually, many authoring system products were originally "macros" or "routines" that were developed by people initially programming in a general purpose language. The developers realized they could help other people improve productivity, so they packaged their "routines" in a product. (After all, that's what keeps America strong!) Ultimately, all authoring system commands translate into some programming language that the computer can recognize.

Authoring languages, such as *Coursewriter, Pilot, Tutor, TenCore,* and *Pace* are "special purpose" programming languages with commands that are specific to the needs of interactive instructional designers. They are analogous to other special purpose languages like Cobol or Fortran. Commands such as "test," "retest," and so forth make the programming job easier.

When courseware developers want to include sequences that are beyond authoring system capabilities and structures, they program that part of the course. In fact, powerful authoring systems permit you to "call external programs," which are typically written in an authoring or general purpose language (such as Basic) and execute in tandem with course materials developed under the authoring system. This important capability permits developers to gain productivity through authoring systems while permitting the flexibility and creativity that only a programming language will provide.

Remember, developing powerful and sophisticated courseware frequently requires programming all or part of the instructional sequences in an authoring or general-purpose language. This is almost always true with complex situational simulations and games. It's a part of the power-simplicity trade-off.

Another clear trade-off is in graphics. You have probably heard that many authoring systems, especially PC-based systems, have graphics editors. But there are often differences between "internal graphics editors" within authoring systems and software designed exclusively for graphics development. Differences may include

- power, including number and type of development options;
- ease of use;

- ease of maintenance; and

- graphic output quality.

People on your development team may already know how to use powerful graphics packages. To these people, the time investment in learning internal authoring system editors might be unattractive. Or, you may have an existing investment in (or can call upon) a graphics library that you wish to use within courseware you are developing. Or your courseware application may require special graphics (e.g., three-dimensional or rotating objects) which the authoring system graphics editor can't generate.

Some authoring systems get around these trade-offs by permitting "porting" or input of graphics files generated in external graphics packages. There are also differences in display rate and storage requirements between internal and external graphics editors. When evaluating authoring systems for graphics capability, remember there may be additional options. Ask the vendor or other users about them.

Is there other productivity software for CBT development besides authoring languages and systems?

Yes. And making use of this software can enhance both creativity and productivity. Productivity software can be used during development independently of the authoring system, as with automated design tools during design. Or it can be integrated with the authoring system; for example, word processing software can be used during development, with text files entered into the authoring system during programming to create lesson files. Let's look at the various types of productivity software you'll want to consider. Refer back to Exhibit 4.1 for when to use them and for their associated deliverables.

Idea or Outline Processors. Outline processors permit productive development of course content listings, including topical outlines. They assist in structuring and revising ideas or listings flexibly. Their output can be traditional outlines, tables of contents, and so forth that are simple to revise. Many times we don't add items or change their original location because it's so tedious and time consuming to change the outline numbering scheme. Idea processors like *ThinkTank* [2] can be helpful in creating, documenting, and maintaining CBT materials. They are well worth the price in terms of added productivity. Be sure, as with any software you select, that the characteristics and functions match your particular situation. New software is released daily, and the software mentioned in this book is simply some of the software that is available as I write it.

Automated Design Software. CBT design is a time-consuming and creative process. The process is *both* more creative and productive when appropriate software is used to generate, revise, and document designs. We often hear developers speak of "design documents," but we rarely see more than either general narrative descriptions or general high-level design flowcharts or learning maps. Sometimes we see very detailed flowcharts for linear programs or course sequences. From my perspective, neither of these approaches is entirely adequate.

Keep in mind that we are developing *software* as well as instructional programs. We should use proven techniques and software tools from the software development industry. These include

- idea or outline processors (e.g., *ThinkTank*);

- action diagramming software (*Action Diagrammer* [3]);

- flowcharting software; and

- word processing software.

These special purpose products are powerful and flexible. They permit easy revisions to your documents, which benefits productivity. They overcome the problems associated with changing design, whether the design is represented in narrative, flowchart, or symbolic terms.

The design process is an iterative one. We express our ideas, review them, and then change them. Others then review them and make more changes. Many people get better ideas as they review theirs or others' work but hesitate to recommend or incorporate them due to the difficulty in changing manually developed design documents (e.g., those produced with a plastic template and ink pen or those developed within the authoring system itself while scripting on-line).

I strongly recommend use of whatever automated design or representation tools are available. If your design is linear and can be represented with traditional flowcharting techniques, you could use flowcharting software. If nonlinear design strategies are employed, action diagramming concepts and software are more appropriate. As a matter of fact, action diagramming is optimal for most design structures, be they linear or nonlinear. I urge their adoption as standard representation techniques and accompanying software tools.

Word Processors. Word processing is the most productive way writers can develop, edit, revise, and maintain text. Many learning experiences are entirely or predominantly text-based. Even software application simulations have significant amounts of text describing the software or providing feedback to learner inputs. The best tool for developing scripts within CBT programs is the word processor with its accompanying spell-checker and thesaurus! And many developers are already skilled in using one.

Most authoring systems have text editors within them. But like internal graphics editors, the internal text editors are usually far more limited in function, ease of use, and flexibility than commercial products designed for the full range of text creation, editing, and revision. For example, many authoring system editors are screen or line editors and restrict editing activity to the specific screen or line the writer is working on. They rarely incorporate powerful productivity features such as block moves, global search and change, and spell-checkers. In addition, screen editors create problems during course maintenance: all changes must be found within the software and made on a screen-by-screen basis. Additionally, there is little or no power for setting margins, tabbing, creating hanging indents, and so forth. Control is through the cursor in a specific setting. As a development and maintenance environment, this one is expensive and time-consuming. And, during the editing and review process many reviewers, including project managers, don't suggest desired revisions that will improve course quality and creativity because they know how difficult it is to make editorial changes within the course. Therefore, overall course quality suffers.

Of course, the optimal situation would be a full-featured word processor within the authoring system itself, and some authoring systems are being enhanced to include such features now! In the absence of such, desirable authoring systems permit batch input of ASCII text files produced with word processing software directly into them to create lesson files. Admittedly, this requires developers to structure the word processing files to incorporate relevant commands to be recognized and translated by the authoring system. Or the authoring system format commands must be entered once the text files are in the system. But you will find that authors quickly learn most of the commands they will be using and can enter them while creating the text. Or if your authoring system accepts the ASCII files, you must then format the screens and incorporate the branching and display instructions using the lesson editor within the authoring system. Even if this is the case, it's still often more productive than developing within the authoring system or developing in a word processor and then entering the final text displays again into the authoring system. More about this process in Chapter Five, "Development." But even if your authoring system does not permit batch input of text files, I strongly recommend your developing all your text files in a word processor to get all the productivity benefits during the scripting and writing stages, even if it means entering the text *again* into the authoring system.

What else should I know about authoring systems before I start considering them?

You should know about concurrent authoring systems, lesson presentation systems, and CBT administration systems, for starters.

Concurrent or "Shell" Authoring Systems. A relatively new concept in CBT is that of "concurrent" or "coresident" software that permits learners to easily move in and out of actual applications or productivity software without logging off the software and logging onto a separate and distinct "course." I explain these ideas further in Chapter Eleven, "Software Proficiency Training." It's important to know, however, that there are tools designed specifically for creating such "interactive job aids" or concurrently executing CBT programs.

Some full-blown authoring systems permit such movement in and out of "live" software; others do not. Development tools, such as *Shelley*[4], *Concurrent Development Series*[5], or *Explain*[6], permit creation of on-line reference material, tutorials, glossaries, and so forth without actually simulating the applications software. While each of these development tools provides different capabilities, underlying each is the principle that with simple keystroke combinations learners can move in and out of software without losing their place or having to look information up in the manual. They can then engage in interactive learning experiences while actually working in their applications. These development tools also permit development of interactive job aids or "on-line coaches" (or reference material) with low development costs. This kind of development can be done by subject matter experts rather than instructional designers, since it's essentially a writing task. In addition, having on-line reference material permits users to learn all about the software rather than limit their knowledge to the arbitrarily defined and usually limited content of standalone CBT that typically exists when the costs of actually simulating complex software is involved.

Let me point out that not all concurrent development systems are alike. Some permit easy generation of "hooks" to the live software; others require complex programming to do it. Some permit natural language access; others use "nested" menus. Some are limited to PC hardware and software, while others permit access to mainframe software if there are PCs networked to the mainframe. Concurrent development is also possible with mainframe software via traditional mainframe terminals. This area is rapidly developing and offers great promise in terms of both productivity and quality of interactive learning experiences, including "embedded" training. We may also see some conventional authoring systems develop this ability to interface directly with applications software in the near future. Know your needs and what's involved in meeting them. Concurrent development software will go a long way to solving your problems.

Lesson Presentation Systems. All authoring systems produce lesson code that must be "translated," or communicated to the computer for execution. Sometimes the "presentation code" is actually embedded within the learning materials and its presence is transparent to the user; other times a "presentation" system is required. In the case of microcomputer-based systems, this means the learner must use a separate (and separately sold) "presentation" or "driver" or "individual learner" diskette.

All mainframe-based authoring systems require installation of presentation systems that are priced independently of the authoring systems. These can be purchased or leased for use with commercial products or internally developed courseware presentation. When mainframe-developed courseware is to be executed in a PC environment, there is typically a separate PC "presentation" or "driver" system to translate the mainframe-specific code into terms the PC can understand. For the most part, this "translation" software is too large to embed on a diskette that includes extensive lesson files. These presentation diskettes are required for every PC delivery station to be used for the mainframe-developed courseware and are usually priced separately. Of course, networked PC or PC-mainframe systems may change these requirements.

Finally, some PC authoring systems require separate presentation systems for each individual learner. Others do not. The reasons are sometimes technical and sometimes marketing- or educationally-related. Be certain to ask about this when you are evaluating authoring systems, since it can affect both cost and administrative complexity.

CBT Administration Systems. For some interactive learning experiences or CBT courses it's necessary or desirable to formally "register" learners, track learner performance either within or following the course (e.g., competency tests), or track completion and mastery levels and rates. In such cases, CBT administration software is very desirable. Some authoring systems include partial or full administration systems as part of the package; others require purchasing them separately. Still others don't have them available at all.

In evaluating administration systems, as with other software, know your needs and set priorities. Be certain to consider

• report development capabilities;

• item, lesson, course, and learner analysis capabilities;

• ability to use output in other analytical tools (e.g., spreadsheets);

• upload and download capabilities for mainframe-to-micro connections;

• administrative complexity;

• limits to numbers of learners tracked; and

91

- ability for learners to make context-sensitive or freeform comments for course administrator review.

Netting It Out. In summary, software can be enabling or limiting. It is important to evaluate all the technological tools we discussed, integrating them based on needs and technological compatibility. Involve appropriate technical people (read "resources") if your own technical knowledge or confidence is not sufficient for adequate analysis and decision making. Having the right combination of tools for the tasks at hand makes a big difference in both output and quality. In short, it makes life a lot easier.

[1] Greg Kearsley, *Computer-Based Training: A Guide to Selection and Implementation* (Addison-Wesley Publishing Company: Reading, Massachusetts, 1983)

[2] *ThinkTank* is a software product of Living Videotext, Inc., 2432 Charleston Road, Mountain View, California 94043. (415) 964-6300.

[3] *Action Diagrammer* is a software product of KnowledgeWare, Inc., 2006 Hogback Road, Ann Arbor, Michigan 48105. (313) 971-5363.

[4] *Shelley* is a software product of ComTrain, Inc., 152 Mill Street, Grass Valley, California 95945. (916) 273-0845.

[5] *Concurrent Development Series* is a software product of Vasco Corporation, 1919 South Highland Avenue, Suite 118-C, Lombard, Illinois 60148. (312) 495-0755.

[6] *Explain* is a software product of Communications Sciences, Inc., 100 North Seventh Street, Suite 518, Minneapolis, Minnesota 55403. (612) 332-7559.

CHAPTER

Development

Far less important than the
number of steps involved in
creating CBT is the realization
that there are discrete
steps at all.

You emphasize a structured CBT development process with almost a religious intensity. Describe your idea of a good development process, and tell me why you think it's so important!

One of the basic laws in this business is "You can't wing it with CBT." The very nature of the computer medium requires specificity in articulating design, scripts, displays, and logic beyond that required in any other environment. If you don't plan it, it won't be programmed. If you don't program it precisely, it won't execute. If it doesn't execute, learners can't access the program and therefore can't do *anything* to move themselves along the learning curve.

No other medium is so unforgiving of sloppy planning. With a book or a video, learners can often "tune out" questionable material and move along the learning curve in spite of it. Likewise, you can teach courses that haven't been adequately developed. The dynamic and flexible nature of the classroom permits both the instructor and the learners to compensate for imprecise or inadequate design. Instructors can "branch" online to relevant information, ask learners to repeat material, and present alternative explanations when the initial one doesn't work. Learners can query the instructor for clarification, repetition, additional information, or anything else they think might help them understand. Classes can be presented when there isn't sufficient development time available because instructors can develop as they proceed or call upon related knowledge or experience.

Even when there isn't learning, there's the appearance of training. And that gets political pressure off the training manager's back while actual course development occurs. Typically, the "real course" gets presented after the initial round of training events. We simply call it "advanced topics." Cynicism about some of the realities of organizational politics aside, the fact is that CBT can't be promised without adequate time to develop it. It must be completely developed before it's offered. And there are phases, stages, activities, and deliverables that must be carefully managed to get the maximum result with the minimum effort.

I wish I could give you short cuts. In my experience, there are none. Development of CBT is a "pay me now, pay me later" deal. You either pay up front by following the precise and demanding development steps, or you pay later with less than adequate programs, several passes through the revision or redevelopment process, or poor learning outcomes with resultant poor learner performance on the job. Now, there are several procedural and technological productivity sources that can be employed within the methodology. But the methodology remains the same.

CBT Development Methodology Objectives. The CBT development methodology, or process, has three objectives. The first is to assure timely production of the highest quality CBT courseware that achieves specified learning objectives within the available development time frames.

94

Second, the methodology assures client or program sponsor control of the product content, structure, design, screen displays, and interactivity levels through (1) continuous involvement throughout the development process and (2) review, approval, and sign-off on tangible paper-based deliverables at the end of each major development phase. Work begins on subsequent phases only after written client or program sponsor approval is received on the current phase's deliverables.

Finally, the methodology aims to control the development process to ensure that development team members spend their time in creative and productive activities by clarifying specifications, content, priorities and

Exhibit 5.1
THE SOFTWARE DEVELOPMENT PROCESS

PHASE/STEP	RESPONSIBILITY	ACTIVITY/DELIVERABLE
Phase 1. Project Definition		
Step 1	Client	**Activity:** Provide all existing instructional materials and related subject matter references and documentation.
Step 2	CBT Developer	**Activity:** Review materials
Step 3	Client	**Activity:** Assign accountable subject matter experts, course managers, and approval levels/individuals.
Step 4	CBT Developer/Client	**Activity:** Project scoping—series of meetings/activities resulting in: **Deliverables:** • Learner audience(s) defined • Course learning objectives • Course topic listing • Interactivity level specifications • Course standards • Preliminary Design Schedule
Step 5	Client	**Activity:** Client sign-off
Phase 2. Design		
Step 1	CBT Developer	**Activity:** structure topical sequences, generate specific instructional design strategies, and define supporting graphics. Establish learner paths for each learner population.
Step 2	Client/CBT Developer	**Activity:** Review and revise structure, design, and graphics in joint meetings. **Deliverable:** Course design document.
Step 3	Client	**Activity:** Client sign-off.

CONTINUED

95

THE SOFTWARE DEVELOPMENT PROCESS (cont.)

PHASE/STEP	RESPONSIBILITY	ACTIVITY/DELIVERABLE
Phase 3. Development/Scripting		
Step 1	CBT Developer	**Activity:** Scripting, storyboarding and detailed graphics, and test development.
Step 2	Client/CBT Developer	**Activity:** Review and revise text and graphics in joint meetings. **Deliverable:** Storyboards/script.
Step 3	Client	**Activity:** Client sign-off.
Phase 4. Programming/Entry into Authoring System		
Step 1	CBT Developer	**Activity:** Input to authoring system and programming of graphic images and special routines. Testing and debugging.
Step 2	Client	**Activity:** Courseware review and evaluation, including any representative learner testing.
Step 3	CBT Developer	**Activity:** Revise. **Deliverable:** CBT courseware.
Step 4	Client	**Activity:** Client sign-off.
Phase 5. Evaluation		
Step 1	Client	**Activity:** Conduct learner evaluations and identify revisions.
Step 2	Client/CBT Developer	**Activity:** Decide on revisions and schedule.
Step 3	CBT Developer	**Activity:** Make revisions. **Deliverable:** CBT Courseware
Step 4	Client	**Activity:** Review and approval.
Phase 6. Implementation		

preferences, and roles and responsibilities as early in the development process as possible.

The Nature of the Process. The CBT development process is necessarily a sequential and repetitive one. Design cannot begin before content and learning objectives are defined; programming cannot occur before complete and detailed scripts and storyboards (i.e., scripts annotated with production notes) are created for both text and graphics, including interactions and branching. All deliverables lead to increasingly detailed descriptions of the program that are developed entirely on paper until the material is ready to be "programmed" or input into the authoring system. When an authoring system is used, programming may be a simple data entry activity. When the design is more complex, technically sophisticated people may need to be involved in creating the instructions for the authoring system or programming language instructions.

The cumulative effect of adhering to this process is quality CBT at the least possible cost in the least time possible!

Phases and Steps. The CBT development process can be divided into eight phases. Some project managers feel these basic phases can be further subdivided (for example, making a separate phase of debugging); others combine some (such as when project definition and high-level design are performed as one phase). It's not so important how the different phases and activities are labeled. What's important is that all of the activities occur and that program sponsors review and approve each phase before the project goes on to the next, more time-consuming phase.

Phase 1. Project Definition
Phase 2. High-Level Design
Phase 3. Detailed Design
Phase 4. Development (or scripting or storyboarding)
Phase 5. Programming
Phase 6. Testing and Evaluating
Phase 7. Production and Distribution
Phase 8. Administration

Exhibit 5.1 details the steps, primary responsibilities, and activities that must occur within each phase and the deliverables that are a result of each phase. The methodology presumes that the "development team" is accountable to someone who is the course sponsor or client, even if that client is internal to the development team's organization. The sponsor may even be the development team manager! If there is only one individual doing all of the development activities, that person must either perform or assure the performance of each role during the development steps.

The process is similar to the structured systems development methodologies that MIS and DP have been using over the years to develop data processing systems. The methodology incorporates a blend of both systems design and instructional development processes. The presumption here is that good traditional instructional design activities, such as needs analysis and definition of learning objectives, are necessary but that additional activities are required due to the nature of the computer.

Each step is critical. None can be skipped. To the degree that a more superficial rather than thorough job has been completed and adequately documented, the final product will suffer, or the developer will have to go through the cycle again. Most of the development disappointments or disasters I have seen have been the result of failure to perform all of the necessary activities. Rationalizations such as "we don't have time for this level of detail" or "the client would never do those things" don't

Exhibit 5.2
PARTIAL DELIVERABLE
PROJECT DEFINITION

Preliminary CBT Guidelines

1.   GENERAL CONDITIONS

Hardware:
Course length and ancillary materials:
Audience:
Level of detail and complexity:
Learner outcome:

2.   OBJECTIVES

General objectives of course are stated in workbook. On-line introduction to each unit contains summarized objectives, descriptions, time to complete and materials needed.

3.   INSTRUCTIONAL DESIGN

3.1.   ADDRESSING THE AUDIENCE

Course is geared to new employees with little or no computer experience.

3.1.1.   TONE

Professional but not stiff. Personal pronouns. Touch of humor in examples.

3.1.2.   READING LEVEL

High school graduate. Conversational English.

3.1.3.   USE OF JARGON

Terminology must be explained before it is used, and then used consistently. Acronyms are spelled out the first time, and used as acronyms thereafter. Avoid unnecessary jargon.

3.1.4.   USAGE—STYLE GUIDE

AP Style Guide, assuming no company style guide exists.

3.2.   FLOW AND STRUCTURE

Each unit on separate diskette. Each unit begins with a title screen, an introduction, and a menu of modules in that unit. Modules are presented in sequence unless student chooses otherwise.

3.2.1.   BRANCHING STYLE

a. Menus

Each unit has a menu of the modules including approximate time to complete. Although it is recommended that students take modules in sequence, they can begin with any module and return to the menu to choose another module.

CONTINUED

PROJECT DEFINITION (cont.)

    b. Branching for Feedback

The course branches to another screen to give the student feedback on an answer. The question remains on the screen. When the student has more than one try to get the right answer (for example, multiple choice questions), there is a feedback screen for each possible answer. An exit message is overlaid on the screen when the student has exhausted the number of tries. The exit gives the right answer.

    c. Branching for Remediation

For wrong answer, one summary screen of remediation is presented. Then the text question is presented.

    d. Paging Forward and Back

Student can page back to review material. In paging forward again, student must answer questions to get past the question screens.

    e. Exit to menu available on all text.

    f. Skipping

Student can skip around by choosing modules from menu and paging.

3.2.2. TIMING OF DISPLAY

For graphics and title screens only. Not recommended for text and question screens.

3.2.3. INTRODUCTIONS AND SUMMARIES

Each unit has a formal introduction. Modules may have intro as needed. Each unit and module should have summary—could be in the form of a bulleted list, questions or other activity.

3.3. TESTING AND TRACKING

3.3.1. PRE-TEST

Allows the student to test his knowledge before taking the unit or module. Student may skip material if he already knows the material.

3.3.2. POST-TEST

Post tests reinforce the main point of the preceding material and should reflect the objectives. For each unit, group of modules or module, depending on how much detail and CBT time is involved.

3.3.3. REMEDIATION ON POST TEST

For wrong answer, one summary screen of remediation is presented. Student then continues with test. Additional remediation suggested depending on results.

CONTINUED

PROJECT DEFINITION (cont.)

3.3.4. TIMING OF RESPONSES

Not recommended.

3.3.5. RECORD-KEEPING

For pre- and post-testing only.

3.4. INTERACTION

3.4.1. QUESTION TYPES

True/false, multiple choice, fill-in, and matching as appropriate. Text of case studies can be on-line or off-line; step-by-step analysis provided by CBT.

3.4.2. ANSWER ANALYSIS

Multiple tries, feedback, and exit message are provided by branching.

a. Hints

For complex questions, the student may be cautioned about common errors or reminded about a key on the question screen.

b. Feedback

Non-threatening, constructive, and friendly without being condescending. Always says first what the student's answer was and whether the answer is right or wrong. For wrong answer, explains why the answer was wrong. A lead-in to the next screen may also be given, if necessary.

c. Number of tries

Two for multiple choice; one for true/false. As appropriate for other questions.

d. Exit messages

After the second try, the exit message supplies the correct answer.

3.4.3. SIMULATIONS

For computer entry and functions. Simulations of paper processes are often better on paper. Appropriate prompts and questions relating to the paper simulation are in the on-line course.

3.4.4. COORDINATION WITH ANCILLARY MATERIALS

Student should not go between keyboard and workbook too frequently in one activity, unless simulating actual work process. CBT can wait for student to complete workbook activity.

Workbook may contain forms, charts, crib sheets, etc. not practical for screen display. Can be used for future reference, review, and independent study.

4. VISUAL DESIGN

CONTINUED

PROJECT DEFINITION (cont.)

4.1.   GRAPHICS

4.1.1. COLOR

Limit to four, including black and white. Most text is white on black. White on another background is for special uses such as menus, title screens, charts, and borders. Colors and graphics identify screen elements, such as headings, instructions, and menu choices.

4.1.2. BLINKING

Not recommended.

4.1.3. USE OF CURSOR

Shows student where to type on question screen. Highlight makes cursor stand out.

4.1.4. STANDARD TREATMENT OF LIKE ELEMENTS

Same kind of information has same graphic "look." For example, box feature in red; box benefit in blue.

4.1.5. SPECIAL EFFECTS

Attractive and informative title screen for course and for each unit.

4.2.   SCREEN FORMATS AND STYLE

4.2.1. HEADINGS

Title screens and border information eliminate need for main headings. Where subheads are necessary, use all caps, centered highlight. Subhead is carried through in border.

4.2.2. BORDERS

Top border in Line 1 carries identifying info, including module name and subhead. Bottom border in Line 24 carries instructions, such as press enter to go on, PF1 = menu, PF2 = back page.

4.2.3. IDENTIFIERS

Screen identifiers such as module name go in bar across top of screen. Student will not see any page number or screen numbers.

4.3.   TYPOGRAPHY

4.3.1. UPPER/LOWER CASE

Standard English usage. Exceptions: Subheads are all upper case. Lower border is all lower case, except for key names (example: F1 = menu).

4.3.2. HIGHLIGHTS

Use sparingly in text for contrast and emphasis. Highlight the letter corresponding to a menu choice or an answer choice. Highlight cursor on answer screens. Highlight bullets.

CONTINUED

PROJECT DEFINITION (cont.)

4.3.3. INDENT

Don't indent paragraphs. Indent bulleted info.

4.3.4. BULLETS

Highlighted asterisks are used as bullets.

4.3.5. SPACING

Single space. Double between paragraphs.

4.3.6. MARGINS

For straight text and questions screens, margins are at columns 5 and 75. Screens with graphics may go out to columns 1 and 80.

Text and questions start on line 3. Line 22 is the last available line.

4.4. EXCEPTIONS TO GENERAL STANDARDS

4.4.1. SIMULATIONS

Colors and typography should copy the real thing as closely as possible. Lines 3–15 are available for simulation. Highlighted white line on line 17 separates simulation from CBT material. Lines 18–22 available for accompanying CBT. 80 columns available.

4.4.2. QUESTIONS

Question occupies lines 3–15. Line 17 contains instruction to answer question and cursor. Highlighted white line on line 18 separates question from other material: lines 19–22 for feedback.

Author's note: This document could be described as "standards" or course specifications.

make a difference. They just defer the inevitable problems associated with the program's inadequacies or different expectations between the client and the development team.

Repetitive Process. Rarely does a development team walk through the entire process in a straight line. Typically, especially with new developers, complex projects, or inexperienced or uninvolved program sponsors, there are repetitions of each phase when ideas, changes, or corrections are identified in the walkthroughs following the completion of each stage. The objective is to keep the total number of loops through the cycle to minimal levels while ensuring adequate quality *and* to keep the loops close in phase. For example, it's easier, less expensive, and less emotionally traumatic to repeat Phase 2, high-level design, three times in succession than it is to proceed all the way through Phase 4, scripting or storyboarding, and have to come back to the fundamental design structure and start all over.

Each phase becomes successively more detailed, and each requires almost an order of magnitude increase in the time, expense, emotional commitment, and numbers of people over the previous one. Major revisions at the later stages cost far more money and elapsed time than changes earlier in the project or within a phase. Remember, "There's never time to do it right, but there's always time to do it again."

Exhibit 5.3
SAMPLE CONTRACT CONDITIONS FROM PROJECT DEFINITION

CBT Contract Conditions

1. Any changes requested by the Customer after a section has been signed off, will automatically result in an increase in the personday and elapsed-time estimates. The additional time will be used to analyze the impact of the change on the rest of the project's time frames, which may or may not result in further additional time/expense.

2. If, during Detailed Design, the customer requests or approves a change in scope, the time and cost estimates will be adjusted to accommodate that change.

3. The Customer will be available to the CBT team for consultation on an as-needed basis.

4. The Customer or a representative will attend all content walkthroughs as well as reviewing products.

5. The Customer (or representative) will be given advance notice of all review tasks and specific dates will be agreed upon.

6. If, as a result of any postponement, the assignment of a CBT team member expires, extra persondays and elapsed time WILL be added for orientation of a replacement author, and MAY be added based on the replacement author's skill level. If no replacement author is available, elapsed time will increase and persondays may increase.

Walkthroughs. At the end of each phase, structured and controlled walkthroughs of the deliverables must occur. Walkthroughs are essentially systematic group reviews at key points throughout the CBT development process. As Ginette Purcell of Aetna Life & Casualty pointed out in her article "Walking it Through: Preventive Planning for CBT Courses," (*Training News*, November, 1984):

By implementing the CBT structured walkthrough as an essential step in course development, you can accomplish the following:

• Ensure consistency in tone, format, and style
• Detect ambiguities and errors
• Ensure accuracy of content

Exhibit 5.4

SAMPLE PROJECT DEFINITION: SCHEDULE

ACT III CBT COURSE PROJECT WORKPLAN						
Task	Step	Description	Assigned to	Est P/D	Start Date	Complete Date
I		PRELIMINARY ANALYSIS				
	1	Review Act III as model of new course and intro to subject matter		1.0 1.0 1.0	9/83 9/83 10/83	10/83 10/83 10/83
	2	Define course objectives, approach, coding standard		0.4 0.4	10/83 10/83 10/83 10/83	10/83 10/83 10/83 10/83
	3	Develop course outline and revise			9/83	10/83
	4	Walkthrough case processing on simulated system		0.5 1.5	9/83 9/83	9/83 10/83
II		ADMINISTRATION				
	1	Develop proposal and workplans		3.0	10/13	10/21
	2	Prepare status reports, memos; monitor progress		7.0	9/83	6/84
	3	Team meetings (non-data gathering)		2.0 2.0	9/83 9/83 9/83 9/83	6/84 6/84 6/84 6/84
	4	Supervisor meetings (for project control)		1.0 2.0	9/83 9/83 9/83 9/83	6/84 6/84 6/84 6/84
III		INTRODUCTION TO CBE				
	1	Create format (text only)		0.5	10/83	10/83
	2	Content discussion		0.4 0.4	10/83 10/83 10/83 10/83	10/83 10/83 10/83 10/83

Sample page from project workplan

- Capitalize on prior experience
- Make better use of resources
- Cut down recoding efforts.

To this list I would add the advantages of ensuring appropriate and creative design, ensuring interactivity levels, integrating activities among and between team members, and overall control of the development process at each phase and limiting risk at subsequent development phases.

Purcell continues: "The CBT structured walkthrough is simply a well-planned meeting" with appropriate roles, structures, and rules predefined.

There is an entire body of knowledge developed in data processing called "structured techniques." These techniques elaborate requirements for each development stage. The walkthroughs themselves are critical activities.

All of the key players in a development project must participate, and the role that each plays must be clearly defined. Ed Yourdon, one of the fathers of structured techniques, articulates the roles, activities, outcomes, and political dynamics of structured walkthroughs in his book, *Structured Walkthroughs* (Yourdon Press: New York, 1971). It should be required reading for all involved in a CBT project.

Deliverables and Their Components. It's easy to talk about such

Exhibit 5.5
PARTIAL DELIVERABLE-PROJECT DEFINITION
SCREEN DISPLAY PROTOTYPE
AND SAMPLE WRITING STYLE

Your territory is a large metro area. Your manager suggests you:

- produce a prospect list

- concentrate on medium sized accounting firms.

Best Course of Action:

1. Compile list from local phone book, then call to determine firm's size.

2. Compile list from existing customer files. Files are by business type and installed phone systems.

Enter your selection.

CONTINUED

105

SCREEN DISPLAY PROTOTYPE (cont.)

Module A
Topic B

Think about it more . . .

Which firm would most benefit from "The Accountant"?

1. A firm of 3 account- ants specializing in GL write-ups.

2. A sole proprietorship.

3. A firm of 57 account- ants, a branch of a regional firm.

Enter 1, 2, or 3.

---

1. Not the best answer.

"The Accountant" can improve any firm's efficiency. The larger the firm, the more it will benefit.

Few small firms will use its ability to maintain up to 99 separate billing families or departments per office, linking related entities.

Features such as Accounts Receivables, History, and Work-in-Progress assume many accountants/consultants doing a wide range of jobs.

Options:
A — Access
E — Exit
M — Menu
↵ — Continue

SCREEN DISPLAY PROTOTYPE (cont.)

Topic C

Reaching
the Customer

Ps and Qs
Opportunity

Courses of Action

Consider these courses of action:

1. You compile a list of accounting firms from the local telephone directory, and then make telephone inquiries to determine their size.

2. You compile a list of accounting firms from an internal customer file. The internal customer file is broken out by business type and installed phone systems.

Which would be the most beneficial course of action?

ENTER 1 or 2

A — Access

E — Exit   M — Menu   Y — Continue

things as design or storyboard deliverables that should be the product of a given development phase. It's much tougher to translate that into an operational definition. Many new—and even experienced—CBT developers "wing it" here. And they get into trouble as a result.

There are some definite elements that must be included in deliverables for each phase. I've listed them below. The development team and the program client must know what to expect and must demand it at the appropriate time.

1. Project Definition (Proposal)

- Listing of content topics
- Audience definition
- Learning objectives by audience
- Complexity assessment of each topic
- Program standards
- Interactivity level specifications
- Recommended technical environment
- Role definitions
- Testing specifications
- Preliminary project schedule
- Preliminary cost estimates
- Assumptions

2. High-Level Design

- General narrative description of program structure, instructional strategies, major learning paths, learner options, testing strategies, graphics
- Sequenced topic listing

3. Detailed Design

- Detailed representation of program logic
- Detailed narrative description of instructional strategies and graphics, including content of cases and practice problems for each topic
- Detailed testing descriptions
- Detail of learner options

4. Development (scripting or storyboarding)

- Scripts of all text displays

- Details and logic of graphics display

- Branching instructions for each screen

- Menu structures and options

- Dynamic screen display instructions (e.g., highlighting, windowing)

- Tests, including scoring algorithms

Exhibit 5.6
SAMPLE MODULE FLOWCHART — HIGH LEVEL DESIGN DELIVERABLE

Draft Co. No.: __1__

Page 3 of _____
Date: __6-13-85__
Client Approval: _____
Module _D__   Title _Needs & Solut_ions   Approval Date: _____
Sequence # _1__

NEED/BENEFIT/FEATURE/MODULE

Case/
Need

Which   Which   Which
Benefit   Feature   Module   System
               Response/   Response/   Graphic Used
               Remediation   Remediation in Response/
                                          Remediation

This is the basic structure that will be used throughout the sequence.

Exhibit 5.7
SAMPLE DELIVERABLE
HIGH LEVEL DESIGN AND PROJECT DEFINITION (COMBINED)

Module 1. Internal/External Audit Activities—Content

A. Introduction

B. Objective of the Audit Function
1. Internal
2. External

C. Determine Acceptability of Internal Audit Function
1. Internal Auditors
2. Workpapers
3. Audit Schedule
4. Audit Reports
5. Auditor's Work—acceptable, partly acceptable, unacceptable
6. Audit Program Effectiveness

D. External Audits
1. Types—CPA, non-CPA
2. Competency
3. Independence
4. Procedures
5. Audit Report
6. Scope of Audit

E. Write the Report Comment

Module Overview

Objectives: Student will be able to evaluate the internal/external audit function of a bank by performing examination procedures.

Estimated time:
1 hour

Possible materials:
workbook, handbook

Preliminary treatment suggestions:
drill with questions describing situations that may or may not be acceptable

Module 2. Introduction to UBPR—Content

A. Introduction

B. Analyzing the UBPR
1. Data groups—bank, peer group, percentile ranking
2. Format—summary ratios, income, balance sheet info, other
3. Decision tree approach
4. Source of Data—Call Reports

CONTINUED

HIGH LEVEL DESIGN AND PROJECT DEFINITION (cont.)

5. Variations
6. Peer Groups
7. Tax Equivalency

C. Relate BPR Data to the Bank

1. Assets and Liabilities
2. Trends
3. Summary ratios

D. Principal Uses

E. BPR Priority Review Process

Module Overview

Objectives:
   Students will be familiar with:

   • the overall format of the BPR.

   • using the BPR as an analytical tool in evaluating the financial condition of a bank.

Note: This module will not cover all BPR entries in detail.

Estimated time: 2 1/4 hours

Possible materials: workbook, BPR instructions

Preliminary treatment suggestions: walk-through a BPR, then give student exercises to evaluate the data from another one

Reproduced with permission of The Courseware Developers, Inc. 63 East Center Street, Manchester, CT 06040.

5. Programming

• Executable code using the authoring system or in programming language on appropriate computer storage medium

• Program documentation including program overview, logic, display formats, facilities, course print

6. Testing

• Technical evaluations

• Learner evaluations

• Educational evaluations

• Subject matter evaluations

• Recommended revisions (specific)

7. Production and Distribution

- Physical production of diskettes or tapes and other program materials packaged for distribution

8. Administration

- Registration procedures

- Administrative and record-keeping procedures

- Definition of responsibility for administrative activities

- Physical equipment installation

Samples of Deliverables. Beyond just listing the required elements, Exhibits 5.2 through 5.19 are examples of deliverables, many of which are now in use in business organizations. I offer these to you as models, departure points, and idea generators. There's nothing sacred about any of the formats or terms. What *is* sacred are the components themselves.

One of the major difficulties development teams have is agreement on standards for components, structure, style, and level of detail for the deliverables. The best time to get such agreement is, of course, before you begin. If you wait until one of the reviewers or the project manager deems whatever was delivered "inadequate," defensiveness and conflict inevitably emerge. The temptation is to underestimate the degree of detail required at earlier stages and to jump into what most people view as the "real work," scripting. In fact, the "real work" from my perspective is in the design phases. That's what separates technical writers from interactive instructional designers. It's the more complex, creative, and critical phase of this work. Scripting becomes relatively straightforward once you create the design structures and sequences and logic or display standards.

Some would say that truly experienced designers who also have extensive subject matter expertise can skip stages or create deliverables with far less detail. In my experience, the more experience people have, the more they learn how important detail is.

Considerations in Defining Deliverable Specifications. No given deliverable is right or wrong, too detailed, or not detailed enough as it stands alone. Each organization must define the content, detail level, and style that is appropriate in relation to the following considerations.

- Nature and complexity of the content

- Available time

- Criticalness of the project

- Project length and complexity

111

Exhibit 5.8
SAMPLE DELIVERABLE
HIGH—LEVEL DESIGN DOCUMENT

Introduction

The XYZ CBT consists of a training diskette and an accompanying Student Guide. The diskette presents a case study—a simulated XYZ sales situation—which the student will be able to complete in about an hour. (The actual time frame for the sales cycle in the case is 9 months.) The Student Guide (approximately 20 pages in length) explains how to use the CBT diskette and also describes the two-hour Final Exercise that the student will carry out following completion of the case study.

The case study covers the entire XYZ sales cycle, but particularly emphasizes qualifying customers. Both marketing and technical information concerning the XYZ are reviewed, with cross references to the Marketing Guide. The cost justification model in the Financial Selling Guide is implemented at the appropriate point in the sales cycle.

The CBT is highly interactive. The students will have to make some type of choice every few screens. Many of the choices will be quite challenging. The students will be called upon not only to demonstrate good product knowledge, but also to exercise judgment in reaching qualitative sales decisions.

The students will experience the negative consequences of poor decisions, but they will also have the opportunity to recover from each mistake and proceed to a successful sale.

Some choices will involve optional review of information presented or discovered earlier (e.g., the cost justification of the XYZ solution proposed to the prospect).

To help the students retain the sales lessons embodied in the CBT, there will be periodic recapitulations of the steps the students have taken to develop the account.

The case has been designed to illustrate how the XYZ sales team (sales rep, sales manager, and engineer) will collaborate in planning and carrying out their sales efforts. The intention is to prepare the students for actual XYZ sales action planning.

The Student Guide begins with a very brief summary of basic information about the XYZ and then goes on to an explanation of the major phases of the XYZ sales action training.

Following three short sections providing instructions for use of the CBT diskette, the central portion of the Guide explains the two post-training activities the students will carry out with the assistance of their sales manager:

- Reviewing the CBT and completed sales aids to make sure its main lessons are clear

- Designing and implementing an initial sales action plan

The Guide will then describe and reproduce the three sales aids being provided to sales reps:

- Prospecting Organizer

CONTINUED

HIGH-LEVEL DESIGN DOCUMENT (cont.)

- Qualifying Checklist
- Account Planner

Purpose of the Design Report

This report contains the CBT objectives and detailed design outlines of the CBT case study and Student Guide. The design report offers the client an opportunity to review and approve the content of the case study and Student Guide prior to completion of the first draft.

The first draft will consist of a hard-copy script for the case study and the entire text of the Student Guide, including the Flow Chart for XYZ In-Branch Training and Sales Execution and samples of the sales aids.

See the attached implementation Flowchart and sales aids. The sales aids will be modified for the XYZ.

Audience

The audience for the CBT is:

Sales Reps

Customer Service Reps

Other members of the account team who should be familiar with the content of the training

Objectives

The objectives of the CBT are:

- To let students apply the knowledge they have gained from the Marketing Guide to a realistic sales situation.
- To let the students use the sales aids and Financial Selling Guide in a realistic sales situation.
- To address the sales cycle that the students will follow in the field, particularly prospecting, qualifying, and cost-justification.
- To prepare the students to carry out XYZ sales action planning.

Profile Of The Case Study

1. Description for Companies

KIM Corporation has:

Five major departments (see organization chart):

- Manufacturing and Engineering
- Sales and Marketing
- Materials Management

CONTINUED

HIGH-LEVEL DESIGN DOCUMENT (cont.)

- Planning (and MIS)
- Controller's Office

9000 employees, including 60 salespeople

Plants In:

- Birmingham, AL
- Fresno, CA
- Ann Arbor, MI
- Pittsburgh, PA (headquarters)
- Austin, TX
- Salerno, Italy

Sales currently at $650 million per year and growing at an annual rate of 8%. Foreign sales account for 15% of the total. Profits are $30 million, or 4.6% of sales.

Recently completed a friendly takeover of ABC Inc., second largest U.S. producer of high-speed printing presses for magazines and newspapers.

ABC Inc. has:

- Manufacturing (includes Engineering and Materials Management)
- Marketing (includes Sales)
- Finance (includes DP)
- Human Resources

4500 employees, including 45 salespeople

Plants in:

- Mobile, AL (headquarters)
- Houston, TX

Sales currently at $600 million per year.

Reproduced with permission of Spectrum Training Corporation, 50 Salem Street, Lynnfield, Massachusetts 01946

- Numbers of people involved
- Quality standards and expectations of the management, training staff, and learners
- Knowledge, experience, and skill of development team
- Available training alternatives
- Political issues
- Project control needs

Exhibit 5.9

SAMPLE DELIVERABLE: COURSEWARE FUNCTIONAL SPECIFICATIONS USING THE TENCORE AUTHORING SYSTEM

Reproduced with permission of Scientific Systems, Inc., One Alewife Place, 35 Cambridge Park Drive, MA 02140.

SSI CBT Development Tools, Phase I,
Parts Definition Presentations And Glossary, Revision 1.0, Jan. 6, 1986

The Standard Parts Definition Presentation

SSI's standard sequence for parts definition presentations works as follows:

1. The computer system displays an overall diagram or picture of the machine whose parts are to be defined. This overall diagram or picture may be a TenCORE unit, a PC-Paintbrush file, or a videodisc frame.

2. The student is asked to "point to" the part s/he wants defined. Pointing may be accomplished in a variety of ways, but we are currently leaning towards displaying a box that highlights one part at a time. The student moves this box from part to part by pressing the space bar on the keyboard, and then presses the RETURN key when it is highlighting the part s/he wants defined.

3. The screen changes to the format shown in Figure 1 on page 8. The detailed diagram or other complementary image may be a TenCORE unit, a PC-Paintbrush file, or a videodisc frame. The definition display for a specific part may actually involve multiple screens, with different diagrams and text on each. If so, the student would move from one to the next in a linear fashion by pressing the space bar on the keyboard.

4. Pressing the RETURN key returns the student to the overall machine diagram or picture with the part just defined subdued in some fashion to indicate that its definition has already been seen.

Required Courseware Parameters

The information needed to deliver SSI's standard parts definitions presentations may be thought of as parameters to a standard TenCORE subroutine. These parameters are:

1. the ID of the overall machine diagram or picture that includes all of the parts to be defined (this may be a TenCORE unit, a PC-Paintbrush file, or a videodisc frame)

2. the names of the parts that can be defined

3. the upper left-hand and lower right-hand boundaries (in pixel coordinates) of each part on the overall machine diagram or picture that has a corresponding definition

4. the text of each part's definition

5. (optional) the ID of the detailed diagram or other complementary image to be displayed with the part definition (this may be a TenCORE unit, a PC-Paintbrush file, or a videodisc frame)

6. the starting position (line number) for text on each part definition screen (sufficient room must be left at the top of the screen for display of the detailed diagram or other complementary image; this parameter will have a default but may be changed by the course developer)

CONTINUED

SAMPLE COURSEWARE FUNCTIONAL SPECIFICATIONS (cont.)

Figure 1

Screen Format For Parts Definition Presentations

Part Name

Detailed Diagram of Part
or Other Complementary Image
(Optional)

Text Defining Part Function
or Explaining Its Use
(Required)

Directions

Table 2

Summary of Field Identifiers For Parts Definition Records In Parts Definition Files

Note: There may be up to 99 Parts Definition Records in one Parts Definition File.

Field Identifier	Requirement Status	Use
NAME	Required	text to be displayed at top of definition screen
LOCATION	Required	coordinates of box encompassing part on overall machine diagram format: x1,y1;x2,y2
DEFINITION	Required	text of part definition; may include embedded symbols listed in Table 3
IMAGE-TYPE	Optional	determines interpretation of Image-ID field; allowable values are: "TenCORE" or "T" "PC-Paintbrush" or "P" "Video" or "V"
IMAGE-ID	Optional	ID of image to display with definition text; may be a TenCORE unit ID, a PC- Paintbrush file name, or a videodisc frame number
STARTING-LINE	Optional	number of line on which definition text is to start (in the range of 1–22)
GLOSSARY	Optional	word or phrase to display if student presses Glossary function key (limited to 24 letters and spaces)
END-OF-RECORD or EOR	Required	marks end of record

Author's Note: This sample of detailed technical or functional specifications could be considered standards, output of the Project Definition, or part of the Detailed Design. The complete set was 36 typewritten pages. It represents the level of precision necessary for a large complex curriculum with extensive sophisticated graphics and instructional routines that is being programmed in a powerful authoring language.

The number of variables and the interrelationships among and between them are complex. Trade-offs are inevitable. For example, a situation where there is critical need, limited time, limited political risk, and experienced developers involved would probably call for less rather than more detail. The important thing is to make any trade-offs consciously and up-front rather than unconsciously and realize the consequence after the fact.

Exhibit 5.10
SAMPLE DETAIL DESIGN DELIVERABLE

SAMPLE
Draft Copy #: _____

Page 2 of ___75___
Date: 6-04-85

Client Approval: _____
Approval Date: _____

Module ___C___ Title _Meet System 10_
Sequence # ___1___

LEARNING OBJECTIVES:

At the end of this Sequence, learners will:

- Understand digital PBX Voice Management features
- Identify product features that will solve specific
  business problems or address identified issues

LEARNING LEVEL:

3
3

INSTRUCTIONAL STRATEGY	TOPICS	NOTES
Model: Symbolic representation of generic voice terminal Vignette Strand: - Problem/Solution - Solution/Benefits Vignette strand will be used to illustrate above model.	Digital PBX Features Voice Management - Leave Word Calling - Abbreviated dialing	
Model: Office voice system Vignettes: Problem/Solution Vignettes will be used to illustrate above model.	- Integrated Directory - Autocallback - Call Coverage - Uniform Call Distribution	Incoming Line

117

Exhibit 5.11

SAMPLE SCREEN TEMPLATES — DETAIL DESIGN DELIVERABLE

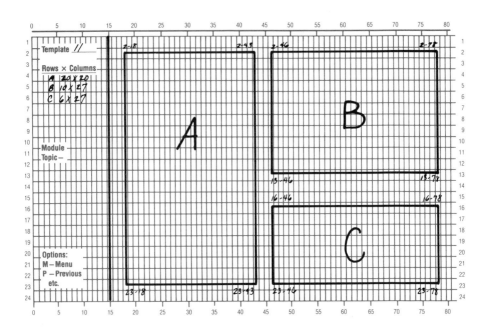

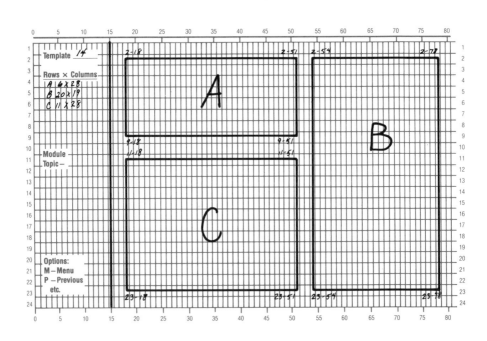

118

Refining Your Process and Improving Your Deliverables. In defining and describing your own deliverables, develop models and then get the team together relatively quickly after the start of the project. Work with the team members to evaluate and revise these models, if necessary, in relation to your task. Following completion of the project, step back and do a review of the entire development process and deliverables and make revisions, as appropriate.

In Summary. A tight development process, clear expectations for out-

Exhibit 5.12

SAMPLE STORYBOARD/SCRIPT DELIVERABLE
USING SCHOLAR/TEACH AUTHORING SYSTEM

```
fn lease130


        INSTALMENT LOANS                                              Leases


        Type an "x" beside the items you would expect to see in
        most lease agreements.


        _  Lessee's promise to take proper care of the property

        _  Leased property must be covered by hazard insurance

        _  Lessee can buy the property or extend the lease at the end
           of the lease term

        _  Bank has the right to inspect the property

----+----1----+----2----+----3----+----4----+----5----+----6----+----7----+----8

ANSWER    RESPONSE
------    --------

x~x~<x|_|%>~x~@
        Okay.  Any of these stipulations could be included in a lease.
        The lessee's option to buy the property or extend the lease is
        sometimes included, while the others are fairly standard
        inclusions.  RETURN to continue...

<_|%>~<_|%>~<_|%>~<_|%>~@
        Type an "x" beside each item for your answer.  (At least on item
        is correct).  Press RETURN and then try again.


alt scanned
<x|_|%>~<x|_|%>~<x|_|%>~<x|_|%>~@
        Type an "x" beside each item for your answer.  (At least on item
        is correct).  Press RETURN and then try again.



    #
        Actually, any of these stipulations could be included in a lease.
        The lessee's option to buy the property or extend the lease is
        sometimes included, while the others are fairly standard
        inclusions.  RETURN to continue...
```

put at the end of each development phase, and a critical and structured walkthrough process of deliverables are necessary conditions for quality and timely CBT development. Of course, there are other factors such as knowledgeable and skilled team members. But a development methodology can go a long way toward compensating for lack of experience. And it certainly provides the control mechanisms to know when and if experience from outside the development team is necessary. As a training or project manager, you should know process is the key critical success factor. Manage it that way.

Exhibit 5.13

SAMPLE DETAIL DESIGN DELIVERABLE

FSA DETAIL DESIGN

LESSON DESIGN

MODULE: Configuration
LEVEL: II
LESSON: Network Configuration Status
OBJECTIVE: Check the Network Configuration Status.
RESOURCES: FSA 2.0 Installation and Operations Guide- Chapter 4
KEY TERMS/CONCEPTS: network monitor module

INSTRUCTIONAL STRATEGY	TOPICS	NOTES
Level II Presentation	-Network monitor module -Network monitor command -Print network configuration command -Partition status command	-Positioning screens remind FE of commands and functions; information on system status presented (graphic of system, logbook information)
Practice Problem		-FE makes decision on correctness of configuration

LESSON DESCRIPTION:

Scene: end of installation. Specialist gives FE information on system status. FE checks that data comm devices are installed correctly. Reasoning behind correct answers is given in feedback.

Presentation	Descriptions & examples of three commands used to check status.	
Practice Problems/ Drill	Screen displays. FE to determine good or bad status. Feedback gives rationale.	

3-18-86

Exhibit 5.14

SAMPLE STORYBOARD/SCRIPT DELIVERABLE
USING SAM AUTHORING SYSTEM

Next you will see various screens displayed by the
status commands.

You will:

- Determine whether the status is good or bad.

- Choose the screen area indicating a bad status.

/BOOKMARK/

PAGE TYPE: Go to and return   PAGE: _____
  starting p: ending p: return to p:

PAGE TYPE: No. of tries:

  Press return   Clear
    Next: 55

SPECIAL FEATURES:
  Assign special keys: Key   Page
              Hint:
           Bookmark:

OTHER:
    Test #:   Question #:   Hint page: Menu page:

COMMENTS:

M.L.L: C.2.5 _____   T/W: _____   DATE: 6/18/86   INITIALS: lma   PAGE: __50__

Reproduced with permission of Unisys

CONTINUED

121

SAMPLE STORYBOARD/SCRIPT DELIVERABLE
USING SAM AUTHORING SYSTEM (cont.)

```
Partition Status 7.0.3                              User name:
Path: [SYS]<SYS>                       Mon Jun 16, 1986 1:30 PM

-------------------------------------------------------------------
Partition  ! #!Totl!Size!Used!    Run File Executing
---------+--+----+----+----+------------------------------------
System     ! 0!181K!181K!181K!t1MstrSpSwp-7.0.3
Primary    ! 1!346K!345K! 21K![Sys]<Sys>PartitionStatus.Run
SysService00! 2! 48K! 48K! 48K![Sys]<Sys>Bmulti.run
SysService01! 3! 79K! 79K! 79K![SYS]<FMCS>MQM.RUN
SysService02! 4! 21K! 20K! 20K![SYS]<FMCS>AGENTBMULTI.RUN
SysService03! 5! 89K! 89K! 89K![SYS]<FMCS>MCS.RUN
           ! ! ! ! !
           ! ! ! ! !
Total      ! !768K! ! !
-------------------------------------------------------------------
  High Bound 7A6A:0000  ! Low Bound 23B0:0000 ! Termination erc 0


      Does this screen show a good or bad status?
      Type g for good or b for bad.   ?
```

PAGE TYPE: Go to and return   PAGE: _____

  starting p: _____ ending p: _____ return to p: _____

PAGE TYPE: No. of tries:

  Single fill-in
  Correct: B or bad   Clear
  Match: 60
  Unanticipated: 65

SPECIAL FEATURES:

  Assign special keys: Key   Page
              Hint:
          Bookmark:

OTHER:

  Test #:   Question #:   Hint page: Menu page:

COMMENTS:

M.L.L: C.2.5 ____   T/W: _____   DATE: 6/18/86   INITIALS: 1ma   PAGE: _55_

CONTINUED

SAMPLE STORYBOARD/SCRIPT DELIVERABLE
USING SAM AUTHORING SYSTEM (cont.)

Right. Now find the problem.

PAGE TYPE: Go to and return   PAGE: _____

starting p: _____ ending p: _____ return to p: _____

PAGE TYPE: No. of tries:

   Press return   Overlay
   Next: 70

SPECIAL FEATURES:

   Assign special keys: Key   Page
             Hint:
      Bookmark:

OTHER:

   Test #:   Question #:   Hint page: Menu page:

COMMENTS:

M.L.L: C.2.5 ____   T/W: _____ DATE: 6/18/86   INITIALS: lma PAGE: __60__

CONTINUED

123

SAMPLE STORYBOARD/SCRIPT DELIVERABLE
USING SAM AUTHORING SYSTEM (cont.)

```
Incorrect. This screen shows a bad status.
Now find the problem.
```

PAGE TYPE: Go to and return   PAGE: _____
    starting p: _____ ending p: _____ return to p: _____

PAGE TYPE: No. of tries:
    Press return   Overlay
    Next: 70   (in window B p.55)

SPECIAL FEATURES:
    Assign special keys: Key   Page
                 Hint:
            Bookmark:

OTHER:
    Test #:   Question #:   Hint page: Menu page:

COMMENTS:

M.L.L: C.2.5 ____   T/W: _____ DATE: 6/18/86   INITIALS: lma PAGE: __65__

Exhibit 5.15
SAMPLE DETAILED DESIGN/STORYBOARD DOCUMENT
USING ACTION DIAGRAMMER

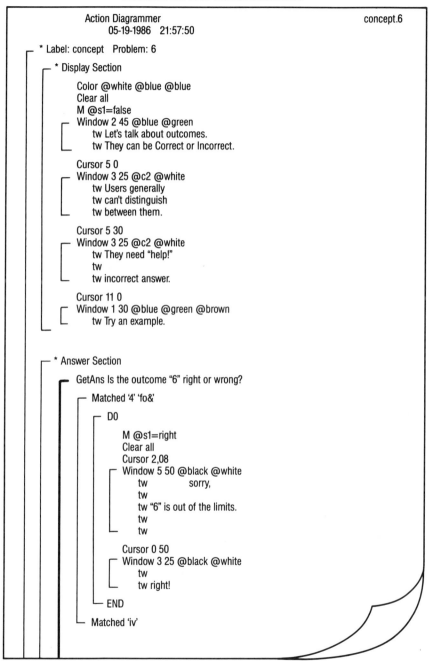

```
                Action Diagrammer                              concept.6
                05-19-1986  21:57:50
  ┌ * Label: concept   Problem: 6
  │   ┌ * Display Section
  │   │
  │   │       Color @white @blue @blue
  │   │       Clear all
  │   │       M @s1=false
  │   │   ┌ Window 2 45 @blue @green
  │   │   [    tw Let's talk about outcomes.
  │   │   └    tw They can be Correct or Incorrect.
  │   │
  │   │       Cursor 5 0
  │   │   ┌ Window 3 25 @c2 @white
  │   │   │    tw Users generally
  │   │   │    tw can't distinguish
  │   │   └    tw between them.
  │   │
  │   │       Cursor 5 30
  │   │   ┌ Window 3 25 @c2 @white
  │   │   │    tw They need "help!"
  │   │   │    tw
  │   │   └    tw incorrect answer.
  │   │
  │   │       Cursor 11 0
  │   │   ┌ Window 1 30 @blue @green @brown
  │   └   └    tw Try an example.
  │
  │   ┌ * Answer Section
  │   │
  │   │  ┌ GetAns Is the outcome "6" right or wrong?
  │   │  │  ┌ Matched '4' 'fo&'
  │   │  │  │   ┌ DO
  │   │  │  │   │      M @s1=right
  │   │  │  │   │      Clear all
  │   │  │  │   │      Cursor 2,08
  │   │  │  │   │   ┌ Window 5 50 @black @white
  │   │  │  │   │   │    tw          sorry,
  │   │  │  │   │   │    tw
  │   │  │  │   │   │    tw "6" is out of the limits.
  │   │  │  │   │   │    tw
  │   │  │  │   │   └    tw
  │   │  │  │   │
  │   │  │  │   │      Cursor 0 50
  │   │  │  │   │   ┌ Window 3 25 @black @white
  │   │  │  │   │   │    tw
  │   │  │  │   │   └    tw right!
  │   │  │  │   └ END
  │   │  │  └ Matched 'iv'
  └   └  └
```

This sample deliverable integrates both detailed structural design with the storyboard using automated design software.

Exhibit 5.16

SAMPLE STORYBOARD/SCRIPT DELIVERABLE
USING THE PHOENIX AUTHORING SYSTEM

FORMS

Course: Attribute bytes: High unmodified – $ Low modified – ¢

Unit/Obj./Level: H05A   High Modified – @   Null – :

Item Number: 17   Low Modified – # Mod. Prot. Inv. %

Indicate highlighting by using   and   .   (Defaults >   <)

```
 ····+····1····+····2····+····3····+····4····+····5····+····6····+····7····+····
1
     >¢_____%/–ON¢_____-
2
3
4
5     Assume you need to add a record to the RLH data base.
6     Cloning seems your best option because you have a record
7     already on the data base whose only difference is location.
8
9     The information you need to start cloning is:
10
11    Key of existing record:        001,45678
12
13    Key of record to be created:  001,87654
14
15    The SCREEN-ID containing the fields that need changing is '02'.
16
17    Please issue the command needed to start the cloning process.
18
19
20
 ····+····1····+····2····+····3····+····4····+····5····+····6····+····7····+····
```

NOINFO – Circle or underline if student entries are to be analyzed.

CU = _____ (default is 1). Specifies the input field for cursor positioning.

                 e.g., CU = 3 would position the cursor at the 3rd input field.

Do you wish to analyze student answers? $\frac{Y}{N}$ NOINFO

(i.e., will you follow this FORM screen with a Question screen?)

Exhibit 5.17
SAMPLE DELIVERABLE STORYBOARD/SCRIPT
(NOT AUTHORING SYSTEM SPECIFIC)

Frame 2030

A man carrying a suitcase comes to the front desk. He says he has a reservation, but you can't locate it. The hotel is sold out.

What do you think you should do?

A. Register him by bumping a guest who hasn't shown up yet

B. Call another hotel and try to find him a room

C. Check with the reservation clerk

PRESS 'A', 'B', OR 'C'

Branch to

A: 2040

B: 2050

C: 2060

Frame 2040

(window)

It's not a good idea to bump another guest. Check with the reservation clerk first, to see if the guest had a Today reservation that isn't at the front desk.

2070

Frame 2050

(window)

Before you relocate the guest, check with the reservation clerk. Maybe the guest has a Today reservation that's not at the front desk.

2070

Frame 2060

(window)

Checking with the reservation clerk is the best thing to do. The guest may have a Today reservation that isn't at the front desk.

2070

Exhibit 5.18
SAMPLE DELIVERABLE — SCREEN DISPLAY DESIGN

CAI SPECIFICATION FORM

DATE _____ MODULE NO. _2_ I.D. _____ DISPLAY NO. _35_

```
Module 2                                          The Nature of Stress

           LIFE EVENT                    UNITS  Y/N
Holmes & Rahe found that
although stress affects          TOP OF LIST              1450
each person differently,     Death of spouse      100  N   900
their relative importance    Divorce               73  N
is remarkably uniform.       Marital separation    65  N
They therefore developed     Jail term             63  N   750
the Social readjustment      Death of family member 63 N
Rating scale to measure      Personal injury or illness 53 N 600
personal stress.             Marriage              50  N
                             Fired from job        47  N   450
Try out the scale yourself   Marital reconciliation 45 N
by using the ↑ and ↓ keys    Retirement            45  N   300
to move the highlighting     Change in family health 44 N
bar up and down then         Pregnancy             40  N   150
typing Y or N to indicate    Sex difficulties      39  N
whether the highlighted      Gain of new family member 39 N  0
life event does or does        29 MORE EVENTS BELOW ↓
not pertain to you recently.

                                          Press RETURN when done
```

BRANCHING (unconditional): _36_

Name of Key	Location	Name of Key	Location	Name of Key	Location
1. objective	24	6. help	5	11.	
2. next	46	7. advice	use the keys to move the bar and type Y to indicate that the highlighted event pertained to you recently		
3. exercises	38	8. menu		13. 3	
4. exit	4	9.		14.	
5. page back	34	10.		15.	

STUDENT INPUTS: SYSTEM RESPONSES (COND.):

The up and down arrow keys move the highlighting bar up and down. The status messages such as TOP OF LIST and 29 more events below ↓ always remain, but they change as the window scrolls. Normal pressing of the ↑ and ↓ keys causes highlighting bar movement, but scrolling (in +6 or −6 increments) occurs when the bar is at the Top or bottom event in the window.

Toggling N to Y causes change in Y/N column in

COMMENTS: Window and proportionate change in thermometer based on number of units for event toggled.

Exhibit 5.19

SAMPLE STORYBOARD/SCRIPT DELIVERABLE
USING PHOENIX AUTHORING SYSTEM

ANSWER GROUP 3:　　　CORRECT/<u>INCORRECT</u> (circle one)

# OF WORDS:	VALUE:	gu001,87654/&
# OF WORDS:	VALUE:	guh001,87654/&
# OF WORDS:	VALUE:	

FEEDBACK: When you 'clone' records, you must start by getting an existing record for update – you specified the key of the record you want to create.

BRANCHING:

ANSWER GROUP 4:　　　CORRECT/<u>INCORRECT</u> (circle one)

# OF WORDS:	VALUE:	&
# OF WORDS:	VALUE:	
# OF WORDS:	VALUE:	

FEEDBACK: To begin cloning, you must get for update an existing record, in this case the one with a key of '001,45678'. It's on the 'RLH' data base, and the best SCREEN-ID to use is '02'.

BRANCHING:

MASSAGE (circle choices):
Convert to <u>lowercase,</u> compress spaces
Remove all: alphabetic numeric <u>spaces</u> punctuation

TRIES: 3
MASTERY:
EXIT MESSAGE: The correct command is:
　　　　　　　COMMAND..GU　001,45678　　　　　　　　　　ON..RLH　02.
HINT:

SIMULATIONS

| Will this question be answer analysis for a form? | Y | NOCLEAR | NOQUES | NOPR | NOINPUT |
| | N | — | | | |

| Is the question used in a simulation in which you want to branch automatically to another screen? | Y | NOINFO | NOSHOW |
| | N | | |

| Do you wish to suppress display of the bottom line? (If you said 'Yes' to the 2 previous questions, this has already been done.) | Y | NODIV | NOSHOW | NOID | NOPR |
| | N | | | | |

How many lines of data are there
on the form associated with　　　　　　　— is the number of lines of spaces you must
this question?　　　　　　　　　　　　　　　　insert as your question.

CHAPTER

Standards

Invest the time up front to
eliminate endless reinvention
and modification down the line.

When people interested in CBT get together, they always seem to talk about standards: in what areas to set them, how rigidly to adhere to them, or even whether or not to have them at all. What's your feeling about CBT standards?

My feelings are mixed. Literally, a *standard* is "something established by authority, custom, or general consent as a model or example." I think it is important for you to establish and define standards, but only after you have sufficient experience to assure that they are reasonable. And we don't have sufficient experience with either commercial or proprietary CBT to feel confident in setting them.

On the other hand, without some defined structures, models, or expectations to work toward, new CBT developers typically flounder. At this point in our individual and collective experience, I suggest that we establish CBT guidelines that are subject to ongoing review, and that we don't simply allow developers to try and err within a given project. I feel strongly, however, that we must come to an agreement on definitions of terms and structures, at least within a given project. You may change them as you proceed or for your next activity, but such agreements create the structure necessary for progress and good team relationships.

The following areas should be considered for establishing guidelines at the outset of a given CBT project:

- Project definition or proposal

- Development methodology

- Walkthrough process and criteria

- Learner options and how to access them

- Definitions of terms, such as *module, sequence,* and *interaction*

- Screen display templates

- Programming instructions or authoring system commands and notes

- Color

- Special key designations

- Graphics

- Interaction structures (e.g., two-option, open-ended, matching), definitions, formats, displays, and learner response

- Learner feedback

- Writing style (e.g., tense, person, case)

- Record keeping

- Instructional paths or sequences to achieve specific learning outcomes (e.g., sequence of types of interactions)

- Documentation

Project Definition or Proposal. The important components in the project definition or proposal are detailed in Chapter Five, which is on the development process. Setting standards goes beyond merely listing the components. The standards should define the variables and the relationships among them to assure a common language for everybody involved. In some ways, the deliverables achieve that. Exhibit 5.2 (see Chapter Five) is an abbreviated version of a project proposal. Representative content, strategies, standards, or assumptions are listed to illustrate the expression.

Development Methodology. Chapter Five details my recommended CBT development methodology. The important thing to remember here is that the stages, phases, activities, deliverables, and roles and responsibilities must be explicit.

Walkthrough Process and Criteria. The topic of reviews and walkthroughs is covered in Chapter Five. Some organizations develop standard walkthrough forms; others simply structure the process. Again, the degree to which you want to structure this is based on similar considerations in determining the degree of detail you require in your deliverables.

Learner Options and How to Access Them. You must create specific definitions of the learner options, and you must define how the learner will access them. In addition, you need to determine how and when the options will be displayed or presented to the learner. How you present learner options will also affect the structure of the program and the screen displays by which you communicate with the learner. You can give learners the following options, but you may develop others:

- Review

- Previous or back (to previous screen)

- Menu (within the section)

- Main menu

- Escape (or quit or exit)

- Hint

- Help

- Bookmark (or notation)

- Exercises or additional practice

- Skip ahead

- Glossary

- More information

- Print screen

- Change previous input or response

- Special purpose options within an applications software program (e.g., accessing program-related data, on-line documentation, interactive job aids or procedures)

Your development team must share a specific understanding of just what such terms as "review" or "previous" mean and communicate them to the learners. To some, for example, "review" means repeat the whole section; to others, it may mean to review the last completed sequence following the last interaction. Meanings must be clear.

When establishing learner options, you must take several things into account. You need to consider the nature and complexity of the content, learner knowledge of the content, learner expectations, available development time, and the ability of your authoring system to achieve various options (or the ease with which it does so!).

As with the establishment of all other standards, trade-offs are inevitable. For example, the program's instructional design might specify that the learner be able to review previous content while making a decision or performing an action during an interaction. Some authoring systems don't permit review on an interaction screen (although I'll never understand why such limitations are built in). Or development time is short and the decision is made not to permit learners to review sequences except at menu choice points. The trade-off will be in learner frustration during the actual CBT program.

Experience will tell you what trade-offs are more or less acceptable. To date, we've had little experience with extensive learner-controlled instruction, but we have learned some things. For example, learners like to review material much more than most CBT permits. As designers we greatly underestimate repetition as a learning strategy. Second, too many options confuse learners. Unless the options are continually displayed on the screen or can be easily accessed through a single key press (e.g., by pressing F1), learners forget how to access them and are frustrated. But too many options displayed on the screen make screen displays too crowded. A sticker or paper-based job aid can sometimes alleviate this problem.

If you try to limit the options by layering them, you will find the learners get "lost" in the program and can't orient themselves to get out and back to where they were. In addition, in complex exercises, case studies, or practice problems, learners strongly prefer paper-based information with on-line interactions. Complex problem solving requires continual reference to information and data, and learners find it too cumbersome and psychologically uncomfortable to be wandering around the software to access it. The print-screen option can solve this dilemma, for learners can opt to print information they view as helpful. But in some learning situations, it is best not to give paper-based information (e.g., when learners are doing advanced simulation of situations in which they would not have available reference material in real life, such as a medical emergency). In addition, the more context-sensitive options are (e.g., access a glossary definition of a term by either typing the term itself or pressing a number that is superscripted or parenthetically next to the term itself on the screen), the better. Providing access to options through "nested menus" (e.g., going to a glossary menu and then choosing a term within the menu) will discourage their use because of the procedure's cumbersomeness.

Definitions of Terms. The need to establish precise definitions of terms and naming conventions in the design process may seem trivial. In my experience, however, the earlier you establish clear definitions, the less difficulty you have. For example, if the developer defines sequences and branches one way and the programmer defines them another, rework is inevitable. Or if one writer defines a display as an entire screen and another defines it as subunits that collectively make up a screen, a mess is likely (mess is a technical term!).

Your work team must define the following terms at the very least:

- Menu

- Main menu

- Submenu

- Display

- Window

- Screen

- Template

- Strand (of displays)

- Sequence

- Module

- Instructional design hierarchy

- Learner mobility options (e.g., Previous, Skip, Review)

- Entry points

- Exit points

- Branch

- Menu-level branch (e.g., menu-to-menu, menu-to-sequence)

- Intra-sequence branch

- Inter-sequence branch

- Off-line branches (e.g., to learner options, such as Glossary, that are not a part of the primary instructional path)

- Decision-point branches (originating from interaction screens)

- Page-naming conventions

- Frame-numbering sequences

These terms, along with others, are defined in the glossary of this book. Those are my definitions, however, and you should use them as departure points. Some developers illustrate definitions with flowcharts.

Again, you have trade-offs to consider in creating your definitions. For example, you must consider the complexity of the project—its scale, instructional design strategy, number of instructional paths, branching complexity, and so forth. You also have to look at the complexity of displays (e.g., static text displays versus dynamic screens with multiple windows) and the number and complexity of learner options. In addition, there are technical considerations: is the course programmed in a language or developed with a highly structured frame-based authoring system? How many people are involved in the development team? What different media are used in combination (e.g., videodisc, audio, workbook)?

For example, a complex simulation where learners input and manipulate variables that will be programmed in a language will require fairly explicit definitions. They need not be so explicit with linear tutorial programs being developed by a single person using a frame-based authoring system with limited branching capability.

Screen Display Templates. A *screen display template* is a pattern to which writers write. It establishes display parameters like margins, window size, display sequences, and screen position of particular elements such as learner options or feedback. Once displays have been mapped out on paper, it's important to prototype them with the authoring system or some other screen generator. Fill them with text; insert some graphics. Get different reactions and modify as appropriate. Obtain client or course sponsor approval before proceeding.

There are many reasons for establishing at least a base number of screen templates prior to storyboarding or scripting the CBT program. For example, writers will *write to* the display rather than simply filling up the entire screen. The use of templates forces conciseness at an early stage and reduces the need for editing of text, compressing numbers of screens, renumbering branches, and reformatting displays. This conciseness is a major source of development productivity. Second, templates force early discussion that generates consistent and optimal display formats to orient learners to their interactions and options. Such early orientation improves writer efficiency in working through the program. Bringing the authoring system expert or programmer into these discussions can dramatically reduce the amount and complexity of programming required to generate certain displays (e.g., numbers of "calls" to display windows and so forth). Productivity benefits from the latter stem from the relative ease or difficulty of programming certain display structures and sequences with the authoring system or language being used.

In addition, template margins and structures can be programmed or formatted into the word processor or editor the writers use for scripting. They can then be "called up" by the writer, who inserts specific text or graphics. The time the writer spends on purely mechanical activities like margin setting and boxing screen areas is minimized. You can generate specific routines for translating ASCII text files or even manually enter text and graphics into the authoring system. Either approach will limit the amount of formatting decisions required when displays are input into the authoring system. If such decisions aren't agreed upon in advance, each data entry operator will make them independently in order to get the job done, and then you have to make edits and changes for consistency. And if the operators don't make independent decisions, they will keep interrupting other work to get the decisions made, a frustrating and time-wasting approach. If your writers are not using a word processor (God forbid!) and are manually writing storyboards, you can provide preprinted paper forms for particular templates or simulation screens. This improves efficiency, clarity, and completeness.

Exhibit 5.11 (see Chapter Five) offers some samples of screen templates. They are no big deal to do but are very important to your effort.

Programming Instructions or Authoring System Commands and Notes. Before you do any scripting, you must agree on all terms, details, positioning of commands on storyboards, and the use of function or special-purpose keys. These include:

• Branching instructions

• Display formats

• Frame or page numbering

• Display components (e.g., highlighting, flashing, sound, animation)

• Color annotations

• Special programming instructions

• Key functions

To the extent possible, these should be incorporated in the template formats on the word processor to be certain that the writer includes all required production notes. This provides a writer's job aid on which all displays, anticipated and unanticipated responses, feedback, and programming notes can be on one sheet. Typically, writers "script" the content and focus on getting all the information and displays expressed clearly, concisely, and in the proper sequence. They then must fill in the programming instructions or production commands. This should be done relatively quickly following the writing, at least once a day, or the writer will forget intentions about branching, screen display, and so forth.

By obtaining agreement on, and including a place for, programming instructions and keeping them with the screen templates in a writer worksheet (either paper-based or stored in your word processor), you gain writer efficiency, design and display clarity, editor efficiency, and early detection of inadequate or incomplete instructions. Reviewers need these instructions to see what will occur under various conditions within the program before programming or input to the authoring system has occurred. Having these instructions offers major productivity advantages.

Color. The development of standards for color generates some interesting discussions. Some will argue that specific colors or color combinations should be defined and reserved for specific purposes (e.g., blue boxes with green text for interaction screens and yellow text for feedback on an incorrect response). Others feel as strongly that a limited number of color combinations of boxes, text, and symbols should be available to authors and that color standards should be chosen with aesthetic appeal and readability or clarity in mind. Research has repeatedly indicated that use of color has little impact on learning. Intuitively, we know that we can use color to draw the eye to a particular point, as when we want to point to a particular area in a graphics display that we wish to emphasize or discuss. To that extent, it might speed up the learner's identification of the item. I doubt if this discussion will settle the controversy. Jesse Heines[1] discusses this issue in more detail.

Without settling the controversy, however, I can give you some rules of thumb and general observations. Less is more. Too much color on a single screen is distracting. The resolution of the video monitor (i.e., RGB as opposed to composite) affects character readability. Using color in text displays on low-resolution monitors makes reading difficult, if not impossible. Next, adding lots of color decisions that must be made for each screen adds writing and programming time. Be sure the color adds sufficient value to make the extra time required worthwhile. Another rule is that "pretty" does not translate into "more effective." Finally, developing screens for a given type of color monitor does not always enable you to provide good display in a monochrome environment or with color monitors with different characteristics.

Special Key Designations. You must designate in advance the use of specific keys for special purposes (e.g., F1 for help, ESC to quit the program). This assures accurate programming instructions and consistency for the learner, and it limits interference with the actual software system function if you are executing CBT programs concurrently with live production software (see Chapter Eleven for more information on "concurrent" CBT).

Typically, special key designation ties into the learner mobility options. Be sure key designation is clear to both developers and learners. And try to make the designations as similar as possible to those for other uses of the keys to avoid confusion and error. If you are using an authoring system, some key designations may be predetermined. Some keys are programmable as defined by an authoring system procedure. If there are conflicts with key designations for your applications software, contact the authoring system vendor for assistance. One more thought: when deciding whether to use the enter key or the space bar for progressing through the program, remember that the space bar is a repeating key on most personal computers. If the learner holds it down just a bit too long, screen displays flash by and can't be stopped. If the learner can't page back easily, it's a mess.

Graphics. Graphics are the least likely candidate for standards as we usually think of them. Typically, graphics are individualized to a particular sequence or display. We can, however, think through in advance the primary graphics we are likely to use within a project and be certain that they are designed for ease of design, re-usability within this or other programs, and visual effectiveness. For example, the development team can decide whether graphics are to be symbolic or representational. *Representational* graphics mean a complete and realistic likeness of a specific real object, like a computer terminal with visual details exact. *Symbolic* graphics would mean something that looks like a terminal. Clearly, symbolic graphics are less expensive. But they may not be appropriate to the content or the specific learning objectives. Deciding up front which to use can save a lot of time, money, and aggravation.

You can also create a graphics "library" that developers can use as a form of "electronic clip art." Once the graphics have been developed, they can be called upon for a given sequence. This has enormous productivity benefits, since each person is not re-inventing the wheel. And besides, many of us aren't artistic and would welcome the chance to avoid such work. These graphics can be used across courses when they are appropriate.

You must make decisions about the value added by graphics to the educational experience. Some members of CBT development teams simply like the complexity and variety associated with graphics design and programming, so they build them into programs to meet their own needs for satisfying work. That's fine if productivity and time frames are not a consideration. But graphics are expensive to generate and require considerable storage. Complex and animated graphics can dramatically affect display rates and response time. I feel strongly that graphics for their own sake are irrelevant. The criteria for whether or not, how much, and what quality graphics will be included should be based entirely on whether or not they add educational value. For the most part, my experience with adult learners is that "cute" is not appreciated and delays are not tolerated unless something meaningful is at the end of the wait. In short, it appears that the graphics-per-se-add-variety notion is a fallacy. Interactions, not irrelevant displays of images, are what engage adult learners. Enough said. No poison pen letters from graphics advocates, please!

Learner Feedback. Feedback structures should be discussed and generally agreed upon in advance at least to the point where base level feedback is defined. Feedback can be categorized into the following types:

- Acknowledgement

- Confirmation

- Prompt or hint

- Judgment or reinforcement (positive or negative, statement of acceptable or unacceptable, right or wrong)

- Correction (statement of acceptable or correct response)

- Explanation (augments the statement of acceptable response or provides explanation of unacceptable response)

- Consequence (the result that would have occurred had the decision been made in real life)

- Referral (directs learner to another source, such as documentation, for information)

Your feedback standards require decisions on how many feedback interactions at which level should be used for (1) a minimum level of feedback or for (2) specific types of interactions or learning objectives. You must also decide when and how to use prompts and hints, what form the reinforcement should take, and what is appropriate feedback for initial interactions, practice, simulations, and so forth. Finally, you must decide whether you will repeat the learner response in the narrative feedback or whether the system will display the learner feedback with your feedback on the same screen. This last decision is affected by your system's capabilities.

There are no hard and fast rules for learner feedback, but the following considerations and observations should be helpful.

- The amount and type of feedback and restatement of content should vary according to position in the program. Generally, more of all types should appear earlier in the program. As learners demonstrate mastery, less feedback is necessary.

- Positive feedback is important and should be used often. A simple "good," ' 'that's right," or "correct" is enough. There is no need to scream "outstanding" in large flashing letters to reward an adult learner. Let's ship the happy music and smiling faces too, please!

- Learners like summary feedback that indicates how they are doing overall (e.g., following review exercises or quizzes). It increases confidence and decreases uncertainty. (Note: the required programming or CMI instructions increase development time.)

- Learners get very upset when there is no indication about whether their response was correct or acceptable, although you should remember that the indication might simply be advancement to the correct screen (as in an applications software simulation).

- Prompts and hints are best used at beginnings of sequences in early practice activities or questions. Their use should decrease or be more controlled by the learner as the content is repeated. They are inappropriate in mastery or competence tests.

- Good hints are time-consuming and expensive to develop.

- Learners should not be allowed to make the same unacceptable responses repeatedly. Inappropriate responses should be corrected.

- Complex or lengthy explanations should not be used as feedback. If complex explanations are needed, you can branch learners to remedial or alternate loops or to new sequences.

- Humorous or demeaning negative reinforcement should not be used.

- Learner names should not be used in giving feedback to unacceptable responses.

- Feedback is an important part of the learning process and can be used to repeat previously expressed material with repetition in the primary learning path.

- Associations between concepts or pieces of information are helpful.

Writing Style. Far be it from me to tell you what person, case, tense, or voice is best. Of course, I have my strong preferences and can be as determined as the next person that my way is the *right* way. Just ask me. I've listened to endless debates about such things as whether the computer should ever speak in the first person ("I'll now show you how to. . ." or "Let's review. . ."). They've reminded me of college dormitory discussions about the issues explored in Philosophy 101! Existentialism as a philosophy doesn't seem to be anywhere near as controversial as the subject of writing style in CBT programs.

There is, however, universal (almost!) agreement on some things. Concise is better than wordy. Simple is better than complex. Displays should limit the number of ideas or "chunks" of information to one or two. Humor is difficult to achieve. And, finally, sarcasm is a disaster!

In all other areas of style, it's best to have some discussions among development team members, develop some "test scripts" using alternative styles, and discuss them some more. And then someone must decide on the style and enforce conformity. It should be the customer or, in the absence of an external customer, the project manager. Without such a decision (which will never be accepted unanimously!), each writer will write with his or her preferred style. The program will be choppy and look like multiple writers wrote it (which they did). Or the editor will have a heck of a job integrating styles. And the ensuing arguments and defensiveness will be endless.

Once the decision about style is made, it must be clearly communicated to all parties. And the editor's decisions must prevail. In my experience, writers will conform reasonably quickly if you require them to submit scripts early and frequently and have editors "red pencil" them and return them quickly to the writers. If long time periods elapse and volumes of work are produced that must be revised (and revised), conflict and defensiveness ensue. Productivity and morale suffer. And if the writers don't adapt their style to the standards under red-pencil feedback, the program manager must play "watch my lips." This is an important area. Determine style early, and monitor and reinforce writers quickly once the project gets underway.

Record keeping. You should base record-keeping standards on educational requirements, organization culture and customs, and employee relations practices. There may be reasons to set record-keeping standards in advance of program development, especially when technological considerations make record keeping more or less difficult, or impossible. For example, some authoring systems permit detailed tracking of learner performance by keystroke or interaction. Programs coded in a programming language such as Basic (and some of those created with concurrent authoring systems) don't incorporate any record-keeping activities unless the developers write code to permit it, an expensive and time consuming process.

In determining your record keeping standards, keep the following in mind:

- The nature of the program (e.g., a required course with mastery or

142

competence requirements versus a practice program to improve fluency)

- Educational need and impact

- What will be done with the records

- Who cares about the records

- Privacy considerations

- Required storage (disk space or DASD) for both the records and the record-keeping programs themselves

- Technological issues (e.g., micro-to-mainframe links and networks) and complexity

- Administrative issues and complexity (e.g., learners mailing record-keeping diskettes to a central location where the data is aggregated)

- Record-keeping payoff

- Length of time records will be retained

- Legal requirements (e.g., EEO record-keeping or your organization's requirements on course completions related to promotions)

- Objectives of the training program (e.g., pilot program records will help in evaluating program effectiveness while a stable production course is unlikely to be changed)

In my experience, more records are kept than are ever used. People seem to keep them because they can, not because it makes sense. I've seen record-keeping activities slow mainframe system response time. Beyond pilot evaluation, be sure the record keeping is worthwhile and that you keep only what you need and will really use.

Instructional Paths or Sequences. There are times when a given sequence of instructional activities is the best way to teach something. Or time frames may be tight and you may need to reuse certain instructional sequences for design and programming efficiency rather than have each designer or writer spend time on approaches that have only incremental benefit or no benefit at all other than variety for its own sake.

Writers can "fill in the blanks" with specific material. Such standard sequences can be used in many areas such as how you will teach applications software or procedures. Once an instructional strategy has been designed and demonstrated to be effective, reusing is a powerful source of productivity. And it's a real boon to inexperienced developers who can use these instructional prototypes to acquire skill and understanding of effective interactive CBT while actually producing something.

Two for the price of one!

Documentation. Documentation becomes very important during walkthroughs and maintenance. Much of the MIS and DP world is plagued with poorly documented programs that have to be maintained or enhanced. Such work is endless and thankless. Much can be saved through appropriate documentation. The elements of documentation include:

- Program overview, with instructional strategies

- Logic (flowcharting or other design representations)

- Facilities

- Screen formats

- Course or program print

- Notes and correspondence

- Adjunct materials

- Administrator or monitor's guide

Documentation should be completed at the end of each phase. It won't be done adequately or at all if you wait until the end of the project.

In determining the nature and degree of detail associated with documenting your CBT , consider the number of people on the development team, anticipated program or course life span, and the stability of material. In addition, look at whether the course will be maintained, technical considerations (such as the documentation capabilities of the authoring system or content of the course), the available time, and your organizational policies and practices.

Obviously, courses that have long life spans and that must be maintained by people other than the original development team require much more extensive documentation than a program to be used as a one-shot training event. Use your common sense, but never underestimate the need for documentation. You'll be sorry if you do!

In summary. . . Your standards will evolve as you gain knowledge and experience. Take every opportunity to get learner feedback and incorporate it into your standards and guidelines. But don't use the fact that you haven't developed any CBT before as an excuse for not talking through the issues described above. Analogous experience, common sense, prototype development, and diverse reviewer reaction can make major contributions to early standards development. The quality, specificity, and durability of your standards can be a major source of development productivity, staff satisfaction, and program quality. They also assure that the development team spends most of its time in the creative aspects of the CBT development process, a much more satisfying activity than the case-by-case decision making on such matters as screen display components. Standards development is a leverage item in your management arsenal.

NOTES

[1] Jesse Heines, *Screen Design Strategies for Computer Assisted Instruction* (Bedford, Massachusetts: Digital Equipment Press, 1983.)

CHAPTER

Roles

There are fourteen separate and
distinct jobs in the production of
a CBT program, even when the
development team has only
one member.

The term "author" is frequently used to describe a CBT developer. Just what is an author, and what does one do?

I don't know how the term *author* came to be used in CBT, but I don't think it accurately reflects anything other than the writing or scripting component of the CBT development process. Literally, an "author" is a writer of a literary work—a far cry from the varied activities associated with CBT production. I personally think the term is misleading, and I prefer not to use it. This chapter details the jobs of the people involved in developing CBT, and you will notice the word *author* is not used anywhere in these descriptions. In this section we'll explore fourteen roles that must be filled at various points in the development process. These roles must be tied into the activities detailed in Chapter Five, "Development." But let's look at each role and some of the characteristics required to successfully fulfill it.

Be clear that the existence of fourteen roles does not imply that each role is filled by a different person. As a matter of fact, the fewer the number of people, the better. In some situations, one or two individuals must perform all of the roles or be certain that someone else does. In other cases, defined responsibilities are divided among a number of individuals within a CBT program development team. Situations vary enormously. What is important to remember, however, is that to the extent that the roles are not adequately filled by individuals with appropriate skills, the CBT product will suffer.

Using this Information. Managers and individual developers can utilize the detailed descriptions of activities and critical skills in this chapter to structure development team efforts or to compensate for the limited experience of an individual developer working alone.

The more of the requisite knowledge, skills, experience, and characteristics each of the players brings to his or her role, the more complete the team. Rarely, if ever, does a candidate bring everything to a position. Trade-offs, as always, are necessary. A strong motivation to achieve in this field often makes up for a lack of experience!

At some point—and the earlier in the development process the better—it's important to assign these roles to people. Then the project manager must make very clear that team members are to respect one another's roles. Without a clear definition of responsibilities, team members will constantly try to redo each others' work, which can add enormously to development time and cost while decimating team morale and cohesion. For example, the programmer can spend considerable time challenging the instructional design (which is clearly not in the programmer role), but these challenges are expensive and not productive. Unless there is a software limitation preventing reasonable implementation of the design, the programmer should not be criticizing the instructional design. Editing is another case in point. Absolutely everyone is the

Exhibit 7.1
SAMPLE JOB DESCRIPTIONS, UNISYS

UNISYS   Position Description

Classification Title	**Classification Code No.**
Senior CBT Instructional Designer	
Corporate Unit **Date Approved**	☒ Exempt
U.S. Marketing Group	☐ Non-Exempt
Functional Activity **Approved By**	
Field Engineering Education	

A. Basic Purpose

The Senior Computer-Based Training (CBT) Instructional Designer is responsible for the design and development of interactive courseware which is directly related to student job tasks. Applying instructional design techniques, the Senior CBT Instructional Designer analyzes actual and desired performance, and designs courseware which trains students to achieve desired performance objectives.

B. Job Responsibilities

1) Analyze content, target audience job tasks, and learning environment, and identify the training strategy which will direct students toward the achievement of course goals.
2) Define course objectives and design/develop courseware presentation and practice activities which train students to achieve performance objectives.
3) Attain a level of subject matter expertise which will enable a designer to create meaningful, accurate, and challenging training for the target audience.
4) Design and develop testing schemes which measure the student's mastery of course material, and which evaluate the student's ability to perform targeted job tasks.
5) Design and participate in the development of non-CBT materials which supplement computer-based training courseware (e.g., video, print, audio based material).
6) Participate in the courseware qualification process with members of the target audience; recommend and implement courseware revisions where required.

C. Qualifications

Bachelor's or Master's Degree in instructional technology with emphasis in CBT; two to three years experience in course design using a formal instructional systems design approach, preferably with one to two years experience in CBT design. Teaching experience and the ability to apply various advanced media to technical training are required.

SAMPLE JOB DESCRIPTIONS (cont.)

UNiSYS

Position Description

Classification Title
CBT Instructional Designer

Classification Code No.

Corporate Unit
U.S. Marketing Group

Date Approved

☒ Exempt
☐ Non-Exempt

Functional Activity
Field Engineering Education

Approved By

A. Basic Purpose

In this entry-level position, the Computer-Based Training (CBT) Instructional Designer gains proficiency in designing and developing interactive courseware which is interesting, challenging, and directly related to student job tasks. This person works under the guidance of experienced designers to develop skills for designing effective training using state-of-the-art authoring tools and techniques.

B. Job Responsibilities

1) Under supervision, analyze training needs and design/develop CBT courseware which achieves course goals for the target audience.

2) Attain a level of subject matter expertise which will enable a designer to create meaningful, accurate, and challenging training for a specific audience.

3) Under supervision, design and participate in the development of non-CBT course materials which supplement computer-based training courseware (e.g., video, print, audio based material).

4) Under supervision, design and develop testing schemes which measure the student's mastery of course material, and which evaluate the student's ability to perform targeted job tasks.

5) Participate in the courseware qualification process with members of the target audience; recommend and implement courseware revisions where required.

6) Gain proficiency in the use of author tools, including the CBT development system, the authoring software, and the word processor.

C. Qualifications

Bachelor's or Master's Degree in instructional technology with emphasis in CBT, or Bachelor's Degree in education with one to two years experience in designing/developing computer-based training.

SAMPLE JOB DESCRIPTIONS (cont.)

UNISYS   Position Description

Classification Title
Senior CBT System Analyst

Classification Code No.

Corporate Unit
U.S. Marketing Group

Date Approved

☒ Exempt
☐ Non-Exempt

Functional Activity
Field Engineering Education

Approved By

A. Basic Purpose

The Senior Computer-Based Training (CBT) System Analyst is primarily responsible for the input of CBT scripts and logic structures into the CBT authoring system. This person will acquire, disseminate, and maintain expertise in the CBT authoring and delivery system, and will determine the most efficient and cost-effective means of applying specific instructional strategies within the CBT system.

B. Job Responsibilities

1) Produce CBT courseware from word-processed scripts using authoring software.
2) Monitor status of production phase tasks and recommend actions necessary to ensure completion of CBT production on schedule.
3) Formally evaluate courseware design documents to determine the feasibility of design strategies within the current authoring system environment.
4) Complete the programming, testing, and documentation of simulation exercises identified by CBT instructional designers as required for CBT courseware.
5) Complete the analysis, design, programming, testing, and documentation of author productivity tools required to maximize the efficiency of the CBT development team.
6) Define hardware/software resources required for CBT development and delivery.
7) Perform interim and final testing of all courseware modules produced by the CBT development team.
8) Provide internal training and support on the current authoring software to other CBT team members; recommend the most efficient system utilization for specific design strategies.
9) Act as the interface between the CBT development team and the authoring system vendor support staff; identify and resolve software problems with vendor.
10) Evaluate outside authoring/delivery tools for compatibility with the system currently in use; recommend tools which will improve training effectiveness and/or author productivity.

C. Qualifications

Bachelor's Degree in Computer Science or equivalent formal training in systems analysis, programming, data base design, and data communications. Two to three years in program design and development at the application level, and knowledge of delivery system hardware requirements. The person in position must have excellent written and verbal communication skills effective program documentation and vendor interface.

SAMPLE JOB DESCRIPTIONS (cont.)

UNISYS

Position Description

Classification Title CBT System Analyst	Classification Code No.

Corporate Unit U.S. Marketing Group	Date Approved	☒ Exempt ☐ Non-Exempt

Functional Activity Field Engineering Education	Approved By

A. Basic Purpose

In this entry-level position, the Computer-Based Training (CBT) System Analyst gains proficiency in courseware production responsibilities, including software design and programming, authoring software application, courseware testing and debugging, and courseware packaging. The CBT system analyst works under the guidance of senior CBT system analysts while developing skills in software design and development.

B. Job Responsibilities

1) Gain proficiency in production tasks; produce courseware from word-processed scripts using an authoring software package.
2) Under supervision, formally evaluate courseware design documents to determine the feasibility of CBT design strategies within the current authoring system environment.
3) Under supervision, complete the programming, testing, and documentation of simulation exercises identified by CBT instructional designers as required for field engineering courseware.
4) Under supervision, perform interim and final testing of courseware modules produced by the CBT development team.
5) Under supervision, provide internal training and support on the current authoring software to other CBT team members; recommend the most efficient system utilization for specific design strategies.
6) Recommend hardware/software resources required for CBT development and delivery.

C. Qualifications

Bachelor's Degree in Computer Science or equivalent formal training in systems analysis, programming, data base design, and data communications. Strong communication skills are required for effective program documentation.

world's best editor—in their own opinion. The project manager's responsibility is to clearly state that writers write, designers design, and editors edit. And the editor's word is final unless the changes make the content inaccurate or affect the design structure. Naturally, this role assignment should not preclude reasonable discussion among team members, but the discussions should be focused at early stages of a project or phase. At some point, each person must do his or her own job.

Integrating the Activities and Blending the Backgrounds. Orchestrating and integrating the activities is a critical project management activity. Each of these roles must be filled at one time or another in the CBT development and delivery process. Typically, however, individuals in given positions play multiple and sometimes overlapping roles. Exhibit 7.1 gives samples of job descriptions adapted from those actually in use by Unisys in articulating their CBT responsibilities. Note that this is an organization in which there is centralized responsibility for interactive instructional design. In organizations where CBT development is a part-time activity, elements should be institutionalized in job descriptions and performance plans to assure results.

Careful creation of specific expectations, roles, and accountabilities is crucial to the CBT effort. The CBT development methodology (see Chapter Five) is the structure through which the roles are integrated. Sound knowledge, skills, and experience do not guarantee to create successful computer-based training: they are necessary but not sufficient. Good process management controls the outcomes.

CBT Development Roles. The fourteen roles in a CBT development and implementation effort are project manager, program or course sponsor or client, instructional designer, subject matter expert, writer, editor, programmer, data input or entry specialist, media expert, graphics designer, technical systems expert, learner, production administrator, and CBT administrator.

Let's look at each in terms of skills, responsibilities, and activities. Remember, the larger the CBT development group, the greater the probability of more functional and activity specialization. And the larger the particular project, the more likely it is that you'll have several people performing the duties of the same role (e.g., several writers).

Project Manager. This person oversees the project from beginning to end. In my view, the project manager has the most critical role.

Activities

- Defines project: scope, time frames, responsibilities, schedules, development activities, evaluation criteria, approval process, reporting relationships, accountabilities, budgets.

- Selects staff and develops full-time, part-time, or "borrowed" people for particular roles (e.g., subject matter expert to review program content). Defines roles and has decision-making authority for each team member.

- Obtains commitment from managers of team members to permit timely and attentive participation in the project. Logistical and political components must be considered, including building accountabilities into performance plans.

- Creates and obtains agreement on the development process, including explicit definitions of deliverables and accountabilities at the end of each phase (see Chapter Five, "Development"). Communicates the procedures to everyone concerned.

- Develops and monitors CBT standards (see Chapter Six, "Standards").

- Creates and maintains an atmosphere conducive to creativity and productivity.

- Manages communications among and between team members and with the CBT program sponsor or client.

- Manages activities during each development phase, including building consensus or making decisions as the project manager.

- Establishes priorities; manages the review, evaluation, and approval of each deliverable; makes or recommends necessary trade-offs. Manages specification changes and modifies or gains agreement on resultant schedule and budget changes.

- Negotiates support and enhancements with authoring software vendor.

- Evaluates and obtains tools to improve team productivity (anything from hardware and software to procedures and work flow).

- With client, defines implementation requirements: hardware, software, administrative, communications.

- Manages team and client relationships; communicates, manages conflict, recognizes, rewards, and so forth.

Skills, Characteristics, and Knowledge

- Team building
- Organizational skills
- Communications skills
- Negotiation skills
- Coaching (developmental, performance improvement)

- Conflict management skills

- Assertiveness

- Ability to learn quickly and to deal with complex abstractions

- Ability to propose and sell change

- Tolerance for ambiguity and ability to create structure

- Tolerance for pressure and working under deadlines

- Process orientation

- Work-flow management skills

- Ability to set goals and monitor performance

- Ability to handle multiple activities simultaneously

- Listening skills

- Ability to incorporate diverse views into the best solution; problem-solving skills

- Task orientation

- Commitment to quality

- Ability to manage detail

- Whole-brained: both creative and analytical

- Knowledge of instructional design, structured design or development techniques, computers and programming management very desirable

- Sense of humor

Program Sponsor or Client. This person authorizes the program's development and provides the logistical, economic, and political support necessary to orchestrate all the variables and the individual involvements necessary for success.

Activities

- Requests or approves the project.

- Allocates necessary resources, including human, economic, technological, logistical.

- Assures that individuals meet their responsibilities if they are not within direct control of the project manager; requires that the project manager involve him or her as necessary when problems or needs arise.

- Provides or delegates the responsibility and authority for input, review, and approval for program specifications and design and development deliverables; assures the program will meet intended objectives.

• Monitors project activity from a customer perspective.

• Signs off and accepts the program following completion.

• Performs post-implementation evaluation in conjunction with project team.

• Identifies whether future maintenance will be required; plans for when and how maintenance will be accomplished.

Skills, Characteristics, and Knowledge

• Understanding of relevant business needs

• Willingness and ability to use position power and credibility to manage resources during project activity and to authorize, review, approve, and accept deliverables

• Knowledge of learning audience and criteria for product

• Ability to learn quickly

• Commitment to controlled development

Instructional Designer. This person determines the strategies and techniques for imparting the content to the learners.

Activities

• Participates in or conducts a job task analysis.

• Develops learning objectives for each learner audience.

• Evaluates content, audience, media requirements, and objectives to develop program specifications.

• Develops content program structure and sequence and interactive or traditional instructional strategies to achieve learning objectives.

• Develops detailed programming structure and logic, including specifications for learner control versus course control, learner options, and instructional techniques to a level of detail that permits scripting by the writer(s).

• Works with writers, programmers, client, and technical specialist to optimize both program creativity and development productivity.

• Designs formative or summative evaluation instruments.

• Conducts a program qualification with target audience learners; identifies learning obstacles and recommends appropriate revisions.

Skills, Characteristics, and Knowledge

- Experience in developing instructional materials in the related program content desirable; understanding of adult learning theory and instructional design or ability to learn quickly

- Experience with interactive media highly desirable

- Creativity; no deep ties to a past tradition or procedures; open to ideas

- Attention to detail

- Oral and written communications skills

- Ability to operate in a team environment

- Listening skills

- High tolerance for ambiguity

- Ability to create structure

- Ability to work under pressure and deadlines

- Familiarity with technical considerations in the authoring system, programming, and delivery environment

- Ability to "dig into" technical authoring software in order to maximize its capabilities

- Familiarity with, or ability to quickly learn, subject matter of training program

- Ability to compromise

- Ability to accept and incorporate critical comment

Subject Matter Expert. This person consults on content for the training.

Activities

- Educates and provides input to team on program content, including scope, complexity, and learning objectives.

- Reviews deliverables at completion of all design and scripting phases for technical accuracy, completeness, clarity, and an assessment of whether the approach and content will achieve anticipated learning objectives.

- May be actively involved in the instructional design activity if time permits, particularly if he or she has experience in teaching or coaching others in the area and has developed ways of communicating the content to others effectively.

- Assists in program testing to respond to challenges related to technical detail.

Skills, Characteristics, and Knowledge

- Adequate knowledge of the subject matter in relation to the program objectives and the learner population
- Experience in communicating the subject matter to others
- Knowledge of the learner audience
- Time and motivation to participate throughout the project, particularly during the demanding period of script reviews, revisions, and edits
- Ability to work in a team

Writer. This person composes the "script" of the training program.

Activities

- Translates design specifications into scripts for text and graphic screen displays to effect learning.
- Revises scripts based on editorial, technical, client, and learner comments.
- Describes or creates appropriate graphics to reinforce content.
- Develops specific production notes describing branching instructions and screen dynamics (such as highlighting, motion, sound) to be executed by the data entry or programming staff.
- Participates in design and technical decisions to assure programming quality.

Skills, Characteristics, and Knowledge

- Ability to write concisely, clearly, and coherently for the visual medium of the screen display
- Analytical and logical skills
- Attention to and tolerance for detail
- Ability to accept critical comment and incorporate ideas into his or her work
- Ability to assimilate large amounts of information quickly

158

- Knowledge of, or ability to learn about, authoring system or the computer programming required to execute designs, scripts, and displays
- Creativity
- Ability to work independently
- Ability to work under pressure and deadlines
- Ability to work in a team
- Flexibility
- Commitment to quality
- Ability to produce large volumes of work in short time periods
- Knowledge of instructional design helpful
- Knowledge of subject matter or experience writing about it very helpful

Editor. This person reviews the project for communication effectiveness.

Activities

- Reviews, alters, adapts, and refines scripts to conform to CBT standards and to assure clarity and conciseness from learner's point of view.
- Reviews production notes and programming instructions for completeness, clarity, and appropriateness (last cut before programmer involvement).
- Evaluates appropriateness and clarity of graphics or combinations of text and graphics.
- Evaluates introduction and instructions to learner for ease of use.

Skills, Characteristics, and Knowledge

- Editorial experience; CBT editing helpful
- Ability to communicate, especially with writers
- Interpersonal and persuasive skills
- Assertiveness
- Ability to operate under pressure and deadlines
- Attention to and tolerance for detail
- Commitment to quality
- Knowledge of the subject area and learner population helpful

Data Entry Specialist. This person feeds the scripts into the authoring system.

Activities

• Enters program scripts into authoring system, including programming instructions, if appropriate.

Skills, Characteristics, and Knowledge

• Has keyboarding skills

• Can work independently

• Pays attention to and tolerates detail

• Knowledge of the authoring system internal editor helpful; strong word processing experience is typically a good foundation

Authoring System Specialist or Programmer. This person prepares executable code or runs the authoring system to create the actual program and consults on the capabilities and limitations of the computer system.

Activities

• Reviews storyboards and scripts for clarity and completeness in programming and production notes (e.g, branching, screen displays).

• Develops programming instructions or authoring system commands to translate production notes or programming instructions on scripts and storyboards into executable code.

• Consults with designers and writers on technical requirements for implementing design structures in relation to the authoring system or programming language, available time, and ongoing maintenance.

• Educates project team members on technical issues, authoring system capabilities and limits, and complexity in implementing design alternatives.

• Recommends alternative design approaches when initial approaches are not feasible or affordable.

• Writes project requirements and schedules.

• Conducts technical review of the program.

• Tests and debugs the program.

• Develops and maintains program documentation.

• Develops and maintains communication with authoring system vendor to resolve system bugs and to request problem resolution and enhancements.

- Participates in the selection and implementation of technological tools to address program development.

- Develops and maintains technical interfaces between software tools (e.g., word processing and authoring system software, graphics packages) to ensure development productivity.

Skills, Characteristics, and Knowledge

- Analytical skills

- Skill in use of authoring system or programming

- Understanding of programming logic

- Knowledge and skill in systematic software testing

- Ability to project requirements and schedules

- Orientation to detail

- Communications skills

Media Expert. This person serves as a link to various presentation media which may be included in the program.

Activities

- Consults with designers and writers on media capabilities, limitations, costs, and production requirements.

- Participates in the design process.

- Manages production of other media, as required (e.g., develops video sequences).

Skills, Characteristics, and Knowledge

- Understanding of interactive and other media involved in the program (e.g., video, audio, print)

- Creativity

- Communications skills

- Ability to operate in a team

- Ability to work under pressure and deadlines

- Ability to accept critical comment and incorporate it into his or her work

161

- Commitment to quality
- Tolerance for ambiguity and ability to create structure

Graphics Designer. This person designs the visual layout of the presentation.

Activities

- Participates in creation of screen display standards, including development of prototypes.
- Creates computer graphics displays to support instructional program.
- Consults with designers and writers to indicate when verbal message can be more concisely and effectively presented via graphics display.
- Reviews initial screen displays for conformance to standards and with regard to visual impact.

Skills, Characteristics, and Knowledge

- Graphics skills
- Knowledge of and skill in creating computer graphics
- Communications skills
- Ability to operate in a team
- Tolerance for detail work

CBT Authoring System Specialist. In PC environments, the CBT system technical expert's activities are typically performed by the programmer. In mainframe environments, the role is frequently separated from the development team itself; it is located in a staff function charged with CBT system administration and operations.

Activities

- Provides technical consulting, advice, and problem resolution for the hardware and software under which the CBT program is to be developed, installed, and implemented.
- Evaluates technical requirements of the authoring and presentation systems from a development and implementation perspective.
- Installs and maintains CBT programs (if mainframe).
- Develops necessary security, backup, and control of programs.

Skills, Characteristics, and Knowledge

- In-depth knowledge of the technical environment
- Ability to work in a team
- Availability
- Communications skills
- Attention to detail

Learner Evaluator. This person is a representative of the intended audience who tests the effectiveness of the CBT program.

Activities

- Reviews and evaluates CBT programs and provides feedback to developers.
- Participates in the design or script reviews, as possible, to evaluate approach and specific content from a learner perspective.
- Identifies confusing areas in courseware.
- Identifies content and activities that are not relevant to actual job environment.
- Identifies supplementary materials, such as job aids, that might help the learner.

Skills, Characteristics, and Knowledge

- Representative of the learner population
- Commitment to the project
- Communications skills

Production Administrator. This person oversees the actual production and distribution of the media bearing the software.

Activities

- Produces or manages the production of program materials, including diskettes, tapes, print, and packaging.
- Distributes program materials.
- Maintains appropriate inventories.
- Manages production budgets and costs.

Skills, Characteristics, and Knowledge

- Organizational skills

- Attention to detail

- Ability to work in a team

- Knowledge of production techniques

- Commitment to quality

CBT Administrator. This person makes the training program available to the learners who need it.

Activities

- Develops and implements CBT administrative procedures, including program communications, registrations, and record keeping.

- Provides assistance to learners with questions and technical system or program problems.

- Maintains liaison with other training units, line managers, CBT development team.

- Monitors use of equipment and implements changes as required to optimize utilization.

Skills, Characteristics, and Knowledge

- Organizational skills

- Oral and written communications skills

- Patience

- Ability to operate in a team

- Attention to detail

- Knowledge of the audience background: keyboard skills, software operations skills, if appropriate

CHAPTER

Fielding a Team

Your chances of hiring CBT
talent and expertise are pretty
small; you had better plan on
developing it.

I'm overwhelmed by the description of all of the roles that must be played and the knowledge, skills, and experience that go into a successful development team. Where can I find such people?

Well, people with the necessary skills and experience aren't standing around waiting to be found. As a matter of fact, people with more than a few of the specific skills and experience necessary for CBT development are rare. That's why team development produces far superior programs. But if you want new employees to fill the bill, there are places to look for experienced CBT folks.

Let's look first at external recruiting sources.

Conferences and Professional Meetings. Conferences are good places to recruit because lots of informal networking goes on. Typically there are bulletin boards where people seek opportunities. Recommended conferences include:

- CBT, a conference sponsored by *Data Training* magazine

- The ADCIS (Association for the Development of Computer-Based Instructional Systems) annual conference (or the organization's local meetings)

- The NSPI (the National Society for Performance and Instruction) national conference (or local meetings)

- SALT (Society for the Advancement of Learning Technology) Conferences (there are several of these specialized conferences annually)

- Training, the national conference sponsored by *Training* magazine

- The ASTD (American Society for Training and Development) national conference (or local meetings)

- Society for Technical Communications (or local meetings)

Some of these organizations have special interest group sessions to focus on particular disciplines or applications. National meetings are typically a better source than local ones, but don't miss any opportunity. Local professional association newsletters might also be helpful if you feel you must find someone locally and don't want to pay relocation costs. And don't miss the hospitality suites at professional meetings! Lots goes on at them besides the consumption of hors d'oeuvres.

Informal Networks. They might not provide a very structured resource, but informal contacts and referrals are typically the most fruitful way to find people. Consider contacts in companies already doing CBT, custom or commercial courseware development houses, vendor organizations, professional groups, your current training and CBT employees, universities with active CBT efforts, and independent consultants.

166

Authoring System User Groups and Vendors. Vendors and users cultivate user groups for many purposes. No matter the stated intent, these groups create a network within which people find jobs and jobs find people. User groups can be a particularly good source of people with skills in your specific technical environment. Vendor sales reps can also be good sources of candidates.

Advertising. Advertising in industry-specific publications may be fruitful. Recruitment advertising in the general press is typically non-productive unless you are in a large metropolitan area or near one of the areas where the CBT activity level is high (e.g., Minneapolis, Minnesota, or Champaign/Urbana, Illinois, which are historically centers of *Plato* activity). The following specialized publications may generate resumes. Addresses are in the resource guide appended to this chapter.

- *Data Training* magazine

- *Training News*

- *NSPI Journal*

- *Training* magazine

Placement Firms and Headhunters. Few, if any, of these specialize in CBT yet. Try the better known firms specializing in training professionals. I'm not too optimistic about this source right now, but you may have some luck.

I plan to use existing internal staff to develop CBT. What suggestions do you have for developing existing trainers, technical writers, and instructional designers into effective CBT developers?

Sometimes you get to choose new staff; other times you want to or must work with people you have. When you work with the people you have, you're likely to be staffing your CBT project or department with individuals who have insufficient knowledge, skill, or experience with CBT to achieve your objectives. I have seen excellent work produced by relatively inexperienced people when they are provided with the right education, development, structure, and coaching. The key is to be specific in your development and support plans and not to use hope as a strategy for skill and knowledge acquisition.

If you are making do with current staff, don't feel you are facing an insuperable obstacle. Your situation is the norm, and it's very manageable, assuming certain minimum ability and motivation levels are present. Resistant developers won't respond well to even the very best development programs. Without at least some minimum configuration of knowledge and skills in the area of training, content, project manage-

167

ment, subject matter, and writing, you may want to reassess taking on the project. But presuming you either have or have access to people with basic skill levels, let's look at the specific staff development options open to you and how to go about defining a specific staff development plan for your organization.

Assess Current Staff. It's critical to understand exactly what knowledge, skills, experience, and personal characteristics exist on your staff in relation to the task at hand. In the Chapter Seven, "Roles," all of the roles, responsibilities, and associated critical staff experience are discussed in detail. Compare your current staff to these profiles. You might ask them to go through the same process since their participation in structuring the development plan will probably make it an even better one. Their participation in developing the plan will increase their commitment to it, which is half the battle!

Remember, while evaluating the fourteen CBT development team roles, that in most organizations, team members play multiple roles. In more than a few organizations, there is a development "team of one." But if you have a one-person team, it will be likely that you'll need people to work with the developer at certain points. It's virtually impossible, for example, for most people to review and edit their own writing objectively. So you'll be compensating for the limited amount of knowledge or skill in certain areas.

Following that initial evaluation, you'll need to assess the task at hand. For example, graphics design skills aren't anywhere near as important in application software training as they are in other content areas. Different CBT activities will require different staff depth. Following the task assessment, you'll need to come back to the results of your staff assessment to put it in perspective and set priorities for development activities based on the relative needs of all team members.

Development is a process, not an event. All of us would like to spontaneously develop knowledge, skills, and experience in a discipline. Many managers, when faced with production demands in tight time frames, favorably rationalize staff capability in relation to the task and seriously underestimate the required investment in time, money, and resources to bring the team up to speed. If I leave you with no other thought from this chapter, let it be this one: *Do not equate a course about CBT with staff development and skill acquisition.*

Training "events," such as a CBT design course or a workshop by the authoring system vendor on the system's capabilities and use of its basic functions, provide a conceptual framework and basic skill levels that can serve only as a departure point. A course in interactive design can only provide an orientation to concepts, terms, and basic techniques. Learning how to actually develop interactive instructional material is a function of experience, period.

Training programs are necessary, and they can do a great deal to give new development team members a "kick start" in the right direction. Training programs give everyone involved a common understanding, language, framework, and philosophy from which the team can depart, as well as the stimulation to do so. Without them, most people don't know where to start. If you were to simply provide the computer hardware and authoring system software, along with a goal of getting something produced, it would be like putting someone in the pilot's seat of an airplane with instructions to take you to Chicago. It's unlikely that you'll get where you want to go safely. Even if you got there based on the motivated amateur pilot's general skills, intuition, and experience playing with *Flight Simulator* on a PC, it wouldn't be without a lot of false starts and some serious risks to all involved along the way.

Authoring System Training is Not Enough. In my consulting experience, I find that most managers limit their author development to training in the authoring system itself. This training is necessary but not sufficient for effective CBT development. If reviewing all of the roles involved in the activity doesn't make that clear, maybe this analogy will.

You are the manager of a publishing company and you want your staff to write books instead of just editing them. Some of your people have edited books, some haven't done more than read some, and others have hardly read any. None has ever written one. Your production plan includes giving these people the basic resources they will need to be productive: reference material on the book content and a computer with powerful word processing software installed. You bring in the word processing software vendor—or a trainer very experienced in teaching others how to use the word processor. The new authors learn about creating new files, editing files, structuring files, and so forth. You teach techniques like global search, change, and block move. You even demonstrate how to merge files once they're created. The new writers feel confident with the text processor, and they have the vendor hot-line support if they ever get confused. Everyone is happy. You breathe a sigh of relief and go back to your office.

From time to time, you walk about the work area and see productive-looking activity: people staring at screens, people creating text, writers huddled together. You ask how it's going and they say fine. You query whether the training was adequate. They reply, "Yes, the instructor was great, and this really is a wonderful word processor. Thank you for buying it for us." When it comes time for you to review what's been done, you are appalled. Nothing's coherent. Simple sentences are strung together. There's little or no substance. At best, they produce "vanilla" material when you need "Rocky Road" to satisfy your market. What more could you have done?

In staff development, there are numerous alternatives to seminars, workshops, and training programs. But let's start with them and proceed to the alternatives.

Seminars, Workshops, and Training Programs. You can find public and in-house seminars in critical areas such as introduction to CBT and interactive training, interactive instructional design, CBT project management, interactive video development, authoring system skills, graphics design and development, and technical writing skills. Sources for these programs include consultants, professional associations, universities, training companies, and authoring system vendors. Various training publishing houses have produced directories of providers with cross-references by topic (e.g., CBT design, CBT technical training).

It's fairly easy to locate information about public programs. The issue is not whether they exist, but how closely they meet your needs. As with other content areas, public seminars can provide a good introduction, and there may even be one that specifically meets all of your needs. But be certain you do the following:

- get detailed information about the content, time spent on each topic, background and experience of the instructor as it relates to your situation, and other participants;

- obtain at least five references from past participants and call them with detailed questions on the above areas;

- call others whom you know and respect in the CBT field; and

- evaluate what you've learned in relation to your specific needs and budget.

Consider bringing one of the seminars in-house—even if your numbers are few. Many times the instructor's per diem expenses or the cost per participant is less than that of sending people outside, especially when travel and lodging are involved. Expense is less the issue than whether or not you'll get what you need. As your staff gains more experience, bringing experts inside and assuring that they address your needs is frequently a superior alternative.

It's also likely that you can bring someone in to focus on your specific needs for less time than a complete packaged course would take. You have more control, your specific environment and training applications can be addressed, and your staff gets far more concentrated attention. This idea is particularly important when you're trying to develop design ideas. No individual, regardless of skill and experience, has a total overview of all that's possible. I strongly urge clients to bring in a number of experts to address topics from different perspectives. The diversity stimulates discussion and creativity and limits the chance that your staff will prematurely develop a specific approach to CBT design without being exposed to alternatives. These "experts" may not teach traditional workshops, but they can generate lots of ideas.

Remember, the more experienced the staff, the more they will benefit from consulting rather than training. Discussions about alternatives and techniques and specific problem-solving activities associated with consulting do more for experienced people than do lectures and demonstrations. And when your staff is without internal peers with whom to have challenging dialogue, development and growth stagnate.

Consultants (at the risk of sounding self-serving) can be excellent resources for staff development. Beyond their training and idea generation roles, they can work effectively in the following ways:

- As an *advisor or coach* for development staff to get things started in the right direction, provide ideas, criticize work, improve controls, increase confidence, and assist in making conscious trade-offs. The best times to use a consultant in this capacity are before the project starts, at the beginning of it (for stimulation and structure), and at the end (for review and critique) of each phase. Some companies invest in having the consultant work with the team as an advisor or coach all the way through initial development activities—sometimes doing and sometimes reviewing. Whether that's appropriate is a function of available resources, how quickly you want staff development, and whether there's a consultant available who matches your needs.

- As a *producer*, actually doing some of the work and using internal staff as peers or assistants. This is particularly useful when you have tight time frames but want your staff to "walk through" the process with someone.

- As a *validator*, to review materials at specific stages.

- As an *educator or informer* about any range of things, including technical information.

- As a *project manager* to structure and manage the project or to serve as a "coach" to the actual project manager while he or she is learning how to manage CBT development. Sources of consultants vary: peer referrals, industry guides, trade shows, conferences where they are giving presentations, and software vendors. It's always important to check references and be certain that the consultant you select matches your philosophy and has enough experience in your environment to add value. Otherwise, you are paying them to learn.

The client-consultant relationship is one of trust. Professional reputation and references by people whom you trust in your business is always the best measure available.

Conferences are excellent for getting a perspective on the industry, generating new ideas, networking with peers, and assessing marketplace issues and products. They can vary in quality. While there are several excellent programs that present a variety of seminars and workshops where true learning can occur, others are just bazaars. Carefully evaluate program content, speaker quality, and any other information you can glean about a conference. Again, check with your peers. Some conferences run by professional organizations and for-profit organizations are listed in the appendix to this chapter.

Many conferences are best attended by manager types. Very few, if any, specific skill development opportunities occur at conferences unless they present in-depth workshops—typically before or after the traditional conference schedule. Usually, numbers are too large for there to be much more than general overviews of subject areas. Some professional groups, on the other hand, offer sessions that go into considerable detail. Regardless, the entire conference experience can be an important one for idea generation and perspectives. One of the best outcomes is the development of relationships with peers in similar types of organizations or doing similar work in similar technical environments. These peer networks will serve developers well over time.

User Groups. Authoring system user groups can be very helpful. Particularly useful are those groups that try to present in-depth educational or informational content, rather than limit themselves to product announcements for the next release of the authoring system, which are often the preoccupation of vendor-sponsored organizations. Some authoring system vendors see development of client knowledge as a high priority and they retain speakers, organization member presentations, and have their own staff leading specific and very helpful discussions. User groups can be important sources of staff development.

CBT Courseware Review. One of the very best ways to get staff up and running is to make available a range of commercial CBT products (or proprietary programs, if you can get them) for review. For truly inexperienced staff, having an experienced person walk through a program helps them to identify what is happening in the program, why, what could be better, and so forth. Sometimes reviewers react positively or negatively to something but don't know exactly why. Creating conscious understanding is an important part of learning.

One of the best investments you can make is to spend several thousand dollars and buy copies of a range of things in the marketplace. This is easy to do for micro courseware. With mainframe programs, it's more difficult and expensive. In addition, many of the mainframe programs are extensive curricula (e.g., a thirty-hour course in a fourth-generation language) that wouldn't be easy or appropriate to review. Demo disks or tapes are a good way to get ideas, as vendors tend to put the best work on demonstration products.

You can also get demonstration diskettes that many custom CBT development houses use for marketing. You can certainly use them to make the evaluation the vendor wants you to make, but also view them as an educational opportunity. Review them at conferences or bring them in-house if you can.

Reading. The good old book. Nothing wrong with it! As a matter of fact, you're (I hope) learning from one now. There's a bibliography on books and magazines in the appendix to this chapter. Structure the reading process for your staff. Assign chapters, articles, and other readings.

Discussion Groups. Conduct structured discussion groups around particular topics or issues. Ask specific staff members to do reports on highlights from particular books, meetings attended, design alternatives, and courses reviewed. Create and legitimize opportunities for mind-stretching discussions. Encourage your people to shoot the breeze on these topics.

Professional Organizations. There are many professional training organizations. Some are dedicated to interactive learning, such as ADCIS. Others, such as NSPI, have broader charters but have special interest groups that focus on interactive learning. Still others, such as the Society for Technical Communication, have a very specific focus. A list of national organizations is included in the appendix.

Aside from their national conferences, many organizations have local chapters. It's usually worth the dues to check them out and get the publications. The quality and relevance of local chapters varies widely. Attend a few meetings to see if they're worthwhile.

Putting the Plan Together. Be sure to make a plan. Development will occur without one, but not necessarily in the direction or pace necessary to achieve your objectives. When obtaining sponsorship for CBT, be sure that you achieve understanding of time frames, effort, and investments necessary for staff development if you are going to begin CBT development seriously. Be certain that there's sufficient budget money available to fund external and internal development activities or the use of consultants. And, equally important, make sure that *time* is budgeted for staff development activities.

Remember, staff development is a pay-me-now, pay-me-later deal. The up front investment has an enormous payoff for both your staff and your organization.

Appendix. A
Selected CBT Resources

This listing of books, articles, publications, and conferences only highlights the primary resources available. The selection is largely based on how they complement the material in this book and is not intended, in any way, to be an exhaustive listing.

Books

Burke, Robert; *The CAI Sourcebook* (Prentice-Hall: Englewood Cliffs, New Jersey, 1982).

Dean, Christopher and Whitlock, Quentin; *The CBT Handbook* (Cogan Press: London, 1983).

Heines, Jesse; *Screen Design Strategies for Computer Assisted Instruction* (Digital Equipment Press: Bedford, Massachusetts, 1983). Order from J. Heines, 18 Courtland Drive, Chelmsford, MA 01824.

Kearsley, Greg; *Computer Based Training: Evaluation, Selection and Implementation* (Addison-Wesley Publishing Company: Reading, Massachusetts, 1983).

Marsh, Patrick; *Messages That Work* (Educational Technology: Englewood Cliffs, New Jersey, 1983).

Martin, James and McClure, Carma; *Action Diagramming* (Prentice-Hall: Englewood Cliffs, New Jersey, 1985).

Steinberg, Esther R.; *Teaching Computers to Teach* (Lawrence Erlbaum Associates: Hillsdale, New Jersey, 1984). Lawrence Erlbaum Associates, Inc., 365 Broadway, Hillsdale, NJ 07642.

Yourdon, Edward; *Structured Walkthroughs* (Edward Yourdon Associates: New York, 1984). Edward Yourdon Associates, 1501 Broadway, New York, NY 10036.

Articles

Carroll, John M. "Minimalist Training," *Datamation*, November 1, 1984.

"Computer Based Training for End Users." *EDP Analyzer*, October, 1983. Order from *EDP Analyzer*, 925 Anza Avenue, Vista, CA 92083. $7.00.

Endriss, Carol, "Screen by Screen–Training Lessons from Poetry and Television," *Data Training*, March, 1985.

Gordon, Jack and Lee, Chris, "The Future of Computer Based Training," *Training*, September, 1985.

Heines, Jesse, "Interactive Means Active–Learner Involvement in CBT," *Data Training*, March, 1985.

Jonassen, David H. "Interactive Lesson Designs: A Taxonomy," *Educational Technology*, June, 1985.

Judd, Wallace, "Beyond the Menu Screen–What a Help System Can Be," *Data Training*, July, 1986.

Judd, Wallace, "What, Exactly, is Your Problem?–An Introduction to Dynamic Help," *Data Training*, August, 1986.

Kearsley, Greg, "Embedded Training: The New Look in Computer Based Instruction." *Machine-Mediated Learning*, Vol. I, No. 3, 1985. Crane

Russak, 3 East 44th Street, New York, NY 10017.

Quinn, Herb, "Why CBT Doesn't Work," *Data Training*, November, 1986.

Rockart, John, "Computers and the Learning Process." Massachusetts Institute of Technology, 1975. Order from Sloan School of Management, Center for Information Systems Research, MIT, 1 Amherst Street, Cambridge, MA 02139. $3.00.

Zemke, Ron, "Evaluating CBT: What's Hot, What's Not and Why." *Training*, May, 1984.

Publications

Data Training (monthly). Weingarten Publications, Inc., 38 Chauncy Street, Boston, Massachusetts 02111.

Training Magazine (monthly). Lakewood Publications, 50 South Ninth Street, Minneapolis, Minnesota 55402.

Journal of Computer-Based Instruction (quarterly). ADCIS, 409 Miller Hall, Western Washington University, Bellingham, Washington 98225.

Conferences

Data Training. Annually in November, rotating site. For information, contact Weingarten Publications, 38 Chauncy Street, Boston, Massachusetts 02111.

CBT. Annually in March, rotating site. For information, contact Weingarten Publications, 38 Chauncy Street, Boston, Massachusetts 02111.

Association for the Development of Computer-Based Instruction. Annually in November, rotating site. For information, contact ADCIS, 409 Miller Hall, Western Washington University, Bellingham, Washington 98225.

National Society for Performance and Instruction. Annually in Spring, rotating site. For information, contact NSPI, 1126 Sixteenth Street, N.W., Suite 315, Washington, DC 20036.

Training. Annually in December, New York City. For information, contact Lakewood Publications, 50 South Ninth Street, Minneapolis, Minnesota 55402.

Appendix B

Professional Organizations for CBT Developers

ASTD
American Society for Training and
Development
  1630 Duke Street
  Alexandria, Virginia 22313
  (703) 683-8100

AECT
Association for Educational
Communications and Technology
  1126 16th Street, NW
  Washington, DC 20036
  (202) 466-4780

ADCIS
Association for the Development of
Computer-Based Instructional
Systems
  Miller Hall, Room 409
  Western Washington University
  Bellingham, Washington 98225
  (206) 676-2860

NSPI
National Society for Performance and
Instruction
  1126 16th Street, NW
  Suite 214
  Washington, DC 20036
  (202) 861-0777

SALT
Society for Applied Learning
Technology
  50 Culpepper Street
  Warrenton, Virginia 22186
  (703) 347-0055

176

CHAPTER

Cost
Estimating

How long does it take to develop
an hour of CBT? How many
angels can dance on the
head of a pin?

How many hours does it take to develop an hour of CBT?

I know you need to know, but if I hear that question asked that way one more time, I'll scream. The question frustrates me since there's no straightforward answer. In many ways, the question's not even valid because in extensively branched, learner-controlled, or inquiry-based instructional programs, we can't define "an hour of CBT." The learning experience is too individualized for that kind of time measurement. In any case, when I do respond to the question, the answer is "It depends." And what it depends on is a substantial number of situational variables that can be evaluated and determined only on a case-by-case basis.

But my saying that doesn't help you, does it? So let's take a more specific—and I hope helpful—look at the CBT estimating issues, the factors influencing development time and cost, and how you can apply them to your CBT application.

Estimating CBT development time and cost is a problem. We lack models and a language for describing course specifications on which to base estimates. We have yet to build a body of experience; there is little published information. Most people don't even know where to start. Of course, humanity has done lots of things for the first time and has marched into new situations and gotten them under control without as much anxiety as the CBT estimating problem seems to be causing.

The main reason for all this churning is fear. Fear of writing a blank check; fear that the outcome won't be worth whatever it costs, because we've seen some pretty boring and trivial lessons developed; fear that— even when money is no object—the courses won't be done within the available time. Fear, in sum, of the unknown. Additionally, we worry that even if we intuitively arrive at a reasonable estimate or schedule, we can't consciously defend or explain our estimate to others. The political issues here loom larger than the economic. And so we seek simple formulas with accompanying testimonials from those who've developed CBT before.

Now, nothing's wrong with seeking information from the experience of others. We all do it. But there's a big difference between finding out for information's sake what it has cost other people and using their experience to predict your own. Others' experiences may have nothing to do with your situation. It's best to diagnose your own case and go from there.

At conferences and in the press, you often come across people quoting ratios of hours of development per hour of CBT instruction. I have seen ratios of 25:1, 150:1, and 400:1. These ratios have been derived primarily through hearsay or some unsubstantiated "industry average," and are nearly useless. Even if these broad ratios are "accurate" or generally applicable, they produce indefensible figures. Try justifying a budget based on something as vague as an "industry average" when demands for detailed explanations or pressures to reduce an "unacceptably high" estimate are being put on you. And when they don't trust the grounds on which the original estimate is based, clients and internal management frequently do apply pressures.

You can use these industry averages, but only as ball-park figures. By that I mean to use them when you are making the initial decision of whether or not to proceed with CBT development. Perhaps use them cautiously as "order-of-magnitude" figures on which to screen out the grossly unaffordable or impractical. At each stage in a project's cost justification and development process, you must increase the precision of your development cost and schedule estimates. These estimates are crucial to key management decisions such as whether to proceed with the project, how to handle internal political pressures, and when to plan release of courseware.

In other cases, when estimates are unacceptably high, developers and course sponsors need to be able to make conscious design compromises. Or, preferably, they must bring productivity gains to bear so that time and costs are more acceptable. Knowing the real contributing factors permits better decision making and courseware than do general development ratios.

Clearly, a time- and cost-estimating methodology is important for successful CBT management.

Does such a CBT time- and cost-estimating methodology exist?

Well, the groundwork for one does. I've isolated the factors contributing to CBT development time and cost and put them in an initial framework. I'll leave it up to you figure out how you should calculate the weight of each factor, but I will explain where they come from.

Thirty-seven factors individually and collectively contribute to the total time expended in courseware development. Although there are some other cost factors (such as the choice of delivery medium), development time expenditure translates pretty directly into development cost. The thirty-seven factors can be grouped into four major categories: courseware variables, technical variables, human variables, and other variables.

Courseware Variables. Of all the sets of variables, what you build obviously has the greatest impact on cost. There are fourteen variables related to course content, complexity, learning objectives, design, and structuring that contribute to development time and costs. They are summarized in Chart 9.1.

In order to decide whether a variable's contribution to the development time and cost of a particular program is low, medium, or high, you must first analyze the program itself in detail and then judge each factor individually against it. And you must also look at each factor in relation to all the others. As a way of simplifying this process, I recommend

Figure 9.1
RELATIONSHIP OF COURSEWARE VARIABLES

		• Multi-media courseware • Complex, conceptual, or non-linear material • Highly individualized and conditionally branched program • High-level learning objectives requiring synthesis, analysis, and extrapolation • Complex response analysis • High interactivity • High level of learner control • Complex testing or learner assessment • Highly creative • Instructional strategies include simulations, games, highly branched tutorials, or branched case studies and dialogues
	• DP simulations • Branched tutorials • Case studies (linear) • Dialogues (linear)	
• Standalone CBT (single medium) • Simple material • Low-level learning objectives (recognition/recall, knowledge) • Proscribed learning paths • Low interactivity • Simple testing • Basic low-level reponse analysis • Limited feedback • No graphics (or line graphics) • Instructional strategies limited to drill and practice or linear tutorial • Limited to interactive job aids (co-resident with applications software)		

DEVELOPMENT TIME — High / Med / Low

DEVELOPMENT COSTS — Low / Med / High

Chart 9.1
COURSEWARE VARIABLES

- Nature and complexity of learning material
- Learning objectives (level)
- Instructional design strategies
- Nature and frequency of interactivity
- Conditional branching
- Response analysis: complexity, feedback, and branching
- Nature and depth of feedback
- Nature and depth of testing
- Creativity desired or required
- Nature, complexity, and volume of graphics and animation
- Testing requirements
- Courseware specification standards: quality, specificity, stability
- Other media integration (type and complexity)
- CMI (record-keeping and administration) requirements

plotting the final judgments about each factor's contribution on a grid. Figure 9.1 illustrates my judgments about courseware variable costs *in general.* Judgments for an individual course may vary considerably from those shown here.

More complex material with higher-level (and therefore more difficult) learning objectives will take more time to develop than will simple material with low-level learning objectives. For example, achieving understanding of the concept of virtual memory in data processing is more difficult than gaining familiarity with the difference between hardware and software. And enabling learners to apply a concept is more time-consuming than simply leading them to recognize it. More sophisticated learning objectives cannot be achieved without repetition and more complex situations, interactions, and response analysis. And these take a *lot* longer to develop.

Creative and complex design structures such as gaming take longer than "text-and-test" tutorials because of the number of design variables used and the interrelationships that must be constructed among them. Complex branching, access to options such as glossaries, extensive learner mobility options such as back-paging, and fixed start and restart points, among many other things, take substantial time to incorporate.

Some of these factors weigh more heavily in the equation than others do. Designing complex, branched games is considerably more time-consuming than simply inserting paging or start and restart instructions in the code. Therefore, the estimator must make judgments and weight them appropriately. That's what makes this process so difficult. You should recognize, however, that the cumulative effect of lots of smaller variables can also make an enormous difference in the total development time and cost. Seconds add up to minutes, and minutes to hours, and hours to weeks. Designing and writing two-option versus four-option multiple-choice interaction structures alone (given learner options, response analysis, and feedback for each option) can decrease significantly the time spent in design, development, programming, testing, debugging, and revising for an extensive course.

Here, you are going to create a scatter gram for the application as you evaluate and plot each group of variables on the graph. To make the grids clearer, different people find different techniques helpful, so play with them to work out approaches that will be meaningful for you. You might want to choose different symbols or colors for different categories of variables and weights.

Once you have identified the courseware variables and plotted the evaluations for your specific application, you can start on the technological factors.

Technological Factors. The five technological variables contributing to courseware development time and cost are listed in Chart 9.2. Many of these variables have to do with the authoring system and other available software tools. Be aware that the characteristics of these tools are not the significant factor. What is important is the closeness with which their capabilities and limits match the design requirements for the courseware and the knowledge and skill of the development staff.

For example, if you were to propose having inexperienced developers build complex, branched courseware requiring flexible displays, graphics, and other features with a simple and limited-capability authoring system, the programming time required would be substantial. Your developers would spend a great deal of time figuring out how to achieve the complex design with a simple tool. Indeed, you would have a complicated project ill-matched by limited tools and unskilled designers. If, on the other hand, the same project were to be tackled by a team of experienced developers using a very powerful and sophisticated authoring system or language, the development time might be much less. Another comparison should drive this point home. Say you were creating CBT for applications software training. If you had access to a concurrent or shell authoring system, you wouldn't have to create simulations since you can move in and out of the actual software to create instructional sequences. Eliminating the need to create simulations would cut your development time by fifty percent or more.

In summary, if you were to base your cost estimate solely on the simplicity of the authoring system without taking into consideration its appropriateness to the task at hand, you would go badly astray.

Another factor is the availability of auxiliary tools. Most authoring systems have limited internal line or screen editors rather than extensive internal word-processing capability. When this is so, you will save much time if you can batch input text files previously produced on a powerful word processor into the authoring system to create lesson files. In my experience, the use of external word-processing tools with block move, global search, and spell-checking features can decrease development costs for text-intensive courseware by up to twenty-five percent. The limited capabilities of most authoring systems' internal line or screen editors cannot even compare to the routine operations of most word processing programs.

Having a powerful and flexible editor within the authoring system itself is most desirable—especially when editing is not limited to single-screen content. The ability to revise text files during maintenance or course enhancement activities also substantially reduces maintenance costs. You will find it much easier to work with flexible lesson text files than with compiled code in an authoring system with a limited internal screen editor. Remember that maintenance costs are really "ongoing development costs" and must be considered in the formula.

Finally, new automated design tools are becoming available that have enormous potential for compressing time spent in representing and revising courseware design activities throughout the process (see chapter four

Figure 9.2
RELATIONSHIP OF TECHNICAL VARIABLES

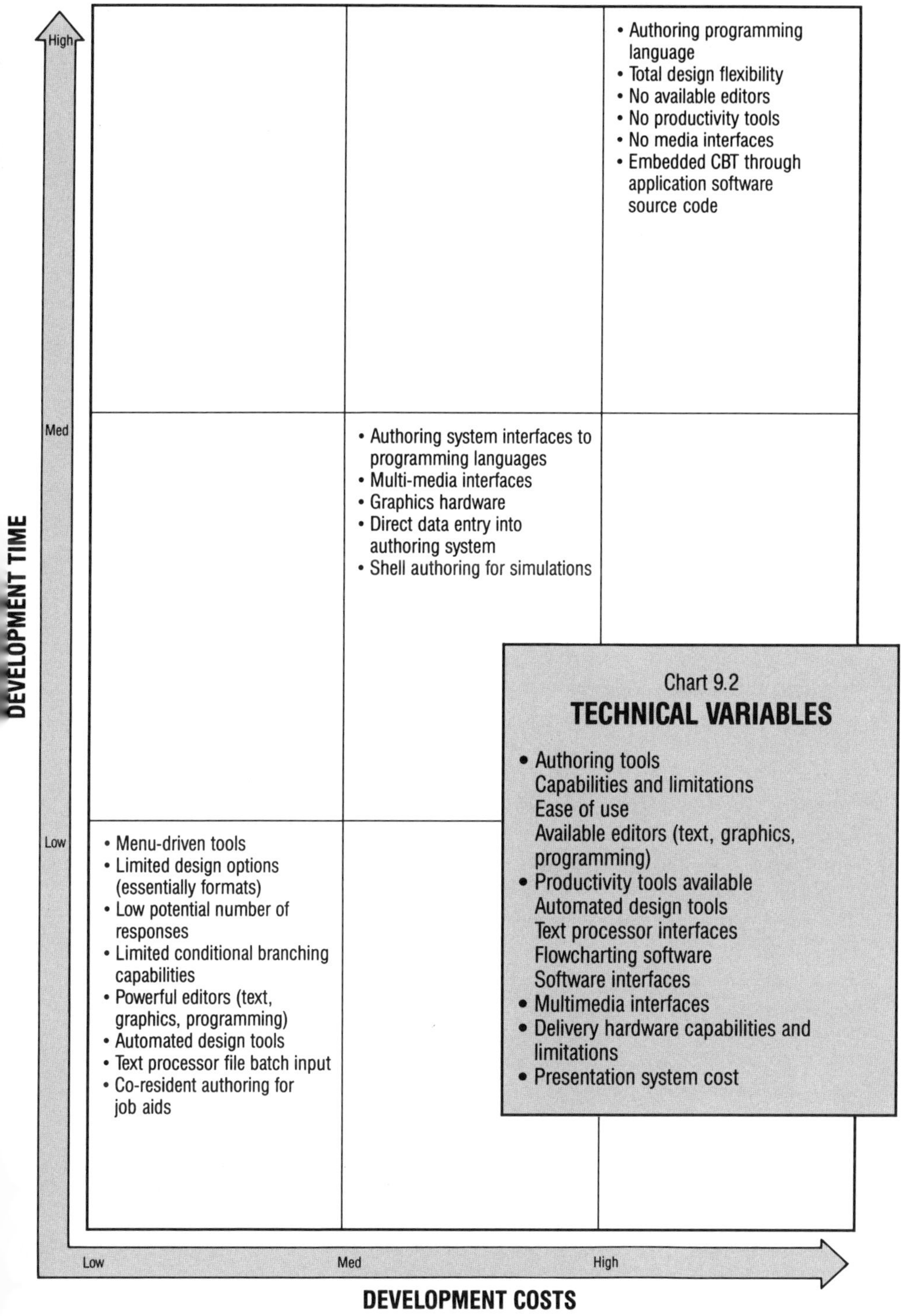

	Low	Med	High
High			• Authoring programming language • Total design flexibility • No available editors • No productivity tools • No media interfaces • Embedded CBT through application software source code
Med		• Authoring system interfaces to programming languages • Multi-media interfaces • Graphics hardware • Direct data entry into authoring system • Shell authoring for simulations	
Low	• Menu-driven tools • Limited design options (essentially formats) • Low potential number of responses • Limited conditional branching capabilities • Powerful editors (text, graphics, programming) • Automated design tools • Text processor file batch input • Co-resident authoring for job aids		

DEVELOPMENT TIME (vertical axis: Low, Med, High)

DEVELOPMENT COSTS (horizontal axis: Low, Med, High)

Chart 9.2
TECHNICAL VARIABLES

- Authoring tools
  Capabilities and limitations
  Ease of use
  Available editors (text, graphics, programming)
- Productivity tools available
  Automated design tools
  Text processor interfaces
  Flowcharting software
  Software interfaces
- Multimedia interfaces
- Delivery hardware capabilities and limitations
- Presentation system cost

on CBT technology). These tools will enhance both quality and productivity. Although they haven't yet been used extensively for CBT, I expect that they'll help bring development costs down for most courseware.

Figure 9.2 illustrates the judgments I've made about how various technological alternatives affect development time and cost.

Naturally, developers must diagnose their own situations and evaluate the effects on the specific CBT applications development activity. Again, judgments are necessary and not all of these factors will carry equal weight. You should plot the technological factors right on the same grid with the courseware variables.

Human Variables. The characteristics of the people developing the course make a big difference in time and cost. Experienced CBT developers who know the course subject, the authoring system, and CBT design principles (*and* who like working with the medium of CBT) will take considerably less time than a team of inexperienced people who have never worked together and whose commitment to the project is low. Chart 9.3 lists the human variables that must be considered in estimating time and cost.

Again, you must consider the relationship between the people and the technological environment. If developers must learn how to use the technological development tools at the same time they are learning the course content and designing the course, you are in for a longer and more expensive process. Figure 9.3 plots some general assessments of how the human variables affect development time and cost.

Many managers grossly underestimate the time it takes to learn all of the tools, techniques, and processes associated with CBT development. As much as two-thirds of the time in initial CBT projects is spent on educationally related activities and in developing standards, terminology, production forms, and other indirect or supporting activities. More about that later.

Plot your judgments about the human variables on your graph with the courseware and technological variables. By now you might be starting to see a pattern in where the variables are clustering.

Finally, other processes and factors come into play, not the least of which is the development methodology employed during the project. Chart 9.4 summarizes these other variables.

I can't over emphasize the importance of a structured development methodology in timely and affordable CBT development. (See Chapter Five, "Development.") In their desire to "get screens written," many developers try to skip steps. They try to design using on-line, prompted authoring systems without first having developed an overall integrated instructional design strategy for achieving learning objectives and engaging the learner. Project managers are seduced into mistaking all the activity they see for progress.

The major contributor to CBT development time and cost is repetitive

Figure 9.3
RELATIONSHIP OF HUMAN VARIABLES

DEVELOPMENT TIME (vertical axis: High, Med, Low)

DEVELOPMENT COSTS (horizontal axis: Low, Med, High)

High / High cell:
- Inexperienced authors or team
- Limited or no experience with authoring tool
- Many or complex changes
- High team or client turnover
- No defined development methodology
- Low role clarity
- Highly political environment
- Low client commitment
- Large number of team members
- High learner expectations
- Conflict or disagreement among team or client members

Med / Med cell:
- Small, stable, balanced development team
- Some development team experience
- Moderate specification or content changes
- No experience with particular authoring system

Low / Low cell:
- Experienced author with subject knowledge
- Small, stable team
- Limited specifications or content changes
- Experience with authoring tools
- High role clarity
- Structured development methodology
- High client commitment
- Strong project management skills
- Small number of development team members
- Low learner expectations
- Stable client interface
- Experienced with authoring or other productivity software

Chart 9.3
HUMAN VARIABLES

- Number of development team members
- Author or team members' individual knowledge, skill, and experience
- Number of projects team has worked on together before
- Percentage of team members' time dedicated to this project
- Project management skills
- Role clarity
- User or client skill, commitment, and time
- Team synergy
- Political factors
- Management pressure
- Team and client turnover
- Learner expectations

cycling through the development stages. In weighting this development methodology factor, bear in mind that it may be responsible for as much as seventy-five percent of the total cost if there are low levels of structure and control. Design and development of CBT is a "pay-me-now-or-pay-me-later" proposition, the payment being in the form of delays and expense or compromised course quality and staff commitment or morale.

Earlier I mentioned the importance of the CBT "infrastructure" of standards, terminology, and production processes. Over time, you can expect to dramatically reduce development expense when terminology is clear and universal (e.g., What is a lesson "sequence" or "module"? What are we calling a particular type of instructional sequence?) and when there are standard display templates and interactive approaches. Realize that few new developers, their managers, or client reviewers have a common language on which to base discussions, design documents, or any other communication about the process. Fewer yet have experience in visualizing actual interactive lesson execution from scripts or storyboards. Expect to spend considerable time during your initial development work on this type of activity. Productivity will increase significantly, and you'll be less likely to hear "That's not what I thought you meant" when the final lesson is on the computer. At that point, it's either too late or very expensive to make changes. There is more about these productivity-oriented items in Chapter Five.

Figure 9.4 illustrates the positioning of the other variables. It should be obvious that things like availability of existing training material on which to develop courses can make a big difference.

Putting It All Together. The matrix on which you've plotted your CBT course application is probably now filled with markings at all points on the continuum. The next step is to combine, or synthesize, these many individual judgments into a single integrated perspective. There are several alternative approaches, but everyone will want to start by eliminating irrelevant or low contributory factors. For instance, if you really don't need or realistically can't include graphics, eliminate that element. Plot only the major contributing variables in courseware, development process, and staff experience levels. Include an overall judgment about how the available technological variables contribute to the process. If there's a strong match between the technical environment and your needs, you will plot it on the low side; if not, it will be a greater contributor.

The "left-brained" estimators will likely establish weights and point values for each factor and approach the situation mathematically, establishing ranges for "low," "intermediate," and "high" factors. They will then plot all of the factors and come up with numbers. I've even seen folks use a spreadsheet to do this. We "right-brained" estimators will look at all the graphs, synthesize them unconsciously, and then use our overall

Figure 9.4
RELATIONSHIP OF OTHER VARIABLES

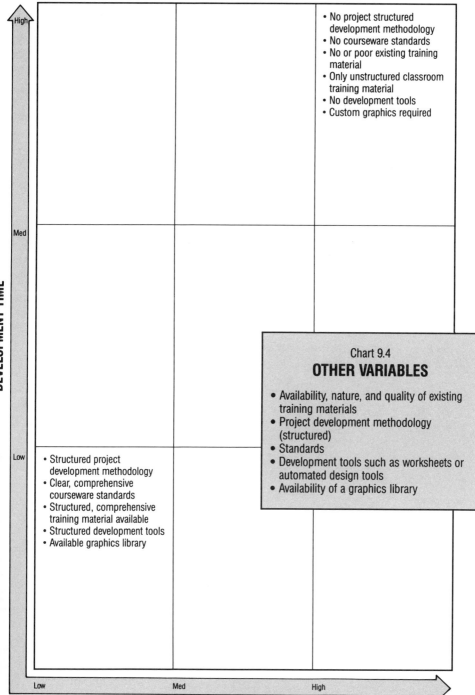

DEVELOPMENT TIME (vertical axis: High, Med, Low)

- No project structured development methodology
- No courseware standards
- No or poor existing training material
- Only unstructured classroom training material
- No development tools
- Custom graphics required

Chart 9.4
OTHER VARIABLES

- Availability, nature, and quality of existing training materials
- Project development methodology (structured)
- Standards
- Development tools such as worksheets or automated design tools
- Availability of a graphics library

- Structured project development methodology
- Clear, comprehensive courseware standards
- Structured, comprehensive training material available
- Structured development tools
- Available graphics library

DEVELOPMENT COSTS (horizontal axis: Low, Med, High)

judgment about the entire set of interrelationships. The project will "look like" a certain amount of time.

Whatever your approach, recognize that your outcome will be only as good as the quality of the data going into the process. And I caution you against presenting your results as if the process were a science. Remember the old saying "Measure it with a micrometer, mark it with chalk, and split it with an axe." Making judgments is what you're going to be doing in estimating until you become experienced with a given type of instructional material development to base your estimate on reality-based data.

The main value of this estimating process lies in the certainty that you haven't left anything out. Simply going through the exercise will force more thoughtful discussion and decision making about the course, the development environment, the tools, and the people who will be doing it. You will know that you're considering all of the important contributing factors, and you can begin discussing with confidence how to approach the major factors for productivity-enhancing or time-consuming possibilities. These might include making the design less complex, using additional productivity software, tightening up the development process, and so forth.

Development Ratios. In my experience, when these factors are put together they tend to group on a particular sector of the time and cost grid. Your final step, then, is to look at the pattern of your completed scatter gram against the graph shown in Figure 9.5. This graph illustrates the number of development hours, and thus the cost, that will be required to produce an hour of CBT instruction. For example, if most of the variables that apply to your situation fall on the medium to high portion of your scatter gram, you can expect to spend 300 or more hours of development time to produce one CBT delivery hour. And if they fall at the lower end, it's more like 100 hours.

Bear in mind that a CBT delivery hour can be defined in many ways. For purposes of this estimating grid, it is defined as an hour of instruction at the computer in a course that is linear in nature, includes conditional feedback, and restricts the use of conditional branching to review segments. This definition represents the bulk of courseware currently under development. Truly conditionally branched instructional materials are rare because of their development complexity and the time limits imposed on most developers.

What I propose is that time and cost estimates be made with greater discipline and definition than most developers and project managers currently use. To improve the quality and credibility of your estimates, you must relate one by one the factors described above, and their interrelationships, to a given application. As a result, more projects are likely to be funded, fewer developers will lose personal and professional credibility, and CBT development and implementation will be more successful.

Figure 9.5
DEVELOPMENT RATIO GRAPH

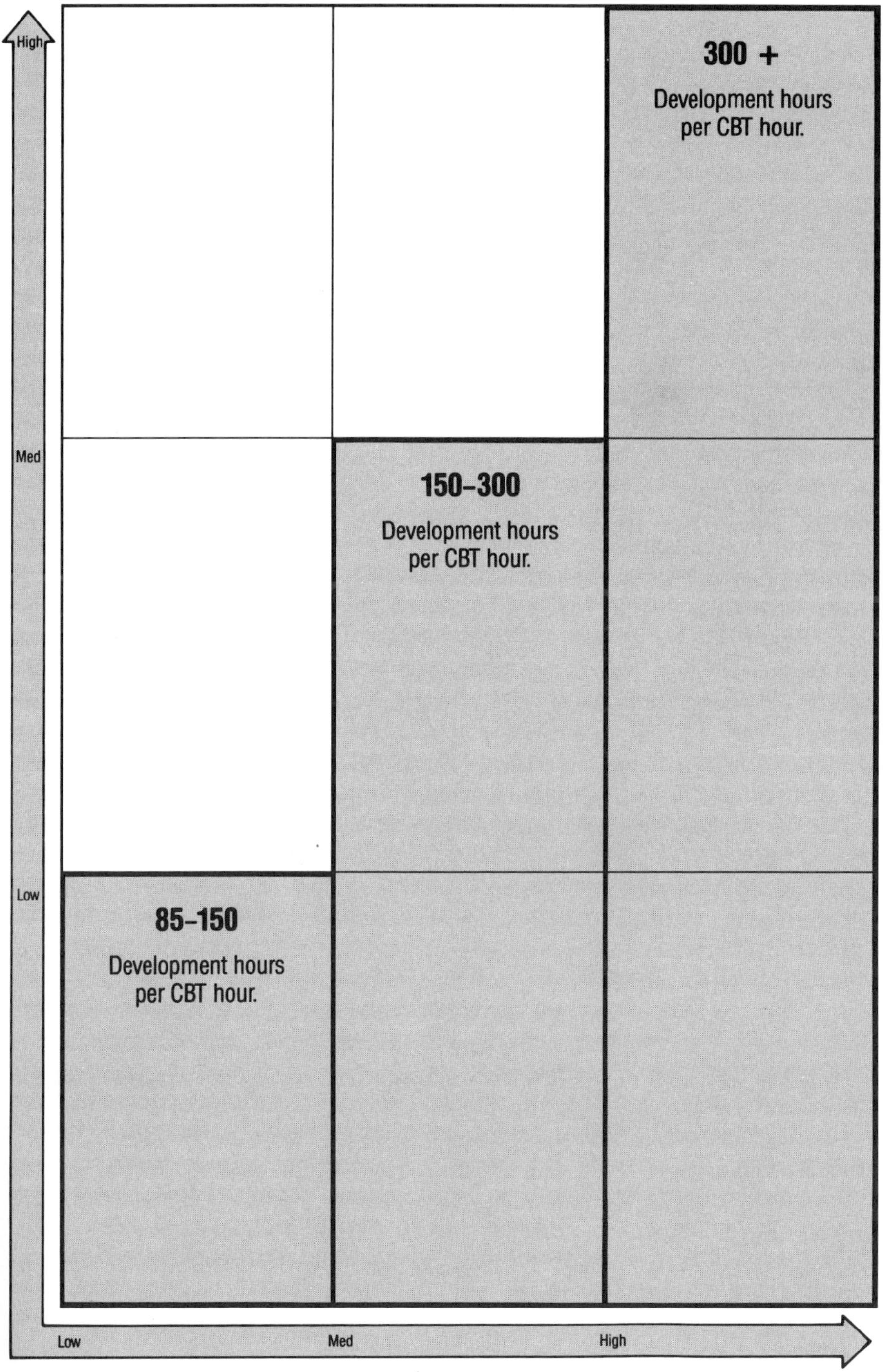

189

Remember that some factors will extend schedules but not necessarily increase costs. For example, if the person who must review and sign off on the technical accuracy of the course content is not committed to your schedule and turnaround times, it will stretch the schedule out. Or if you need content information that's still under development, expect delays in your production.

I can't promise you that it's a simple matter. Nothing is ever simple when it comes to computers and people. Whoever believes that it is believes that "the check is in the mail," "the system is on schedule," and "it's only a simple programming change." Develop some realistic perspectives and don't oversell or undersell what's involved. Make very sure you keep records of the time it actually takes for the various activities so you can do a better job next time. Keep separate the categories relating to standards development and other one-time activities. You can leverage that expense over future courses.

Finally, remember how to ask the question about what it costs by being specific as you can be about the thirty-seven factors. You'll get a far better answer!

CHAPTER **10**

Evaluation

Measure CBT both as
software and a training
program, and be as hard
on it as you would be with
any other medium—
but no harder.

How do you evaluate CBT courseware?

There are both similarities and differences between evaluating CBT courseware and evaluating traditional instructional media. As you might suspect, the most critical differences relate to interactivity levels and the nature and degree of learner control over the courseware. In addition, the interfaces between the learner and the software (e.g., screen displays, mobility commands) become important.

Let's explore both the traditional and CBT-specific considerations. As with any instructional materials, your first and foremost consideration in evaluating CBT is whether or not the material in fact *teaches*. There are lots of resources available in this area. Reams have been written about evaluating educational effectiveness.

Learning Effectiveness. The main point here is that CBT, because of our relative inexperience with it, seems to be under more critical scrutiny than are traditional media. I see more people concerned about educational effectiveness with interactive instruction than with any other kind, and they are putting courseware to the test. On one hand, I say it's about time we looked at whether (and what) we are teaching since we are spending our organization's resources. On the other hand, I have concerns when people conduct exhaustive validation activities looking at CBT where a classroom learning experience would be evaluated using a one-page "happiness sheet" or student critique. And we all know that the student critiques reflect participant *feelings*, not necessarily learning.

Sometimes it appears as if evaluators were trying to *disprove* CBT's learning effectiveness, as opposed to making reasonable comparisons with traditional media. It may, however, be that the visibility and up-front nature of CBT development costs, not to mention the novelty and political risk associated with the medium, creates an understandable critical eye. My point is make fair and even comparisons using reasonably objective assessments of learning outcomes or resulting knowledge and competencies. Separate the emotional reactions of learners and your own media preferences from effectiveness. Those preferences are important, but they shouldn't be confused with instructional outcomes.

Interactivity Dimensions. The nature, depth, and frequency of the interactions within the course are the most critical dimensions to consider in evaluating CBT. Interactivity is explored in depth in Chapter One. CBT courseware reviewers should be very familiar with its content. Without sufficient interactivity to add value beyond what's possible with traditional, more passive, media, there's little purpose in using CBT, unless courseware distribution (i.e., getting it to people) is the main reason for choosing CBT. In general, the following interactivity dimensions should be evaluated. Of course, all must be judged in light of the particular course audience and the specific learning objectives desired.

- Nature of the interactions

- Complexity of the interactions

- Appropriateness and value of the interactions (i.e., are they nontrivial and relevant?)

- How learner responses are analyzed (including flexibility in learner input and the number and nature of learner responses the system can handle)

- Feedback to learner for acceptable and unacceptable responses during instruction

- Feedback to learner for acceptable and unacceptable responses for navigating through the system

- The nature and amount of branching within instructional sequences (i.e., conditional feedback only versus conditionally branched sequences)

- Nature and degree of learner control within the courseware (e.g., menu options, instructional pathing, learner inquiry, hints, mobility options such as paging backward or forward, HELP)

- Ability to hold and manipulate variables (e.g., data within a spreadsheet).

A sample set of evaluation questions relating to the unique considerations of CBT is summarized in Exhibit 10.1.

Learner Interfaces. What the learner sees or hears when using the course affects both learning and emotional reactions. Important considerations are those of clarity and the aesthetic elements of screen displays, menus, learner mobility instructions (e.g., how to escape or review while in the course), and the nature and appropriateness of the use of sound. I described some of these considerations in Chapter One. In addition, however, *Screen Design Strategies for Computer Assisted Instruction* by Jesse Heines[1] details considerations such as spacing, font styles, upper- or lowercase text displays, and resolution.

Questions for courseware reviewers to ask when evaluating CBT are listed in the exhibit. In general, the following considerations are important.

- Intelligibility of screen displays

- Consistency of screen displays

- Clarity and completeness of instructions to learners for interacting with the program

- Learner mobility within the course

- Graphics clarity and resolution

- Use of color

- Clarity and conciseness of text displays

- Appropriateness and learner control in use of sound

- Simplicity of learner mobility and expected responses

- Ability of learners to stop and restart within a sequence (to "bookmark" sections)

- Ability of learners to review sequences

- Clarity and appropriateness of scoring mechanisms

Administrative Considerations. Getting in, around, and out of courseware can be more or less difficult. Some courseware is administratively complex and requires a facilitator for such things as registering a learner, setting up I.D.'s, or loading courseware. Other courseware just requires learners to log on. Some administrative demands are a function of the technical delivery environment; typically, mainframe courseware requires more advanced setup by knowledgeable course administrators. Some administrative requirements are a function of course design or given organizational policy. Naturally, the simpler you can make access and use, the more likely learners are to use and reuse the courseware. Ease of reentry following course completion is also a priority when use of the course for refresher training is anticipated. Relevant administrative considerations are detailed for reviewers in the exhibit.

Required Learner Time Frames. It's generally believed that CBT programs take less time for learners to complete than traditional instruction. That may or may not be true, however; one must always assess learner time frames in context with evaluating learning outcomes. When such time comparisons are made between CBT and other media, apples-to-apples comparisons can occur only when material is comparable in both content and structure (and that means linear). If the CBT courseware is nonlinear or the learning strategies are dramatically different (e.g., instruction through simulations of situations and tasks as opposed to simple presentation of material), time comparison are more difficult and probably less valid. When CBT courseware takes less time, it's typically because of the increased precision and conciseness in expression of material. Writing is more terse to accommodate the visual medium. Scripts are subject to more editing and review, so content is more precise, less unintentionally redundant, and structured more carefully than in the relatively freeform, live-instructor environment. In addition, the irrelevant material, war stories, and personal material that always creep

194

Exhibit 10.1
QUESTIONS IN EVALUATING CBT PROGRAMS

The following questions relate primarily to the software, interactivity, and learner control aspects of your evaluation. You should use these questions as a supplement to the normal evaluation you would make of any training materials (e.g., accurate content, adequate depth of content in relation to learning outcomes, appropriateness of instructional strategy). These questions are designed to evaluate the areas in which CBT adds unique considerations to the educational evaluation.

Technological Issues

What are the technological and hardware requirements for implementing the software (e.g., memory requirements, disk drives, monitors, input/ output devices)? How do they match installed equipment? If additional equipment or software is required, is it compatible with the installed technological architecture?

Does the program require a separate software presentation system, student "driver," or individualized learner diskette? If so, what are the economic, logistical, and administrative considerations in relation to the organization and training or record-keeping needs, budget, and so forth?

Does the vendor (if there is one) provide technical support for the program?

CBT-Specific Educational Components

Do the instructional strategies used take advantage of the computer's capability for conditional branching and variable manipulation?

How interactive is the program (i.e., frequency of interactions)?

Are the interactions related to the educational objectives (i.e., more than simply administrative interactions to enable the learner to progress through or move around the course such as with menu choices)?

Are the interactions appropriate to the content, learning objectives, and learner audience (e.g., complexity, type of interactions, interrelationships among and between the interactions)?

Are the program-controlled interactions placed within the program appropriately to achieve desired learning outcomes?

Are interactions repeated sufficiently to achieve desired learning objectives (e.g., with practice problems or simulations)?

Is the analysis of the learner response to questions, decisions, inputs, and variable manipulation adequate? Can it handle a sufficient range of acceptable, unacceptable, or unanticipated learner responses?

Is the feedback adequate and appropriate for the type of interaction, learning objective, learner populations? Is it always clear to the learner about the acceptability (i.e., right/wrong) or consequence (i.e., outcome) of the response?

CONTINUED

QUESTIONS IN EVALUATING CBT PROGRAMS (cont.)

Is the feedback conditional based on learner input or request?

What is the branching structure of the program (i.e., linear, conditionally branched based on learner performance or choices, linear with conditional feedback, and so forth) and is the structure appropriate to the learner audience and content?

Can the learner select learning paths within branches? How (e.g., menus, on-line options)? Are the options sufficient, meaningful, appropriate, and clear to the learner?

What is the balance between learner control and program or course control? Is it appropriate to the content, learning objectives, and learner audience?

What specific options for learner mobility exist (e.g., sequence review, back-paging, skipping sequences or interactions, glossary, hint, help, on-line documentation, more detail, bookmark, examples, page-forward, or scan without completing interactions)? How does the learner access them? Are access methods clear to the learner and usable?

Can learners maintain an orientation to where they are in the program? How?

Is it clear what learner records are being maintained? Is the learner clear on what is being recorded and its use?

Are screen displays clear and appropriate (e.g., layouts, text size, font size, graphics quality, readability, use of highlighting or inverse video)?

Is the writing style concise and appropriate to the visual medium of the terminal or monitor?

Are graphics meaningfully and appropriately used? Do they contribute to learning? Could they be used better? How?

Are audio and video appropriately used?

Are input devices and their use appropriate to the program, delivery hardware, and learner needs?

Are keyboard key uses clear (e.g., function keys, control keys)?

into instructor-led courses is avoided. The learner spends more time covering the required material. As a result, significantly more material is often covered in the CBT.

We know from experience, however, that learners frequently repeat and review sequences when they are given the choice. As instructional developers, we probably grossly underestimate repetition as a learning strategy, and typically learners can't control the number of times they review things in classroom or on-the-job experiences. But with self-paced interactive instruction, they can. Learners often take advantage of the opportunity to repeat questions, activities, practice exercises, content sequences, quizzes, and tests. As a result, the *amount* of time a learner spends in the course may not decrease, but the depth and retention of learning achieved in a given time is likely to improve. In addition, the computer permits much more simulation as an instructional approach than do traditional media. Students learn faster by working through real-life situations than by merely reading or hearing about them. And with simulation techniques, learners confront applications problems sooner, more frequently, and in a more controlled sequence than they would on the job. It is also possible to present the material as a part of a simulation or case-study approach. You can do this by presenting the information either within the simulation itself or as a learner-accessed tutorial sequence of the simulation program. If you use instructional strategy and structure, one-for-one time comparisons are nearly impossible.

But Do They Like It? We all want learners to feel good about the instructional delivery. So when you evaluate CBT, you should ask questions about how they "liked" the courseware. It is equally important to find out what they liked or disliked and why. In my experience, when learners don't like CBT, they describe it as "frustrating" or "boring," which relates back to the interactivity and learner control and clarity dimensions discussed above. In some cases, their reactions relate to the learning context: there may have been distractions in the work place or they are frustrated with their inability to study at home or on the train. Or a learner may have had difficulty interacting with the equipment (e.g., low resolution monitors, technical problems).

Sometimes negative reactions relate to a strong preference for live instruction. While I haven't seen any research, my guess is that when given a choice, many (if not most) learners would prefer live instruction with a good instructor to almost *any* other medium. But that's not always practical. In some cases, going away to class gets people away from their jobs or is seen as a reward, and learners may not view sitting at the terminal in the same way. In addition, many learners do not yet have confidence that they can learn via the computer simply because they have not had experience with it before. We see strong differences in reactions between experienced and inexperienced CBT learners. In any event, you must determine the reasons behind the emotional reactions and take them into consideration when making your ultimate decision. Or you might be able to modify the things that gave people problems, such as where they take the course. Don't underestimate the importance of people liking the experience, but don't confuse their liking CBT (or any other instructional medium) with learning. Sometimes the judgment of a method must be made based on effectiveness and practicality, not its emotional appeal.

Costs. The CBT evaluation process must include absolute and relative cost assessments. Cost considerations unique to CBT are detailed in Chapter Nine. Be sure to compare apples to apples if you do comparative costing. For example, some evaluators fail to include instructor preparation time in the cost equation for instructor-led programs. When making your decision, be certain to consider the relative merits of delivery consistency and learning outcomes.

Ultimately, you must remember that CBT is *both* computer software and a training program, and it cannot be judged solely on a single set of criteria. Too many organizations make the mistake of leaving CBT evaluation in the hands of either the content experts, the trainers, or the learners when none of them can do an adequate job alone. As is the case with CBT development, evaluation is an interdisciplinary project and should be managed that way.

NOTES

[1] Jesse Heines, *Screen Design Strategies for Computer Assisted Instruction* (Bedford, Massachusetts: Digital Equipment Press, 1983).

CHAPTER

Software Proficiency Training

New technology and
concepts have made it
possible to produce variations
of CBT that promise a faster
push up the software
learning curve.

199

What's the matter with conventional ways of learning how to use software?

Learning how to use software is a process, not an event. In Figure 11.1, I present a model showing the stages of learning to use a software package. Progression through the stages is a function of time and experience with the software as well as access to learning experiences. Some of the learning experiences are training events, such as a course. A course can be delivered in virtually any medium (e.g., instructor-led classroom, video, programmed instruction, or CBT tutorial). Other learning experiences are more informal and less structured and include access to experts, the use of documentation, trial and error, embedded resources such as internal system HELP and error messages, paper-based or interactive job aids, and so on.

The computer, alone or in combination with other instructional media, can dramatically accelerate the rate and learning depth associated with software knowledge and skill acquisition. Figure 11.2 compares three alternative learning curves: user exploration with no formal training, a "training event" approach (regardless of media used), and a computer-driven proficiency training approach. Chart 11.1 provides more detail on the learning outcomes and approaches in my recommended computer-enhanced proficiency training approach.

Most of this chapter will be devoted to an explanation of computer-enhanced proficiency training, which has become possible only recently, as a result of the development of new authoring tools. I believe computer-enhanced proficiency training dramatically improves the learning rate and skill acquisition over traditional "event" instruction (such as classroom or video) for several significant reasons. Learners have:

- significantly greater practice opportunities;

- ability to access HELP, procedures, definitions, and so forth continuously while actually using the software itself in real and meaningful applications;

- ability to control pace, sequencing, repetition rates, and content in close conjunction with actual need; and

- continuous access to assistance for complex, little-used, or never-used software functions following formal training activities without the need to call for human help or look things up in a manual.

The traditional methods of training people to use software don't make the most of the software learning curve, as I can testify from personal experience. The problem lies in the relationship between the available media and software itself. Few of us have problems learning *about* software. Lots of articles, books, manuals, workshops, and interactive CBT

Chart 11.1

LEARNING TO USE SOFTWARE

Learning Outcome	Definition	Training Approach	Measurement or Testing Technique
AWARENESS OR FAMILIARIZATION	Having general consciousness or acquaintance with software functions, procedures, use, etc.	Tutorials about software features and functions. Guided walkthroughs or demonstrations of software function or its use for specific activities.	Multiple-choice or true/false questions in test form. Attitude questionnaire.
KNOWLEDGE, COMPREHENSION OR UNDER-STANDING	Full understanding or comprehension of software function, procedures, use; a meaningful grasp of the nature of the software and its use.	Tutorials (in depth) about software function, concepts, structure. Explanations and interactive questioning of user, including use of open-ended questions requiring recall from memory. Interactive walkthroughs of software function or use.	Open-ended questions in test form requiring learner recall.
LEVEL I SKILL Deliberate, considered conscious actions at a slow pace	Ability to perform given software functions in the presence of considerable resources external to the system. External resources include: • Hotlines • User Documentation • Other knowledgeable users Skill requires deliberate and conscious application of specific steps, commands, etc.	Guided simulations requiring users to perform functions from memory when presented with applications tasks (e.g. register a guest; change a guest's room). Concurrent interactive job aids.	Test exercises requiring independent learner action or recall using computer simulations with response trapping, response analysis and feedback. Or close human observation of learner performance.
LEVEL II SKILL Conscious action at a moderate pace.	Ability to perform given software functions using HELP within the system or limited reference to documentation or other users. Independent action with conscious thought.	Performance of a sufficient number of practice exercises on required activities using a test data base with live software. Activities can be paper-based, audio or instructor led. Active use of concurrently executing expanded system HELP. Alternatively, exercises can be done under direction of live instructors who reinforce performance, guide, etc.	Extensive test exercises using computer simulations described above or human observation.
LEVEL III SKILL Unconscious competence; rapid execution.	Proficiency or fluency in software operation with little or no use of external resources except use of internal HELP for new or infrequently used functions. Executes functions without conscious thought.	Use of the system over time. Powerful internal HELP or concurrently executing interactive job aids facilitate the process. Typically requires extensive short term drills/ practice or extended use of the system over time.	Observation Competency monitoring. Post-training evaluation: 1) learner self-evaluation 2) administrator evaluation of performance standards (performance criteria established earlier)

201

tutorials teach about what a program can do, demonstrate what it takes to make it do things, or actually assist the learner to do an interactive walkthrough of the software. The commercial CBT courses I've taken even let me press some of the buttons and perform software operations like setting up a data base or formatting a disk; however, this doesn't result in my learning the software to any level of proficiency. Rarely are there enough practice problems for me to do in the classroom or with tutorial CBT. Or the practice exercises barely resemble what I will be using the software for. Or they cover functions I already know, like copying a disk. They hardly ever deal with more advanced topics, like creating subdirectories in MS DOS. As a new user, I thought *I* was the problem. Since becoming more knowledgeable and experienced, however, I've concluded that the real *problem* is this: training experiences—even the interactive CBT software simulations—are *events*, while learning how to use and becoming proficient in software use is a *process*.

Figure 11.1

SOFTWARE LEARNING STAGES

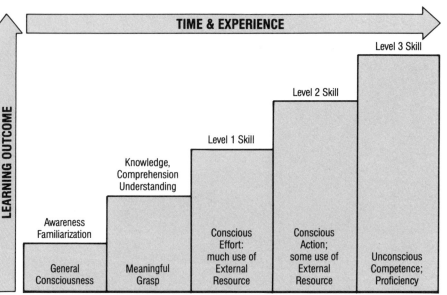

TECHNIQUES OF THE PROFICIENCY TRAINING APPROACH

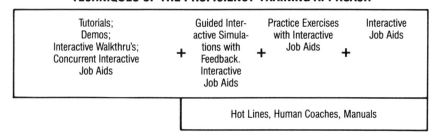

The very best technique to speed my learning is a master user sitting right next to me (or immediately available, at least) who can answer my questions or figure out what I've done wrong and show me how to correct it. I know, however, that few of us have such a luxury. Certainly no organization can afford such hand-holding or human-driven interactive job aids for any but the few very top executives who can command it even when it's not justified! Yet, when it comes to learning software, we all need it.

Any software learner can tell you that you learn fastest when

- you have a real reason to use the software for an application that is personally meaningful and has a payoff for you (*not* an artificial classroom or self-paced exercise that someone else constructed!);

- the timing of the learning experience coincides perfectly with your need;

Figure 11.2

THE SOFTWARE LEARNING CURVE

MEASUREMENT OR TESTING

Multiple-Choice or True False Questions in Test Form	CBT Test Exercises Requiring Recall	Extensive Test Exercises with Human Observation	Human Observation; Job Performance

- the learning experience addresses only what you need (or want to know) and does not involve learning superfluous options, commands, or information;

- you can go at your own pace, learn in the sequence that makes sense to you, and explore paths that interest you without regard to the "average" learner; and

- the teacher doesn't impose herself or himself on you but responds to your inquiries, is patient and able and willing to repeat the information as often and whenever you need it, never makes you feel dumb, and essentially acts as an "on-line coach."

In real life, these conditions rarely come together. For the most part, we are subjected to structured, inflexible learning situations like formal classroom workshops. These are sessions where the instructor must teach to what someone determined was the norm, cover predetermined content in a predetermined sequence, and permit only limited practice using contrived—and frequently irrelevant—workshop exercises. To further frustrate optimal learning, classes are scheduled at times when it is administratively feasible or when classrooms are available, rather than when they are right for the learners. And we usually must sign up for such sessions weeks or months in advance.

Real-life formal training programs don't conform to real maximum or optimum user learning cycles. I call concentrated traditional classroom instruction on software use "a week at software camp." At the end of such a week, I've walked through all of the aspects of the game, including those I'll never need or don't think I'll ever need. Which means I never learned them. Following software camp, I'm "over-dosed" on content: "Is it Control-Shift-P or Shift-Control-F1 and Enter?" At best I've learned about the nature of the game and maybe a few of the rules. But I haven't mastered much, if any, of it, and I certainly don't feel prepared for a serious real life match under time or competitive pressure!

As bad as it is, "software camp" is better than no formal learning situation at all, which is what many users face in real life. We get the software and the manual and try to figure it out. That's a perfectly adequate approach for an experienced software learner who has a conceptual framework about how software is structured and who understands terms and concepts (like the difference between memory and storage, how to set up a file and why, and what a format command is). But for the novice or less-experienced learner, it's a disaster:

- We can't read, interpret, locate, understand, or apply what is (or isn't) in the manual. I once spent an afternoon trying to find the command for a page break in my word processor. I wound up having to call my computer store, who had to call the software vendor, who informed us that it was listed under "embedded format commands." Come on!

- We don't have experienced users or consultants who are readily available to get us started or work us through the rough spots. If we do have access to such people, they are busy answering questions from fifty other users or they run out of patience with us, or we don't want to look as dumb as we feel. Few information centers are staffed for or inclined toward such attention giving. Listening to Muzak while we're on "hold" doesn't soothe us, either.

- We become anxious and frustrated as our learning proceeds at a snail's pace. And if we are learning the software while we must be producing something, we become convinced that our old way of doing it is much faster. Finally we reject the software as a tool. We also become resistant to learning other software since the pain associated with our trial and error learning was so great.

- We learn only part of the software's functions and don't advance to higher mastery levels on more advanced and powerful functions. Much of the PC-user world believes MS DOS has only a few commands since all they were taught is FORMAT, COPY, DEL, DIR, and CHKDSK (whatever that is!). In fact, that's all that most introductory workshops or fifty-dollar tutorials can hope to cover. What then happens to the hard-disk user with 500 files on-line? Looking through the sequential file listing that DIR generates can fill up an entire afternoon! That user must learn the MK DIR command and understand how to create sub-directories to be efficient and effective. And where can the user go to learn it? There are few advanced topics classes, and it would probably take months to get registered for one. By then, who cares?

Many of us hoped that computer-based training tutorials or simulations would solve these problems. And, in fact, they do address some of our needs—like making training available on demand and providing good basic introductions to the software products. But currently, many CBT simulation tutorials have most of the same problems of classroom instruction. The medium just happens to be electronic. (An exception to this generalization, some of the CBT available for mainframe-based products, often encompasses a comprehensive curriculum. Mainframe CBT software has typically been developed for products with core stability that have been on the market for many years, such as *Focus* or *SAS*. Most of my comments apply to PC-software tutorials, although there are exceptions in this category as well.)

CBT tutorials and software simulations are generally linear and sequential and force a learner through a particular sequence with only menu selections as options.

They rarely go beyond the walkthrough or guided simulation levels of interaction. There are insufficient numbers and types of practice exercises for achieving mastery at any but the most rudimentary skill level. Rather, exercises are usually limited to the basic software functions or tasks. They are typically simple and require little more of the learner than following written instructions appearing on the screen. Almost never do exercises require recall or integration of tasks beyond the immediate question-and-answer or stimulus-response cycle. These CBT exercises are so limited because of simulation courseware's development complexity (especially in response analysis), expense, required lead times, authoring system or author limitations, and so forth. The fact that there are good reasons doesn't make me feel better as a learner, however.

After I've completed the tutorial and go "live" with my production software, I still have the same problem of trying to remember and integrate everything at once. I'm unable to "suspend" my actions while I'm "in" the actual software. I must log off, find the CBT tutorial, boot it up, work my way through the menus (if I have such options!), locate what I'm looking for (if it's there), and go through the sequence. "That's it!" I recall. And then I must log off the tutorial, boot up my software, load my files, and begin my transaction again. I'm beginning to think it was faster to wait on "hold" for my information center consultant or my brother-in-law!

Computer-based training tutorials aren't easily and quickly changed, if we even have that option. As new software releases, enhancements, and versions are introduced, considerable time is required to add to tutorials—and some commercial courseware vendors aren't committed to such maintenance. Even if they are, there's considerable time associated with ordering, exchanging, and distributing it.

Please don't get me wrong. I think there is a place for CBT software simulations. They are excellent for giving new users a cognitive framework about the software's structure and functionality, and they are good for interactively demonstrating operations with the software. Interactive walkthroughs are also great for getting new users or "shoppers" to touch it and see whether they want to "buy" it, increasing their confidence that they in fact will be able to learn it, and so forth. These simulations and "guided tours" may even be adequate for basic skill acquisition. They provide a "kick start" to get people going. And that is very necessary. But it's not sufficient to get full utilization or benefit from the powerful software we've acquired.

The computer-enhanced proficiency training approach is designed to eliminate the problems of traditional software training. It wouldn't have been thinkable a few years ago, but new tools make it possible to create electronic interactive job aids. The electronic interactive job aid allows learners to work with, ask questions about, or obtain quick instruction on their software as a supplement to traditional, formal training experiences. For sophisticated software users, it may eliminate the need for formal training programs. In many ways, this tool can automate the human coaching activities we all wish were available and affordable. There are lots of ways to define and structure interactive job aids, but let's assume a basic definition:

> *Interactive job aids are resources such as quick reference tools, glossaries, expanded HELP procedures, and quick, subject-limited tutorials that are immediately and easily accessible to a software user actively engaged in the software itself.*

What this means is the users—whether novice or experienced—have ready access to an expanded version of HELP that goes beyond the limited HELP available in most software. Exhibit 11.1 shows screens from two software products that generate on-line help.

Developers of interactive job aids can create glossaries defining or describing commands, functions, error messages, options, fields, input requirements, or displays. They can go beyond glossaries to create text tutorial sequences, develop interactive walkthroughs or demonstrations, windows overlaying fields, sets of instructions and procedures, and so on.

The user can call these options (or whatever others the developer has the imagination to create) via keyboard toggle keys (e.g., pressing the plus or minus key) while simultaneously working in the software. Without quitting the software, the user can learn new procedures, processes, functions, or information; refresh a memory of a function that is somewhat or even vaguely familiar but not used frequently or recently enough to generate recall; validate the proper step before actually executing it; or explore the software's capabilities to determine whether it fits an application (i.e., "playing with" the software and trying to fit it to the desired activity).

Essentially, the interactive job aid serves as an on-line coach. Naturally, it must be clearly structured and comprehensive if it is to stand alone or if it is to be a primary resource to a heterogeneous user community with a full range of competence, confidence, and needs. But you can define it much more narrowly to meet targeted objectives, such as that of familiarizing new or casual users with the simple commands needed to work with Lotus *1-2-3* macros for annual salary budgeting or territory management. Increasingly, companies are developing special-purpose programs that require little or no knowledge of the underlying software. It isn't necessary for users to learn more than the specific input commands or data requirements. No need for elaborate paper-based instruction, instructional meetings and seminars, or whatever. Just develop the job aid that executes concurrently or coresidently with the software, put the log-on instructions on the diskette, orient users to access techniques and structure, and let them go. This significantly reduces hotline activity.

Exhibit 11.1

SAMPLE SCREENS OF CONCURRENT
AUTHORING SYSTEM PRODUCTS

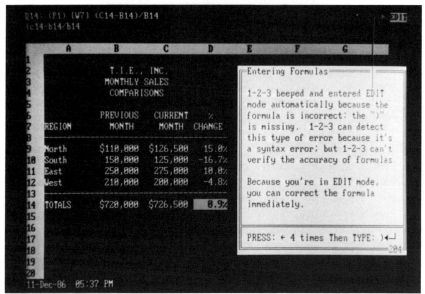

Vasco Corporation's *Lotus 1-2-3 QuickRef,* which runs concurrently with *1-2-3,* can open a window (here labeled "Entering Formulas") to explain a user's error and advise corrective action. *Lotus 1-2-3 QuickRef* is available from American Training International, a Vasco Company. Figure courtesy of Vasco Corporation.

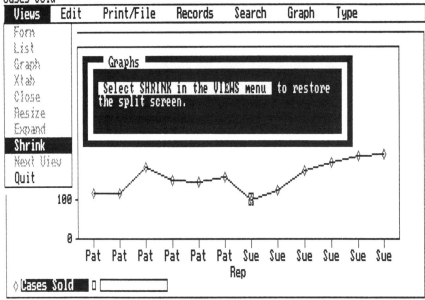

ComTrain, Inc.'s *Shelley* authoring system can be used to create lessons for application software users. Here, *Shelley* has superimposed an instructions box labeled "Graphs" on a *Reflex* screen and will monitor the user's selection in the pop-down menu at the left. Figure courtesy of ComTrain, Inc.

How can interactive job aids be used for instruction if they don't have the ability to direct learner sequences, trap and analyze learner responses, or do some of the other things you have said are so important?

In fact, some of the concurrent, shell, or coresident authoring systems used for developing these materials do have some traditional CBT capabilities like response analysis. However, that gets you back into more complex development, and with the more powerful, open-ended applications software, it's harder to anticipate all of the learner possibilities.

Consider this approach to end-user training: develop paper-based activities or exercises relating to the particular user situation (e.g., making or changing hotel reservations, adding new patients to a customer file, calculating rates). Then have the learner interact with a training version of the software using a preloaded data base with the relevant records. This can be a very effective training method if the system has adequate HELP or error messages and if there are human resources available when the learner gets stuck. Unfortunately, many (if not most) systems have inadequate HELP. Error messages are frequently obscure (e.g., "Invalid Entry" or "MG08KJ"). Terrific.

And then there is the user who never gets to go to training programs at all and the user who simply prefers to "fly live" with the software and disregard the formal training options. In the real world, many software users are too far away from the training site, there are no more or no currently scheduled classes, and the self-paced materials were never updated. Even more users are poorly trained (e.g., Sally showed Mary the system on her last day of work between the going-away luncheon and cleaning out her desk). And finally, some people just haven't the patience or learning style to deal with any training approach structured by others—or they have the confidence to go it alone. They can and will only learn by doing.

Enter the on-line electronic interactive job aid. It permits the use of this paper-based exercise approach with fewer or no human coaches available. And it is effective in helping untrained or poorly trained users. It permits users to begin actual work transactions with limited or no training because they can quickly pop out of of the software and get expanded help, explanations, or quick instruction. It also permits more flexible use of personnel who might be needed to fill in during emergency situations but whom you normally would not "train" on the system. Used in combination with the traditional CBT or self-paced tutorials that orient the user to the system's overall capabilities, the electronic interactive job aid adds tremendous leverage to our systems, and increases productivity through more rapid and timely knowledge acquisition. Until recently, creating these tools was only a dream.

Traditional authoring systems don't permit development of interactive job aids or references accessible from within the actual software being used. They create standalone training events. To create an on-line interactive job aid, you use a concurrent, coresident, or shell authoring system.

The concept of concurrently executing software is a relatively new one in the user and training world. Within the past several years, there have been introduced several products permitting users to pop in and out of software applications to perform additional functions like checking spelling, making notations, and capturing screens. *Sidekick* and *Turbo Lightning* (products of Borland International) represent such products. For example, a *Turbo Lightning* user can be working in a word processor that has no spell-checker or glossary and employ *Turbo Lightning* to check spelling or call up a thesaurus to identify synonyms. The user can then go back to the word processor and proceed with creating the document— all without any interruption in the primary software's activity. You move to and from concurrent or coresident software with simple commands or by pressing defined toggle keys such as a plus or minus key.

These coresident utilities have grown explosively as a software category, which shows just how much users wanted the convenience they offer. Now development tools that can generate this kind of concurrently executing software are available to trainers, documentation specialists, systems developers, and users.[1] These tools are called *concurrent authoring systems*, and they come in three basic varieties: embedded, coresident, and shell. There is an explanation of the three types and their capabilities in an article by Wallace Judd, "Programs in Tandem" (*Data Training*, May, 1986). Some of these systems require traditional programming. Others are menu-driven. The systems have a range of functionality, special capabilities, and so forth, just like the more familiar authoring systems or development tools. For the most part, however, these concurrent or shell development tools don't permit response trapping or response analysis with conditional feedback. The technical reason for this limitation is that parameters cannot be passed back and forth between the software packages. But for the most part, this option is not necessary. We are not talking about developing conventional CBT courseware here— we're describing on-line job aids, documentation, coaches, and quick reference products.

And costs and development lead times drop dramatically. These new tools haven't been around long enough for anybody to collect data on lead times, but they eliminate the most time-consuming activities in application simulation: question construction, response analysis, and feedback development. My experience with traditional CBT tells me that the design, scripting, programming, testing, and debugging costs of interactive job aids using concurrent tools would reduce development time by fifty percent or more, depending on system complexity, depth of the job aid, and developer knowledge and skill. This brings interactive learning experiences into the realms of both the affordable and the doable for a much broader population of trainers and systems implementers. It also gives us the chance to expand on-line documentation without putting the (generally useless) full-blown manuals on-line.

The concurrent or shell authoring systems hitting the commercial marketplace today are largely PC-based, but we can anticipate their use in all kinds of systems. Some of them permit or expect to permit access to mainframe-resident software when PCs are networked. Personal computers are typically required to store the job aid in memory, and dumb terminals don't have the capability. Some mainframe software vendors, such as SAS Institute, have developed the capability and use it for creating courseware. But I hesitate to comment further on the technical details because I fully expect micro-mainframe links and the new concurrent development tools to catch up with the need for on-line coaches on all kinds of applications. Our main objective right now should be to understand the existing possibilities and to identify needs. Then we can look for the development software that runs in our environment. It's just a matter of time before there's a match between our needs and available options.

Be very clear on what's required to produce the product you want, and make sure your developers have or will be trained to produce it. Nothing new here but the software. The selection and evaluation remains the same.

What will change is our concept of "training." There will be more of a shift to learner-controlled interactive inquiries. Training programs are typically sequenced, prestructured activities or programs covering specific content to achieve a specified learning objective (e.g., "At the end of this lesson, learners will be able to..."). Learners have limited control.

These new concurrent development tools and their resultant products permit us to dramatically expand our possibilities. We can extend our definition of the interactive learning experience from a formal course (an event) to a less structured, learner requested, coached experience that results in learning (a process). These experiences are more controlled by the learner, who learns what he wants when he wants, which is, in fact, the only way that people ever learn, despite our fantasies as trainers.

We must break our previously limited frames of reference and shift our efforts to new possibilities that further enhance the effectiveness and productivity or our learners—which improves our effectiveness and productivity as trainers. And concurrent development tools permit truly learner-controlled learning on the use of applications software. A wonderful new possibility! Remember, we define CBT as "an interactive learning experience" rather than simply as a "course" in its traditional sense. We can use interactive experiences, such as on-line interactive job aids, to move people along the learning curve, whether they use the job aid in combination with traditional linear instruction or with no formal instruction at all.

211

NOTES

[1] Some of the commercially-available products include:

Concurrent Development Series. Vasco Corporation, 1919 S. Highland Avenue, Suite 118-C, Lombard, Illinois 61048 (312) 495-0755.

Shelley. ComTrain, Inc., 152 Mill Street, Grass Valley, California, 95945 (916) 273-0845.

Explain. Communications Sciences, Inc., 100 North Seventh Street, Suite 518, Minneapolis, Minnesota 55403 (612) 332-7559.

Glossary

Animation. Repetitive positioning of the computer's cursor or a symbol to create the appearance of movement across the screen.

Answer Analysis or Judging. See "Response Analysis."

Applications Software or Program. A program or group of programs written to perform a specific function, such as accounts, word processing, or inventory control.

Artificial Intelligence. The discipline of making computer systems imitate human behavior or activity. The common areas of artificial intelligence (AI) research and application right now are expert systems, natural language, voice recognition, vision systems, and robotics. Expert systems and natural language would seem to hold the most promise for CBT applications.

ASCII. American Standard Code for Information Interchange. Under the ASCII convention, 128 different keyboard characters are rendered in different combinations of seven-bit code, which is readable by a wide variety of machines and systems. It is very heavily used in microcomputer systems. Word processing programs often include a function for converting files to ASCII (sometimes described as "text only" or "non-document" files), which can then be read by other word processing programs. Some CBT authoring systems are also capable of reading ASCII files, which gives them a method for importing text files prepared with a word processor.

Authoring Language. Programming language with codes specifically designed to handle major courseware needs, such as response judging.

Authoring System. Enabling productivity software which embodies preprogrammed instructional structures and permits users to input and structure content to create computer-based training.

Authors. A somewhat misleading term commonly used to represent the individuals or teams that create and develop CBT courseware. The de-

213

velopment effort actually involves 14 different (but sometimes overlapping) roles, only one of which is the scripting activity that people usually associate with the term "authoring."

Branch. Any variation from the straight linear path through the displays of a computer-based training program, whether caused by a learner selecting an option or by the program's code itself (e.g., a conditional branch to feedback, alternative learning sequence based on specific conditions or responses).

Branch Statement. An instruction that, when met in a program, makes a move to another part of the program deviating from the linear sequencing of the program. Branch statements are one of two types: conditional statement (command IF . . . THEN) or unconditional statement (GO TO).

Chunk. Any series of displays that achieves the instructional objective of conveying a complex concept; a chunk may be as small as, but never smaller than, a strand. Most chunks will require several loops or passes through a strand to accomplish their purpose.

Computer-Assisted Instruction (CAI). One application of CBT that involves an on-line interactive process between a learner and a computerized delivery system, in which the computer assumes a direct instructional role.

Computer-Based Training (CBT). An interactive instructional experience between a computer and a learner in which the computer provides the majority of the stimulus and the learner responds; progress toward increased knowledge or skill results.

Computer-Managed Instruction (CMI). A CBT application in which the computer manages a learner's progress through a training program or course. A CMI system supports instruction by selecting, presenting, and scoring tests; recording student progress data; providing feedback on learner drill and practice and test performance; and prescribing use of various learning resources (e.g., video, textbooks, slide-tapes, reference materials, activities).

Courseware. Software instructional material for CBT applications.

Data Base. A collection of data stored in computer-readable form.

Decision-Point Branches. Branches which originate from interaction screens requiring a learner input or choice: can be both path-line and off-line branches; can include pathing to alternative learning sequences, menu choices, and so forth.

Deliverable. The product at the end of a development phase; a tangible output that can be handed to others for review or use.

Design. To conceive and plan; to draw the plans for. Also, the plan itself. Computer-based training requires design from the broadest outline of the program down to the specific arrangement of the elements in each screen. See also "Instructional Design Hierarchy" and "Instructional Systems Design."

Design Document. The narrative, graphic, and logical description of the instructional scheme and subject matter content for a CBT program. Detail may vary. Content flow, structure, interactivity dimensions, and learner options must be included.

Development Methodology. The process and rules employed to create a specified result including phases, steps, activities, and deliverables.

Discovery Learning. A lesson design strategy in which the conditions are created to allow the learner to discover basic principles or relationships rather than having them presented explicitly. The assumption is that learners will develop superior understanding and better retention by being required to exercise their reasoning in this manner.

Display. The smallest instructional unit, a display is a single window of text.

Display Logic. The code needed to generate displays on a computer screen; may include computer language statements or commands relating to special character sequences to be displayed in graphics mode, algorithms for graphic displays, or use of special screen capabilities such as flashing, highlighting, and animation.

Documentation. Written descriptive material and instructions that accompany and facilitate the use of computer software, courseware, and programs.

Embedded CBT. On-line instruction which is an integral part of a product or system and encompasses help systems, simulations, and intelligent tutors. It is based on a learner-driven problem-solving style of learning rather than a tutorial or didactic instructional approach.

Entry-Level Test. See "Pre-Test."

Entry Point. Any display into which the instructional path flows from a nonsequential point in the program, such as the first display appearing after menu item selection or choice of a learner mobility option.

Exit Point. A point in the program from which the instructional path flows to a display other than the one which would follow immediately in the linear sequence, such as a display whose standard user interaction takes the learner back to the main menu or a display from which a learner mobility option, such as back, may be selected.

Expert System. A computer application that embodies the diagnostic capabilities and other thought processes of an expert. An expert system typically employs the hunches and rules-of-thumb distilled by an analyst (called a "knowledge engineer") from extensive observation of and interviews with a working expert. Theoretically, almost any expert activity could be converted to an expert system, given the time and resources. Thus it should be possible to create a program that could use the analysis and methods of an ideal tutor in a training situation. This book argues that, while such a development is possible, we don't need to wait for it to create highly effective CBT.

Feedback. The flow of information about the outcome of an action back to the source of the action so that it may be used to improve subsequent actions. Can be an acknowledgement, confirmation, prompt or hint, reinforcement, correction, explanation, or referral to another source for information. For instructional systems design purposes, synonymous with *knowledge* of results.

Flowchart. A diagram consisting of a set of symbols (e.g., rectangles, diamonds) and connecting lines that shows step-by-step progression through a complicated procedure or path.

Frame. The basic unit of programmed instruction in initial learning; used for the incremental presentation of subjects and procedures. The three frame types are: teach frame, practice frame, and the test or criterion frame.

Frame-Based Authoring System. Authoring system which is predicated on the assumptions associated with programmed instruction.

Frame-Numbering Sequence. In frame-based CBT, each frame has a unique number, and the order of the numbers controls the order of the presentation of the frames to the learner. The designer can thus incorporate a conditional branching sequence by making a specification such as "if response A, frame 0300," "if response B, frame 0400," and so on.

216

High-Level Language. A computer programming language that is problem- or procedure-oriented (as opposed to machine-oriented) and therefore resembles English more than the low-level languages (assembler, machine language) that are "understood" more directly by machines. High-level languages, such as Basic, Fortran, and Cobol, consist of statements and instructions which each correspond to several machine instructions.

Higher-Order Questions. Questions which require the learner to use higher levels of thought processes such as analysis, synthesis, and extrapolation.

Highlighting. A process that causes some of the characters on the computer display screen to stand out. Typically, highlighting is achieved by causing some characters to be lighted with a greater intensity or level of brightness than others.

Hint. Usually refers to a delayed attempt to assist the learner in obtaining the acceptable or correct response by supplying additional information or calling attention to certain parts of the information the learner already has.

Instructional Design Hierarchy. The order in which an instructional program is partitioned into progressively smaller groups of displays. A typical instructional design hierarchy would specify, from larger to smaller: modules, sequences, chunks, strands/screens, displays.

Instructional Systems Design. A generic term for the procedures involved in constructing learning activities that make up a solution to a complex set of learning problems. Any type of media or learning approach may be employed so long as the principles and techniques generally accepted to be part of the "systems approach" are used. The approach typically involves (1) written documentation specifying learning outcomes, (2) selection and creation of learning activities to match and accomplish learning objectives, and (3) utilization of feedback to improve the learning activities.

Interaction. The stimulus-response-analysis-feedback cycle programmed into the CBT or generated by the learner.

Interactive. A term describing a learning process in which the learner and the system alternate in addressing each other. Typically, each is capable of selecting alternative actions based on the actions of the other.

Intrasequence Branch. Branches that have both entry and exit points within the same sequence (with the exception of menu and exit); intrasequence branches are defined by the set of learner mobility options available. There are two types of intrasequence branches: (1) path-line branches that move the user forward and backward in the instructional path (e.g., previous, skip) and (2) off-line branches taking the user to displays that are not part of the main instructional path (e.g., glossary, hint).

Job Aid or Performance Aid. A device designed for use on the job and providing guidance on the performance of a specific task or skill. May be printed or on-line. Used in situations where it is not feasible or worthwhile to commit the procedure to memory before on-the-job activity.

Learner Mobility Options. Any option or selection that enables the user to deviate from the straight linear path of displays. Learner mobility options include previous, skip, review, and menu.

Learner Response. The constructed answer or indication of choice among a set of alternatives. Responses can be single choice, multiple choice, constructed (learner-created), and so forth.

Lesson Logic. The code needed to control lesson flow in courseware; it typically takes the form of a computer or authoring system program and does not include the commands necessary to generate screen displays. (Compare with "Display Logic.")

Linear Program. A program that contains little or no branching. Each learner in a linear CBT program sees exactly the same information and questions that every other learner sees. The logical branching which occurs in providing conditional feedback to either an acceptable/correct or unacceptable/incorrect response does not disqualify a lesson as linear.

Mainframe Computer. A large computer with extensive memory and disk storage and many facilities, usually requiring raised flooring and dedicated air conditioning; it is typically installed to carry out the DP functions of an organization. Users interact via networked terminals or personal computers.

Menu. A screen display designed to present learners with a number of fixed options and allow them to choose the option they desire. Can be hierarchically structured, or nested, using sub-menus (i.e., more detailed options within an overall menu).

Menu-Driven. Refers to a program, the running of which is controlled by a menu; presents successive menus to the user as prompts for each step.

Menu-Level Branch. Any branch in the instructional path that directly involves a menu (e.g., menu-to-menu, which involves branching between the main menu and submenus; or menu-to-sequence, which involves branching in either of two directions—from a menu into an instructional path or vice versa).

Module. Any series of displays that achieves the learning objectives of an entire unit in the design document. Modules are represented by single selections in the main menu.

On-Line Inquiry. The inquirer asks a question of a program and the answer, from a data base, is transmitted to the user.

Page. Any display possessing an entry point.

Post-Test. A test assessing the learner's knowledge of the instructional objectives upon completion of the training program.

Practice Exercises. Exercises or activities contained in an instructional program that provide opportunities for the learner to apply the information presented and actively interact with the instructional medium.

Prerequisite Test. A test to determine if a prospective learner has the necessary prior skills and knowledge to enter a training program.

Pre-Test (or Entry-Level Test). A test assessing the learner's knowledge of the instructional objectives of a training program prior to entry into the program.

Program. As a noun, a set of instructions that direct a computer to perform some meaningful task. Such instructions are written in a computer language. As a verb, the act of writing such instructions and storing them on a computer system.

Programmed Instruction. Any instructional materials using the principles of programmed instruction: (1) small steps, (2) active responding, (3) prompt feedback.

Question (or Response) Frame/Display. Any CBT frame in which the learner is expected to make a response.

Response Analysis. A CBT term for the process of analyzing a learner's reply to a question or response to a stimulus. Also called "Response Judging" or "Answer Judging."

Reverse (or Inverse) Video. A graphic technique in which entities are displayed as dark images on a light background.

Rule-Based CBT. Rule-based systems are a development associated with recent research in artificial intelligence (AI). These systems express their decision-making criteria as sets of production rules, which are declarative statements relating various system states to program actions. For CBT programs, system states are defined in terms of a task analysis and student model, and actions take the form of the different teaching operations that the program can perform. These components are related by a set of means-end guidance rules that determine what the program will do next for any given state. (With thanks to Jesse Heines.)

Screen. Any set of displays that fills the monitor.

Sequence. Any series of displays that achieves a coherent set of learning objectives as specified in the design document. A sequence may be as small as, but never smaller than, a chunk. A sequence is the smallest unit that can be represented by a submenu selection.

Simulation. Generic name given to a type of program that embodies a model analogous to some real system or situation and that permits variables to be changed in such a way as to reveal the operation of the system or situation.

Strand. Any series of displays that achieves the instructional objectives of conveying a simple concept or single thought; strands can easily be flowcharted.

Subject Matter Expert. A content expert used as a consultant in an instructional systems design effort to ensure the accuracy of factual material in a lesson.

Template. A pattern to be used as a guide. Templates can be constructed for screen displays (e.g., to include margins, window definitions, and option areas), for instructional sequences (e.g., approach, content, sequence to teach a particular type of material), or entire CBT programs (e.g., instructional design templates for courses or help structures).

Top-Down Design. A programming concept in which the structure of the program follows a strict pattern of hierarchical subordination. The advantage of such a program lies in the ease with which it can be understood and modified, even by someone other than the original designer or programmer.

Transportability. The ease with which a program or course that runs on one system can be made to run on another system of a different type.

Validation. The process of field testing materials and revising them on the basis of field test data.

Walkthrough. At the completion of each phase of a software development project, the relevant players meet for a structured discussion of the progress of the phase and a word-by-word examination of the associated deliverables. This book advocates the use of structured walkthroughs in CBT development.

Window. A defined opening or overlay on a computer screen that can be used to display material which is not a part of the underlying screen or display. Windows can be used to explain or graphically illustrate material on the underlying screen. Or material totally unrelated to the underlying display can be viewed.

Index*

*For information on exhibits, charts, and figures, see pp. xiii-xiv.

About The Author

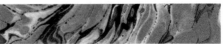

Gloria Gery is an independent consultant specializing in training and the implementation of technological change within large complex organizations. She is an internationally-recognized authority on the subject of implementing computer-based training in business, having consulted extensively in that field, written dozens of articles on it for the trade press, and given hundreds of conference presentations in the U.S. and abroad. She has been a member of numerous courseware development teams, and she conceived and created the first annual *Data Training* survey of CBT authoring systems in 1982. Her corporate experience includes three years at Corning Glass Works and twelve years at Aetna Life & Casualty in Hartford, where she was director of information systems education. Her many consulting clients are predominantly Fortune 500 organizations. She and her husband, Bob (also an independent consultant), live on commercial airliners and at their home in western Massachusetts.